Elvira King holds a PhD from the Department of Politics and International Relations at the University of Leeds.

'While we are familiar with how some Christian groups and organisations in the United States have long lobbied on behalf of pro-Zionist causes, we know next to nothing of how their counterparts in Europe seek to influence policy and attitudes in Brussels towards Israel. In this impressive and highly original new work, Elvira King offers the first detailed analysis over how such groups across Europe have managed to exercise an influence among decision makers in the EU that is often out of all proportion to their actual numbers. Theoretically informed and rich in empirical detail, this book will be essential reading for all those wishing to understand both the scope and trajectory of EU–Israeli relations.'

Professor Clive Jones, School of Government and
International Affairs, University of Durham

'This book is a valuable contribution to the literature on European relations with Israel. It introduces us to new, and increasingly important, research on the relationship between Christian Zionism, policy elites in Brussels and Israel. In particular, it offers a highly useful examination of the key Christian Zionist organisations working in Europe today – their strategies, motives and objectives as they look to engage on Israel and the Arab–Israeli conflict.'

Professor Rory Miller, Department of Government, Georgetown
School of Foreign Service, Qatar

THE PRO-ISRAEL LOBBY IN EUROPE

The Politics of Religion and Christian Zionism in the European Union

Elvira King

I.B. TAURIS

LONDON · NEW YORK

Published in 2016 by
I.B.Tauris & Co. Ltd
London • New York
www.ibtauris.com

Library of European Studies 22

ISBN: 978 1 78453 238 3
eISBN: 978 0 85773 773 1

A full CIP record for this book is available from the British Library
A full CIP record is available from the Library of Congress

Library of Congress Catalog Card Number: available

Typeset in Garamond Three by OKS Prepress Services, Chennai, India
Printed and bound by CPI Group (UK) Ltd, Croydon, CR0 4YY

CONTENTS

LIST OF ABBREVIATIONS

ACCA	Agreement on Conformity, Assessment and Acceptance of Industrial Products
AFI	Anglican Friends of Israel
BDS	Boycott, Divestment and Sanctions movement
BEPA	Bureau of European Policy Advisors
BICOM	Britain Israel Communications and Research Centre
BRIC	Brazil, Russia, India and China
CDU	Christian Democrat Union
CEC	Conference of European Churches
CEEC	Central and Eastern European Countries
CFI*	Christian Friends of Israel
CFofI*	Conservative Friends of Israel
CFSP	Common Foreign and Security Policy
COMECE	Commission of the Bishops' Conferences of the European Community
CSC	The Church and Society Commission
C4I	Christians for Israel
EC	European Commission
ECFR	European Council for Fatwa and Research
ECI	European Coalition for Israel
ECSC	European Coal and Steel Community
EEA	European Evangelical Alliance

EEAS	European External Action Service
EEC	European Economic Community
EFD	Europe of Freedom and Democracy
EFOMW	European Forum of Muslim Women
EFTA	European Free Trade Association
EHF	European Humanist Federation
EJC	European Jewish Congress
EMP	Euro-Mediterranean Partnership
ENP	European Neighbourhood Policy
ENPI	European Neighbourhood and Partnership Instrument
EP	European Parliament
EPC	European Political Cooperation
ESDP	European Security and Defence Policy
ESRC	Economic and Social Research Council
ESS	European Security Strategy
EUMC	European Monitoring Centre on Racism and Xenophobia
FCO	Foreign and Commonwealth Office
FEMYSO	Forum of European Muslim Youth and Student Organisations
FIFA	International Federation of Association Football
FIOE	Federation of Islamic Organisations in Europe
FRA	Fundamental Rights Agency
FSU	Forward Studies Unit
IBCC	Israel–Britain Chamber of Commerce
ICEJ	International Christian Embassy Jerusalem
IDF	Israeli Defence Force
IR	International Relations
JIJ	Jerusalem Institute for Justice
LDFI	Liberal Democrat Friends of Israel
LFI	Labour Friends of Israel
MEP	Member of European Parliament
MP	Member of Parliament
MR	Monthly Report

MS	Member State
NGO	Non-Governmental Organisation
NRMs	New Religious Movements
OSCE	Organisation for Security and Co-operation in Europe
PA	Palestinian Authority
PEF	Pentecostal European Fellowship
PMW	Palestinian Media Watch
PN	Policy Network
PR	Press Release
QMV	Qualified Majority Voting
RTAs	Religious Transnational Actors
RTD	Research and Technical Development
SEA	Single European Act
SEM	Single European Market
SFofI	Saxon Friends of Israel
SWC	Simon Wiesenthal Centre
UIOE	Union of Islamic Organisations in Europe

INTRODUCTION

RELIGION AND LOBBYING
IN THE EUROPEAN UNION

The phenomenon of a re-awakened religion that demands inclusion in the political space is, no doubt, a negative development for a section in European societies that wishes to confine it to a private space. For others, however, this inclusion presents a positive development that can clarify the direction in which the formation of a new European identity is now taking place. So far the relative success of the EU as a political construct was preconditioned first and foremost by the rejection of the Westphalian paradigm, which by extension involves, arguably, repudiation of the old national identities that are heavily built around the religious/Christian element. The universally applicable humanist values, the argument goes, are meant to be sufficient normative building blocks of a new supranational and cosmopolitan Europe, which the EU should actively promote abroad (Diez and Manners, 2007; Manners, 2006 and 2002; Leonard, 2005). Consequently religion has become an issue that is persistently marginalised, or rendered superfluous, in any meaningful debate about European integration. Yet in 1992 Jacques Delors declared: 'If in the next ten years we haven't managed to give a Soul to Europe, to give it spirituality and meaning, the game will be up.'[1]

Clearly the impact of religion on Europe's new identity, and by extension on the EU's political decision making, is an under-researched subject, and consequently there exists a lack of clarity and a gap that prevents a more accurate understanding of the EU as a unique evolving project. Paradoxically the EU's normative values and principles, which are formulated in a context that rejects religion, are meant to sustain and maintain the cohesion in European societies in which religion refuses to be confined to a private sphere. Therefore, given the contemporary trends in Europe, i.e. reassertion of the long-established religious identities and formulation of new ones, which have the capacity to either undermine or enhance those values, it is crucial, not only for the EU's decision makers but for the academic community as well, to engage with the dilemma about the degree of public/political space that the multi-religious factor seeks to occupy.

Of course, the impact that religion in its various forms makes on the new European identity is not confined to the EU's 'internal' issues, i.e. cohesion and legitimacy, but it extends to the EU's external relations also, especially with the Middle East. This is reflected in the fact that the EU's endorsement of religious actors (particularly integrationist-friendly denominational organisations) includes also the establishment of dialogue with the Muslim representations. While contention for political influence in member states from a variety of religious expressions, most notably Christian and Islamic, is a fascinating topic that remains under-explored, this book nevertheless takes primarily into consideration religious egalitarianism in the EU decision-making institutions, particularly how such a level playing field that was afforded to diverse religious actors facilitated the establishment of religious representations in Brussels.

Religious representations, though normatively distinct from the majority of Brussels-based interest representations, constitute in fact a logical addition to a firmly established lobbying culture that over the years continued to evolve along with the decision-making process in the EU. As the EU emerged over the last several decades as a unique economic and political entity so did the lobbying activity increase exponentially, where, according to the website of the Delegation of the European Commission to the USA, there are approximately 15,000 lobbyists and 2,500 lobbying organisations in Brussels, which are broadly grouped into industry associations, NGOs/interest groups and regional representations. Unsurprisingly the explosion of lobbying occurred in the 1990s due to the institutional changes, most notably the extension of Qualified Majority Voting (QMV) on Single Market policies (Coen, 2007; Coen, 2009: 5–12 and 145–54). Such a development was exacerbated through the direct encouragement of lobbying by the

Commission when it issued the 2001 White Paper on Governance. Mindful of the lack of EU legitimacy the document outlined the need for a close institutional engagement with civil society organisations as a way of enhancing the accountability and transparency of the EU institutions to the European electorate. To that end, according to Justin Greenwood, the highly institutionalised Brussels-based NGOs receive 'up to as much as 90 per cent funding' from political institutions, of which the European Commission is the most generous one (2010: 202). Ward and Williams likewise claim that the rapid rise of lobbying arose as a result of the recognition on the part of the Commission that networks contribute towards solving a variety of problems that include administrative, democratic and policy concerns (1997: 443–5).

The proliferation of academic literature about the interest groups that emerged concurrently with the levels of lobbying activities in Brussels was a logical consequence of such development. It ranged from the normative aspect that related lobbying to the EU's democratic deficit (Greenwood, 2011, 2010 and 1998; Kohler-Koch, 2010; Kohler-Koch and Finke, 2007; Karr, 2006; Charrad, 2004; Moravcsik, 2002), studies based on empirical research, which focused on the structural/functional aspect of the interest groups (Kluver, 2012 and 2011; Greenwood, 2010 and 2003; Besussi, 2006; Thatcher, 1998), and perhaps most significantly the impact that the EU interest representations make on theoretical studies (Vale, 2011; Borzel, 2010 and 2007; Coen and Richardson, 2009; Saurugger, 2009; Borragan, 2004; Bouwen, 2004; Grossman, 2004; Beyers, 2002; Peterson and O'Toole, 2001; Richardson, 2000; Kohler-Koch and Quittkat 1999; Peterson and Bomberg, 1999; Moravcsik, 1998; Thatcher 1998; Cowles, 1997; Kohler-Koch, 1997; Sandholtz and Zysman, 1989). The majority of findings and analysis are based on and around the business interests, which should not come as a surprise, given that business interest groups are dominant both numerically and politically in Brussels and the fact that the European integration project was, arguably, conceived, launched and fostered in economic terms. Even as political integration continued progressively with each new treaty, it was always understood that 'ever closer union' among member states is achieved primarily through economic means. Therefore the proliferation of business representations in Brussels is part and parcel of what occurs naturally in any democratic political culture; indeed more than 80 per cent of all registered lobby groups, according to the Commission's registry of civil society organisations (CONECCS) 2009 figures, are business related.

Nevertheless, as dominant as the business-related lobby activity is, the Brussels scene quite clearly encourages and accommodates the existence of normative lobby groups, including religious interest representations, whose legal status was formalised by Article 17^2 of the Lisbon Treaty in 2009. Such substantial changes not only created a conducive environment for the establishment of the diverse religious representations that have a political agenda, but they also broaden the academic debate about the role of religion in EU integration. While research undertaken so far about traditional denominational Christian lobby groups, new religious movements (NRMs), as well as Islamic lobby groups, has provided a greater insight into the organisational competence and strategic savvy of value-driven lobby groups at the supranational level (Massignon, 2010 and 2003; Pastorelli, 2009; Houston, 2009; Steven, 2009, Silvestri, 2010 and 2007; Parker, 2007), there has been no attempt to investigate Christian political support in the EU for the state of Israel. This negligence is surprising given that Christian Zionism is a worldwide phenomenon, and its influence upon U.S. foreign policy in particular has provoked a certain level of academic interest (Lewis, 2010; Marsden, 2008; Clark, 2008; Mearsheimer and Walt, 2007; Cohn-Sherbok, 2006; Sizer, 2004; Weber, 2004). Secondly, although neglected and possibly categorised as inconsequential in social and political science, European Christian Zionism is nonetheless an integral part of Europe's Church and politics, a fact that is exemplified by the formation of the European Coalition for Israel (ECI), a single pan-European Christian Zionist organisation that was officially launched in Brussels in 2004, where the British and German Christian Zionist groups and individuals in particular provide multifaceted and substantial support to its network. Although its arrival on the Brussels scene may have been relatively late compared to the accreditation of other religious interest representations, its successful establishment in the EU nonetheless points to the fact that Europe's original 'economic club' is increasingly comfortable with incorporating diverse religious actors in its decision-making process. By arguing, therefore, that Christian Zionism is a vigorous movement determined to carve a political space for itself in contemporary Europe, specifically in the European Parliament (EP) and to a lesser degree the European

Commission (EC), this book highlights the normative impact that religion can and does have upon the politics of the EU, and more specifically, it narrows a gap in the literature about organisation, strategy, and the level of influence of religious lobby groups in Brussels.

Generally understood, Christian Zionism is an umbrella of Christian groups and organisations from a variety of traditional and contemporary denominations, whose support for the Jewish state is predominantly spiritual and practical, and within some groups political. The convictions of the majority of these groups are rooted in the orthodox Christian doctrines, which include Christian Zionist hermeneutics[3] with a particular emphasis on eschatology[4] and repudiation of supersessionism.[5] In contrast to the American variant, which tends to be homogenous and almost exclusively right-wing, as well as heavily focused on eschatology, European Christian Zionism is politically diverse, less apocalyptic in its hermeneutics, and, on occasion, keen to distance itself from its American counterpart. Some European Christian supporters of Israel contend that the 'Christian Zionist' label itself is problematic given the largely negative appraisal of the movement in various Church denominations, media and academia. The argument extends to the inadequacy of the label to describe correctly some of the more nuanced versions of Christian philosemitism. Nevertheless, the writer's choice of the term was based on the fact that 'Christian Zionism', as a generic expression of Christian support for Israel among all available terms and labels, remains the most accurate one. Moreover, as this book is focused on the philosemitic organisations and Christians that are actively involved in defence of, and agitating for, Israel's interests in national and pan-European politics, the use of 'Christian Zionism' therefore effectively distinguishes these organisations and Christians from those who are theologically anti-supersessionist, but politically inactive. While some politically inactive Christian philosemites may have ambiguous feelings and convictions about the Jewish character of Israel, the politically active European Christian Zionists are fervent promoters and defenders of Israel as the Jewish state, as well as firm contenders for Israel's security.

In light of the fact that Christian Zionism, i.e. the ECI, seeks to establish itself as an influential factor in the politics of the EU, the influence had to be assessed against three criteria: its organisational capability, its normative impact in Europe and, most importantly, its leverage in promoting and sustaining pro-Israel policies. To this end the following questions, or aspects, regarding the ECI advocacy had to be addressed in order to present an accurate picture of Christian Zionist lobbying in Brussels: the extent of the ECI's organisational capacity in influencing the EU agenda shaping and decision making; the ECI's capability in producing a significant normative impact in the EU agenda shaping and policy making; the level of the ECI's efficiency to co-ordinate and streamline national (German and British) Christian Zionist advocacy onto the EU level; and lastly, the frequency of EU's pro-Israel policies that were established directly or indirectly as a result of the ECI's successful lobbying.

It should be noted at the outset that the following analysis, however helpful in a broad sense regarding the politics of religion in the EU, is nonetheless not meant to provide a comprehensive framework applicable to all religious lobby groups that are active in Brussels. The power of a normative factor, which often shapes competing agendas and creates unique strategies among diverse religious lobby groups, may therefore determine different answers for different groups to the above (and similar) questions. It should be noted also that this book does not present a definitive assessment regarding the level of Christian Zionist influence in EU politics, since political influence is difficult to identify, both conceptually and in practice. What this book does show however is that the growth and development of European Christian Zionism illustrates that the proliferation of politico-religious movements is an integral part of the wider trend in twenty-first century Europe, and that religion is no longer content to occupy the margins of the political process but has come incrementally at least to position itself openly and with increasing vigour at the centre of EU politics.

Since moral standards and the political advocacy of all religious lobby groups are grounded in their own distinct religious beliefs, this book therefore presents the existence and activity of European Christian Zionism as a particularly important and interesting political science case study. According to Robert Yin, case studies consist of five components: study questions, its propositions, its unit(s) of analysis, linkage between data and the propositions and, finally, the criteria for interpreting the findings (2003: 21). Given that the ECI is a contemporary politico-religious movement, which has been established and functions in a fluid political system, the latter two components in the case study of the ECI proved to be the most crucial for the purpose of conceptualising Brussels-based Christian Zionist advocacy, but also the most challenging. Firstly, demonstrating the relevance of collected data to the main propositions, such as, for example, the level of inter-organisational partnership/cooperation between, on the one hand German Christian Zionists and the ECI, and on the other hand British Christian Zionists and the ECI, was not identical due to the varying degree of the European identity affirmation. Secondly, the criteria for interpreting the findings (level/measure of the ECI influence) included input from both German and British advocacy, but the criteria for the Christian Zionist influence in each country was selected according to the unique political and historical context in which this influence was exerted. Notwithstanding such challenges, the adopted methodology was clearly the most appropriate in assessing various aspects of the ECI, whose political marginality does not necessarily render the organisation uninfluential or irrelevant in the EU's value system or its politics.

The chapters in this book have been structured with the view that effective explanation of the normative premise and lobby strategy of the ECI is preconditioned by understanding why and how certain issues inform the European Christian Zionist discourse. Therefore Chapter 1 of the book deals with the major contextual themes, firstly the challenges of the Common Foreign and Security Policy (CFSP) and the EU's normative values, and secondly the contentious nature of contemporary European identity, due largely to the long-established and culturally relevant Christianity and an increasingly assertive Islam. The proliferation of religious lobby groups in Brussels is tangible evidence of the religious dimension in European politics, but it is also evidence of the political legitimisation and increasing leverage of the EU. For Christian Zionists, particularly the ECI, there is a deep correlation between the EU's values, foreign policy, and reassertion of Europe's Judeo-Christian ethics, and consequently the ECI maintains that political activism on a domestic level needs to extend to a supranational level, even if Israel prefers bilateral relations.

Chapter 2 presents the normative, political and economic context of the EU–Israel relations by engaging with the issues of Islamism, antisemitism, the peace process and economic cooperation. This is important to include in the book since European Christian Zionist advocacy revolves around all these issues, albeit to a greater or lesser degree contingent on the actual issue involved and the circumstances faced. Sections 5 and 6 of the chapter provide an overview of current German and British relations with Israel and outline the reasons behind the selection of these two national Christian Zionist models in evaluating the ECI. The chapter ends with a section that introduces the ECI or, to put it more accurately, it provides an overview of the ECI's organisational capability, its normative premise, and strategy.

Chapter 3 engages specifically with the internal structure of the ECI – the leadership and nature of its decision making, its membership and network, its ability to use media in its advocacy, and the level of the organisation's professionalism. British and German groups (and individuals) are naturally included in this chapter since their networks enhance the ECI advocacy substantially. Chapter 4 elaborates on the ECI's norms that underpin its advocacy, initially clarifying the normative difference between American and European Christian Zionism. It proceeds to elaborate on, and draw distinction between, the ECI's spiritual, moral and political values and beliefs, and how each one is related to the themes and issues in the first and second chapters respectively. Overall the chapter underlines the importance of the norms that motivate advocacy and underpin the process of lobbying.

Lastly, Chapter 5 conceptualises the ECI by focusing on its lobby strategy, and why certain campaigns are categorised as defensive and others as offensive. It contains information about the ECI's cooperation with Jewish organisations outside Brussels, including those from Israel, and discusses whether the ECI's lobby efforts have gained any recognition by Israel. More importantly, the chapter focuses on key Jewish organisations and the MEPs that the ECI works with in Brussels, and discusses British and German Christian Zionist input into the ECI. In this way the chapter demonstrates the organisation's ability to recognise the most influential national contributors, and to incorporate a range of national lobby practices while presenting a unified voice, an essential element of its strategy, at the EU level. A contextual analysis of several of the ECI's campaigns provides answers to the questions about the success of the ECI's strategy, while the final section discusses specifically the 2010 San Remo Initiative.

CHAPTER 1

EUROPE'S VALUES AND RELIGION

So far the EU's evolution towards a supranational construct, which brought functional changes in social, economic and political institutions, could be described as a relative success (Bohmelt, 2012; Cross, 2012). However, it is the question about the new European identity and consequently the EU legitimacy that is more frequently raised. Within this normative context scholars have only recently engaged with the dimension that religion plays in contemporary European identity and its role in European politics. While the EU normative values provide the Europeans with an attractive political identity, nevertheless, the multifaceted religious trends (such as the rise of new religious movements (NRMs), revival of old religious identities, and formation of religious lobby groups) that are flourishing in twenty-first-century Europe illustrate the reality that Europe is not as secular as political and academic establishments would like to believe. This causes a dilemma, if not a problem, for the EU in light of the fact that the union's nature as a single market could mean that the EU does not have adequate instruments to deal with issues pertaining to religion.

This chapter therefore discusses the nature and importance of the relationship between the EU and religion, not least because the EU's evolving character gradually included social and ethical issues. The ratification of the Lisbon Treaty in 2009 was a milestone that brought substantial institutional changes to the EU, but it also afforded a legal status for religious communities/organisations through Article 17 of the treaty. The inclusion of Article 17 demonstrated that a resurgent religion has itself reached a milestone in its progressive quest for political influence in the EU, but the article also further encouraged proliferation of religious lobby groups. This is evidenced by research conducted so far that religious lobby groups are firmly established in Brussels, with clear agendas, good resources and sufficient insider knowledge that makes them as effective in their lobby strategy as any other well-organised non-religious interest group (Silvestri, 2010 and 2007; Massignon, 2010; Pastorelli, 2009; Steven, 2009; Houston, 2009; Parker, 2007).

Article 17, however, was preceded by other factors that caused the establishment of these groups. Firstly, they emerged as a natural outcome of a development that includes Islamic inroads into European societies and renewed interest in Christian heritage, as well as an exponential rise in the new spirituality of neo-Paganism and NRMs. Secondly, the institutional changes with the Single European Act (SEA) in 1985 created a conducive environment for the formation of lobby groups that went beyond business interest representation. What initially started as harmonisation of business interests across Europe for the purpose of creating the Single European Market (SEM), further evolved into an extension of QMV and establishment of the three pillars in the Treaty of European Union in Maastricht 1992. Two major developments in particular conditioned the proliferation of the non-governmental political participation – the inclusion of the principle of subsidiarity in the European Communities pillar, and, crucially, the emergence of the EP with a significantly enhanced role in the decision-making process.

The enhanced decision-making role of the EP is meant to demonstrate that the federalist agenda need not impede the reduction of the institutional democratic deficit, as the EU is firmly committed to uphold its own values and principles. Accordingly, this chapter reviews the EU's normative values, why they are associated with a post-Westphalian paradigm, and why the inherent contradictions within the EU normative power discourse and the EU's policies draw both criticism and defence from the academic community. Related to this debate is the EU's foreign policy since, if the rise of Christian Zionism in Brussels is to be understood correctly, it must be viewed within the wider context of both resurgent religion in European societies and the EU's foreign policy. The chapter discusses the complex institutional segmentation of the EU and specifically how it generates the structural incoherence in the Common Foreign and Security Policy (CFSP), which, as demonstrated in Chapter 2, undermines the impact that the EU seeks to accomplish in the Middle East, specifically in its relations with Israel through the instrument of European Neighbourhood Policy (ENP).

Having discussed in the initial two sections the CFSP and the EU's normative values respectively the chapter proceeds to the third section that is focused on the (lack of) new European identity. Given that the soft power concept and the EU's rejection of militarism runs parallel to a large measure to the rejection of the American hard power model and its unilateralism, this section of the chapter refers to utilisation of anti-American sentiments as a part of the current search for, and the construction of, Europe's cosmopolitan identity. This is important to emphasise since Christian Zionists who lobby in member states, and particularly those in Brussels, are at times keen to distance themselves from the US-style Christian Zionist lobbying that is widely described as confrontational and unsophisticated.

Further on the chapter addresses the issue of religion in Europe with sections 5 and 6 elaborating Christian and Muslim roles respectively in a multi-religious Europe. While some academic voices are sceptical about the current status of European Christianity (Caldwell, 2010: 142–71), and others are bemoaning its decline in contemporary scholarship (Henry and Agee, 2003), the prevailing academic consensus nevertheless holds to a pragmatic view that the inherent values of justice and peace in Christian religion can be utilised within a secular normative framework, with the role of the Vatican in the integration process as a supreme example. Islam's role in a contemporary Europe, a very important subject for Christian Zionists, also polarises the academic community that argues whether Islam is going to be Europeanised, or whether Europe will be Islamised (Meijer and Bakker, 2012; Hunter, 2002; Ye'or, 2011; Kilpatrick, 2000). Both sections highlight the tension in a secular Europe that has to accommodate the competing demands of two religions – both with inherent expansionist impulses at their core – but have to co-exist in a multi-faith community of European believers.

Demands for a political space that is projected from different religious persuasions are demonstrated most clearly in the formation of numerous religious lobby groups that operate in national settings, but with an increasing significance in Brussels also. This is explained in the last section of the chapter, which does not deal with the ECI and its Christian Zionist political agenda, but demonstrates that there was an identified gap in the scholarship on religion in the EU, and that a number of scholars have addressed it by looking into the religious mobilisation in Brussels. It also demonstrates that the rise of lobbying among the religious communities, and competition for access to supranational institutions of agenda setting and decision making, reflects a growing recognition of the EU's political leverage.

The EU's foreign policy and institutional challenges

The complexities of the EU's institutional functioning, particularly in the area of foreign policy, often presents a puzzle for both the politically astute, for whom the comprehension of international order is largely derived from the Westphalian paradigm, and for the uninformed, for whom the creation of new decision-making offices further confuses their attempt to understand the concept of supranationality of the new Europe (Underhill, 2010). Even though the 2009 Lisbon Treaty established the European Presidency, which is largely expected to represent a united European voice, a rotating six-months Presidency remains intact. The interesting, and somewhat surprising, choice of Catherine Ashton and Herman Van Rompuy for the appointments to the foreign policy chief's office and Presidency respectively reflects the fact that the EU prefers not to rely on personal charisma and wide publicity of political candidates (indeed Ashton was favoured over Tony Blair). Furthermore, these appointments reflect how heads of the member states (France and Germany in particular) still decide who represents Europe collectively. Toby Vogel explains that both were individuals who in fact worked efficiently behind the scenes for pro-EU agendas, and how Brussels is through their election 'signalling its will to create a strong and efficient institutionalisation framework of both Presidency and High Commissioner offices' (2009). Sceptics, however, claim that the reason behind appointments of unknown politicians with very little international clout is a clear signal that member states are not ready to sign over that part of national sovereignty to an institution in Brussels (Charter, 2010). In particular it is the economic crisis that ensued since the Lisbon Treaty that added a considerable degree of distrust towards the EU among the euro-sceptics.

To understand these challenges, it is pertinent at this point to outline the functioning of the EU institutions in foreign policy, namely the Council of Ministers, the European Commission and the EP. Although the 1993 Treaty of Maastricht was a progression from the European Community into the European Union – an agreement that furthered European political unity by establishing three pillars – it was an arrangement, however, that contained a degree of fluidity and, as such, was subject to periodic revision. For this reason the Commission, in itself an autonomous institution since its inception in 1951, used ways and means by which it could solidify its authority in given areas, as well as try to extend its authority in areas out of its scope. The Commission, in terms of decision making in the context of international agreements, has powers to negotiate with third countries and international organisations. These negotiations have to be, of course, conducted according to the Council's approval, with the exception of humanitarian aid, where the Commission has full authority. It is in the area of foreign policy (political and military agreements) where the Commission has been largely powerless, although it has exercised a fair amount of leverage through the Neighbourhood policy. Arguably, its level of influence has increased with the ratification of the Lisbon Treaty. While the Council of Europe remains in control of European foreign policies, it is widely anticipated that the High Representative for Foreign Affairs and Security Policy, an institution that was created by the fusion of the High Representative office with the office of the Vice President of the Commission, will in reality limit the powers of the Council and enhance those of the Commission. In this way, it is expected that the treaty will overcome 'some of the debilitating divisions between the two institutions that have hampered the EU's foreign policy in the past years' (Vogel, 2009).

It is also significant that the Lisbon Treaty increased the powers of the EP, such as the requirement that the Council consults the EP before voting on the Commission's legislation proposal. In its early days the EP was an institution regarded as ineffectual and irrelevant, but its leverage increased in the 1970s when it was granted power over the annual budgetary decision making (Hix et al., 2003a). Largely ignored by member states, the affairs of the EP did, however, manage to create a stir during the European parliamentary elections in 2009. The level of participation across the EU stood at 43 per cent, which was widely publicised as a result of the overall victory of the political right from across Europe, and particularly due to the fact that the extreme right gained a number of seats. Although the EP's powers remain limited when compared to the Council and the High Representative office, the EP is, nevertheless, more than a marginal player in the functioning of the EU (Diedrichs, 2007), which is substantiated by the considerable increase in the number of interest groups in the last two decades (Greenwood, 2010; Kohler-Koch, 1997).

The establishment of the CFSP with the Maastricht Treaty in 1992 arguably added to the existing complexities of the EU governance. The criticism about the limitations of the institutional capacity of the CFSP does not only refer to the complex nature of national and supranational cross-institutional functioning, but also to the area that remains exclusively in the decision-making domain of the Council of the EU, where the repeated question concerns 'how far individual governments try to impose their national preferences during the presidency or whether the experience pushes them towards identifying with collective EU interest' (H. Wallace, 2005: 60). Although national officials are meant to co-ordinate national positions and use ministerial meetings to set unified agendas in the Political and Security Committee, the discrepancies of national objectives remain. Until the Lisbon Treaty was ratified, common strategies needed a unanimous voice in the Council, and joint actions and positions were decided by the QMV. Even though the latest changes now allow for the QMV in the Council on proposals from the High Representative, as well as joint proposals from the High Representative and the Commission, it still remains to be seen whether these latest arrangements will streamline the EU foreign policy to a substantial degree.

Apart from the structural incoherence of the CFSP, it is also its institutional commitment to the EU's normative values and principles that defines its role globally, most significantly in the Middle East (Smith, 2008). For historical reasons the EU is keen to avoid a 'hard power' foreign policy model that is defined by a militaristic approach and determined traditional American role in the region (Mackenstein and Marsh, 2005). It is precisely the opposite 'soft power' approach which, as some EU enthusiasts would like to believe, is going to not only solve the problems in the Middle East, but even define the global politics of the twenty-first century (Leonard, 2005). This defining initially took place in the context of the comprehensive Euro-Mediterranean Partnership (EMP) that was launched with the Barcelona Process in 1995, which aimed at close economic, political and cultural cooperation in the Euro-Mediterranean region, and currently involves the EU and Algeria, Albania, Egypt, Israel, Jordan, Lebanon, Mauritania, Morocco, Occupied Palestinian Territory and Syria, as well as Libya, with its observer status (EuroMed, Partnership). These threefold aspects of proposed cooperation are embedded in legally binding bilateral relationships through association agreements designed to foster greater political and economic reforms, but they also aim to promote multilateral relationships through joint conferences and programmes. For instance, the MEDA programme, the most important economic instrument that emerged from the EMP, invested 90 per cent of its resources in individual countries of the Middle East, but it also included the Palestinian Authority (PA). In the period of 1995–2006 the combined financial aid from the EMP through MEDA I and MEDA II funds and the European Investment Bank to the PA reached 15.2 billion euros, and under the new European Neighbourhood and Partnership Instrument (ENPI) the allocated budget to the PA for the period of 2007–13 stands at 12 billion euros (Huber, 2008: 53).

Given that the EMP is part of an overall EU effort to formulate its own foreign policy, the evolution of the CFSP can arguably be perceived as a process that is gradually establishing Europe's state-like credentials in global affairs. Logically then, the close proximity of the Mediterranean region, as well as its deep impact on Europe's political and economic interests, is a factor that explains the EU's ongoing interest in influencing political outcomes in the Middle East. Although the initial (and existing) structural incoherence of the CFSP prevented the EU from conducting a consistent foreign policy, the ongoing institutional changes are arguably creating a closer political interdependence that is conducive to the making of a single EU foreign policy. Although both sceptics and supporters of a politically more integrated Europe will arrive at different conclusions about the Lisbon Treaty, few would disagree that this particular institutional milestone is an attempt on the part of the EU to assert its credibility in global decision making.

The academic consensus holds that the EU's ongoing regional engagement in the Middle East is clearly not superficial, based on recognition that Europe has deep historic, political, economic and cultural ties with the region. When disagreements and criticism do however arise (and these span from across the spectrum of contemporary political culture and academia), they are almost always centred on the EU's (lack of) political success in the region, and the reasons behind it, of which the most important relates to the fact that the CFSP is still developing (Bicchi and Gillespie, 2011; Holden, 2009). Given the historical, cultural and political differences among the European countries and divergent attitudes and relationships that member states have with countries in the Middle East, which are largely, though not exclusively, a result of past colonialism (Behr, 2008), the continuing intergovernmental institutional functioning of the CFSP and the attempts to streamline the EU's foreign policy are, from the viewpoint of Europhiles, admirable, and, according to Eurosceptics, unrealistic (Underhill, 2010). Such multifaceted ties between the two regions ensure therefore that the differences of opinion are not merely based on the structural analysis of the EU's (incoherent) foreign policy, but they also encompass the debate about the external projection of the EU's values and principles.

EU's normative values

Numerous theories have been developed over decades that sought to explain the complex and unique structural evolution and identity construction of the European Union. The EU's modest beginning in the form of the European Coal and Steel Community (ECSC) in 1951 and its development into a supranational global power at the beginning of the twenty-first century has challenged not only the traditional Westphalian notion of state sovereignty, but also the concept of power itself. The effectiveness of soft power, initially conceptualised by Joseph Nye (2007 and 2004), is a premise that underlines the EU's current quest for global influence (Nye, 2004a). As a framework and narrative, which is meant to underpin the CFSP, it was established by a number of scholars of the European Union, whose conceptualisation of the EU's unique ability to expand steadily in geographic, economic and political terms is based on rejection of the traditional understanding of power defined by military prowess.

John McCormick explains that 'Europe is a superpower, not one that threatens and coerces, but one that offers a new set of interpretations and possibilities to a world that has too long been dragged along behind the increasingly bankrupt philosophy of hard power and militarism' (2007: 174). Similarly Mark Leonard reflects on the EU's lack of statehood and argues that the EU's functioning as a network (2005: 28) guarantees that its success does not depend on hard power, but on the fact that member states bind themselves to the law of the Community and turn 'mutual interference and surveillance into the basis of their security' (2005: 41). Europe's role in the emerging new world order, argues Leonard, will occur as a result of the superiority and spread of the EU's soft power: 'As this process continues, we will see the emergence of a "New European Century". Not because Europe will run the world as an empire, but because the European way of doing things will have become the world's' (2005: 143).

The notion of a global spillover of the 'European way of doing things' is conceptualised as the Normative Power EU that derives most prolifically from the work of Ian Manners, and is currently a dominant discourse within the EU studies, which generates a lively debate. While Nye envisions soft power as an empirical concept, which should be used in foreign policy for the pursuit of national interests (2007), Manners argues that the normative power of the EU is not self-serving, but is a 'theoretical concept requiring an understanding of the social diffusion and normative practices' (2007: 179) that stems from a larger context of multilateralism and adherence to international treaties (2007: 181–2). 'The concept of normative power', explains Manners, 'is an attempt to refocus analysis away from the empirical emphasis on the EU institutions and policies, and towards including cognitive processes, with both substantive and symbolic components' (2002: 239).

Such discourse inevitably singles out traditional understanding of the international system as the most significant aspect of this cognitive process. It focuses on the distinction between a certain set of ethics (i.e. Wesphalian conventions) and power to change what is normal, or perceived to be normal, in world politics. The unique quality of the EU as different from all other 'pre-existing political forms' is precisely the factor that pre-disposes the EU to act in a certain normative way (Manners, 2002: 242). For that reason, Manners maintains, even the creation of the European Security and Defence Policy (ESDP) in June 1999, caused no contradictions to Europe's normative claims. Indeed, as long as militarisation of Europe serves the purpose of diffusing Europe's substantive normative principles, then 'normative and military power are not necessarily incompatible' (Diez and Manners, 2007: 187).

The creation of the ESDP is precisely what gave an impetus to concerns about, and critical appraisal of, the EU's normative power status. Although the widespread consensus among scholars holds that the EU should exercise its soft power through its normative values in both external relations and internal policy making, a relatively small number of scholars persist in theorising the EU from the realist perspectives by singling out militarising of the EU through the institutionalisation of the common defence policy. Alexander Siedschlag (2006) uses a security paradigm of neo-realism and maintains that the ESDP, as an embedded system that is subject to the effects of the world system and balance of power, should be analysed through methodological collectivism (2006: 1–2). Within the Waltzian concept of security maximisation, of which conflict prevention and post-conflict reconstruction are essential components of European security, Siedschlag incorporates Gilpin's flexibility in agency, i.e. pooling European resources in the defence sector authorised by the European Council, as well as Grieco's 'voice opportunity' proposition (2006: 3–4). Siedschlag insists that multilateralism of the ESDP is effectively explained by the neo-realist theory, as long as it is flexible and corresponding to changing national interest. Similarly, Tomas Weiss argues that 'effective multilateralism', which was formulated within the framework of the UN Charter, is unworkable because

> [the] European Union cannot prostitute its security to an organisation which frequently cannot, will not, or is unable, to act quickly, proactively and efficiently. The United Nations may provide a handy framework for diplomatic solutions and negotiations, but it is not going to be the effective or legitimate organisation that is today needed, especially when dealing with the new and dynamic threats outlined in the European Security Strategy (2006).

Adrian Hyde-Price, who dismisses the EU normative power concept as moralistic posturing, specifically analyses the security dilemma of nuclear Iran, and argues that either co-existence with a nuclear Iran or launching a pre-emptive attack on its nuclear sites, demands conflict resolution based on prudence – the parameters of possible – rather than the moral crusade (2008: 35–8). Maintaining that anarchy will remain the dominant principle of world politics, and therefore morality of the states is not and should not be rooted in a rigid constitutive principle, he concludes that when necessary, 'pre-emption and preventive war – not compromise and appeasement – might be the morally right choice when faced with proliferators and aggressors' (2008: 40). Given the realities of the world system in which the balancing of power remains the essential component, Europe's foreign and security policy should not be understood in terms of a liberal cosmopolitanism, but it should be pursued along the lines of 'hard-headed calculation of common "European" interests' (Hyde-Price, 2008: 44). John McCormick rejects such a pessimistic attitude and insists that as the attraction of Europe's values gradually becomes obvious as it engages on different levels (economic, diplomatic and cultural) with the rest of the world (2007: 70), the process will reach the point where Europe 'does not need to use force or threat to encourage change' (2007: 15).

In between the highly optimistic proponents of a demilitarised Europe and a traditional realist concept of power that provides a certain logic to the creation of the ESDP, a range of scholars from the liberal perspective questioned whether the EU is able to retain its distinct civilian power profile. While Diez and Manners do not find the militarisation of Europe a problematic issue that can affect the integrity of Europe's normative standards, mainly because 'the EU's self-binding to international law' (2007: 188) ensures that the EU remains a civilian power, others tend to identify the militarisation trend as problematic. Karen Smith stated: 'An EU military capability would represent the culmination of a "state-building" project' (2000: 27) that could conceivably generate the '"security dilemma" so familiar to realists' (2000: 23), while Lucarelli and Menotti warned that the EU must resolve the inherent dilemma of 'multilateralism and potentially forceful protection of human rights' (2006: 163). Since 'the democratic control of security and defence policy can be considered an essential element of civilian power', Wolfgang Wagner argues, the creation of the ESDP weakens the power of national parliaments to control deployment decisions, damages the legitimacy of the EU-led military missions, and ultimately widens the existing democratic deficit in the EU (2006: 201). Alyson Bailes agrees with this contention in view of the fact that a 'lack of grounding in public opinion and democratic institutions is a normative weakness of the ESDP' (2008: 129).

The criticism of the 'normative power Europe' theory illustrates a twofold issue with which proponents of the theory have to contend – its applicability to European internal security issues and its applicability outside of the European cultural context. Hyde-Price sums it up by asserting that if Europe persists in conducting its foreign policy within the framework of a soft power and the parameters of self-imposed restrictive normative values and principles, it risks being charged with hypocrisy, as well as being sidelined as an influential global actor (2008: 44). Robert Kagan's harsh criticism of Europe's contradictions is aimed at its post-modern rejection of military power: 'The irony is that Europe's new Kantian order could flourish only under the umbrella of American power exercised according to the rules of the old Hobbesian order' (2002). Bailes would not go to such lengths in criticising the EU's idealism, but she nevertheless raises an important point about the EU's duplicity: 'The ESDP deliberately avoided taking over responsibility for Europe's own defence from NATO, an alliance that bases its credibility on strategic union with the very same non-European power – the United States – from whose strategic values the ESS [The European Security Strategy] so delicately distanced itself' (2008: 119).

The attempts to explain (or to explain away) the inconsistencies in the EU's normative power projection and the ability to translate it into all external policies, are perhaps best explained by Bretherton and Vogler (2006). They ascribe the discrepancy between the principles and consistency in practical application to the fact that the EU's actorness is still under construction. The EU is an actor in world politics, and yet it is not defined by statehood, which traditionally determined the actorness. Instead, Bretherton and Vogler maintain, the EU's ability to act and exert its influence is multilayered and, for that reason, the explanation of Europe's actorness must move away from a dichotomy of structure and agency, and adopt 'an approach which emphasises neither structure, nor agency, but the relationship between them' (2006: 20). Given the complexities of these interactive processes, they categorise Europe's actorness in terms of opportunity, presence and capability. For instance, the economic interdependence from the mid 1970s generated a discourse of globalisation, which provided the opportunities and obligation for the EU to act on behalf of its members, while the post-9/11 alternative to US pre-emptive doctrine was an opportunity for the EU to reassert its commitment to multilateralism (Bretherton and Vogler,

2006: 25–6). Secondly, they maintain, the EU's presence is most potently exemplified through the enlargement process and 'unintended external impacts of the Common Agricultural Policy (CAP) and of the Single Market, and the impact of the introduction of the euro' (2006: 28). Thirdly, it is within the capability aspect of the EU's actorness that Bretherton and Vogler evaluate Europe's commitment to normative values and principles. This commitment, they claim, has a potential to increase if public consent in the member states produces a reduction of the democratic deficit, and consequently the cross-pillar cooperation intensifies (particularly in the CFSP) and the external policy instruments (political, economic and military) are utilised in order to achieve coherence and consistency (2006: 29–35).

Given the evolving character of the EU it is unsurprising that theorising different aspects of such a uniquely global actor is done within a constructivist context. Consequently, Diez and Manners refuse to evaluate the 'normative power Europe' through empirical criteria primarily; rather they view it, as already pointed out, as an important discourse that shapes the construction of the European identity (2007: 187). Realist objections to the lack of, or indeed impossibility of, consistent practical application of EU values are misplaced, according to Manners, given the fact that European integration is procedural rather than absolutist (2006: 116). The criticism that normative principles have no substance with regard to security concerns, and that Europe should pursue its foreign policy along hard power parameters, is also refuted by Manners. He insists that in view of the fact that these principles are constitutionalised in the Reform Treaty of the EU, promoted as the objectives in the external relations, and regarded as universally applicable by the UN, they have the power to gradually transform the world into 'cosmopolitical supranationalism', i.e. political participation and interaction of civil society and supranational legal structures across international borders (2006a: 28 and 2008: 60).

Other scholars, such as Bailes, (2008) and Wagner (2006), who are willing to concede that some objections to contradictions in the EU's normative discourse and practice are somewhat problematic, emphasise that such contradictions are the result of the EU's peculiar supranational and inter-governmental decision-making process. Just as the internal structural constraints may prevent uninterrupted diffusion of Europe's values, so the commitment to multilateralism is susceptible to failure as it relies on the benevolence of the most powerful states within the system (Sjursen, 2006: 246). For that reason, when Sjursen questions whether the EU truly is a normative power and, if so, what the power mechanisms are behind it, she concludes that the EU's self-binding through law and commitment to multilateralism are credible indicators that Europe's participation in 'strengthening the cosmopolitan dimension to international law' will continue to distinguish the EU from traditional power politics (2006: 249).

Europe's identity and the EU

In view of the fact that the EU continues to evolve socially and politically, as well as expand geographically, a degree of pragmatism will always be necessary when defending the EU as a value-based community. Mitzen is convinced that the EU's military capability does not diminish its identity as a 'civilising' power because 'the healthy basic trust anchoring intra-European relations makes Europe perhaps uniquely capable of "externalizing" its civilising mission' (2006: 275). Mennotti and Lucarelli use the much discussed and analysed cases of the EU's military deployments in Bosnia and Kosovo. 'There is certainly no enthusiasm for a prominent role of military power', they claim, 'but "crisis management" is all about stabilising Europe's immediate periphery and the Europeans have become pretty serious about this business' (2006: 160). In a similar manner Bretherton and Vogler dismiss the implication that militarisation of Europe is 'an attempt to emulate US approaches to security' (2006: 213), because the ESDP is designed to support Europe's multidimensional civil identity (2006: 214). Karen Smith even adds that the effects of Europe's soft power may make a difference in the long run, but currently, it is Europe's actorness on the global level that is vitally important, and that actorness includes military instruments (2008: 72). Jorgensen makes the general observation that even though the diffusion of European values and principles as well as Europe's projection of supranational and cosmopolitan self images are important, they are not necessarily directly related to policies; instead 'actors are left with the imperative of prudent statecraft, choosing among principles' (2006: 57).

Bretherton's and Vogler's rejection of identifying the militarisation of Europe with the American approach to security reflects a wider rejection of American values, and specifically American foreign policy, on the part of Europe's policy makers (Huber, 2008). Although Europe and the USA share some common values, which effectively place the two continents in a single civilisational unit as Huntington (2002) would argue, there are nonetheless a number of characteristics defining broadly American and broadly European identity that have tended to cause friction at times in the transatlantic relationship. Europe's secularism, the progressive character of its nation states, and its post-war pacifism (Haseler, 2004: 12–35), and perhaps most significantly Europe's preference for social democracy (Haseler, 2004: 129), were aspects of the European society and politics that initially caused no problems for the security alliance through NATO, but it did play a crucial part in a rift that occurred at the beginning of the twenty-first century.

The unequal partnership between the US and Europe endured throughout the Cold War, but was being questioned increasingly after the Soviet threat was removed in the late 1980s and the America's security guarantee was no longer needed. Two decades later, Haseler argues, the split over Iraq in 2003 was a defining moment when a European super-state 'took hold of its "independence", and threw off the yoke of the American "empire"' (2004: 122). Markovits is less admiring of European attitudes and asserts that the anti-American discourse that followed the Iraq invasion is based on a traditional resentment among European elites and intellectuals, whose objections to American moral, social, and cultural values derive from their position that America is brash, prudish and consumerist, while Europe is refined, wise and savvy (2006: 101).

The reaction to the invasion of Iraq was certainly interesting in that it generated a widespread negative response from Europe's political elites and from the popular culture. Initially the response varied from an outrage in France, to a mixed positive and negative reaction in Britain, to the somewhat more positive attitude in the Central and Eastern European Countries (CEEC), while in the aftermath of the war the overall European attitude towards the military intervention was negative (Springford, 2003). This arguably created for the first time a platform for a consensus between the European supranationalists and population at large regarding the question of what constitutes Europeanness and to what extent does anti-Americanism undermine national identities and determine a European one. Antonsich (2008: 516–7), as well as Caporaso and Min-hyung (2009: 29–30), argue that there is a convergence of anti-Americanism between the

European elites and masses which could potentially bridge the gap between the civic/post-national and cultural/national European identity. Markovits agrees, but with an added assertion that the anti-Americanism of the European elites is essentially a nationalist tool in Europe's state-building process:

> A Kulturkampf by artists and intellectuals is one thing. Mass mobilisation of publics is quite another... With the entity of 'Europe' now being on the agenda, anti-Americanism may well serve as a useful mobilising function for the establishment of this new entity and become a potent political force on the mass level beyond the elites' antipathy and *ressentiment* that has been a staple of European intellectual life. (2006: 100–3, emphasis in the original)

A number of academics used the Iraq invasion, which they perceived as morally wrong, as a catalyst to crystallise the inherent incompatibilities between America and Europe that could be used as a demarcation criteria between European and American identity. For example, McCormick lists some 20 plus major differences between the USA and the EU and even doubts whether the future Atlantic Alliance is sustainable given the differences (2007: 167), while Diez and Manners argued that American normative values rest on the assumption of the inherent inferiority of the 'Other' (2007: 182–5). Logically then, Diez and Manners maintain, there is no separation from normative values and military power, which consequently affords legitimacy to the use of military force (ibid.). Likewise Leonard's prediction that Europe will run the twenty-first century is set against the militarism, arrogance and self-interest of the declining American super-power (2005). Krishan Kumar, in contrast, criticises this trend extensively, focusing mainly on the article written by Habermas and Derrida in 2003 in the wake of the anti-war demonstrations across the EU. The two influential philosophers, who optimistically referred to these demonstrations as the beginning of the European public sphere, called on the 'avant-garde' core of the European states to return to European enlightenment values, which America, under the then Bush leadership, obviously lacks. Kumar, however, states: 'The article by Habermas and Derrida was clearly in the nature of a manifesto, a Declaration of European Independence. It was independence above all from America' (2008: 88), an attempt to conceive European identity, which when done so 'against a country like America that shares with Europe so much of the basic Western inheritance' (2008: 98), is self-defeating. Kumar claims this is for two reasons: in the first place their vision of Europe is selective, and in the second place such a stance is contradictory to Europe's cosmopolitanism.

Whether the America has become the 'Other', and whether the 'Other' is necessary to one's identity is arguable from both political and ethical aspects. If the America is Europe's 'Other', than Europe might have to look elsewhere for the 'Other' in years to come. The landslide victory of the Democratic party in 2009, and the election (as well as the subsequent 2012 re-election) of Barak Obama as the President of the US – the most liberal candidate ever in American history, and accused by a section of the Conservatives and Christian fundamentalists of pursuing a futile appeasement policy with the Islamic world – could prove soon that American normative values are fast changing and perhaps even becoming identical to the European in the near future. If, on the other hand, the anti-Americanism is purely of a political nature, then the dilemma that still remains is related to interplay and acceptance of Europe's multiple identities, with the most immediate one relating to the degree of resistance that resides in national identities to a single European identity. Sean Carrey concludes that this degree is difficult to identify given that the relationship between national, sub-national and supranational identities is complex, and that attitudes towards European integration are determined by feelings towards one's country as much as by utilitarian concerns about income and education (2002). Antonsich acknowledges the complexities, but argues nonetheless that the unique interplay, even contradictions, between the national view (held by ordinary people) and post-national views (held by intellectual elites) provide a credible framework in which a new European identity is possible (2008: 517).

A valid point to consider relates to the fact that Europe's countries coexisted most times in history in a perpetual state of war, and consequently strong and diverse national identities have become embedded to the point that a supranational European identity is deemed to be unrealistic. On the other hand, it is possible, as Jon Erik Fossum believes, to view European identity in the context of its diversity. 'The diversity of Europe', he claims, 'has deep historical roots – including supranational ones. These roots are conducive to a wide range of attachments embedded in a complex mixture of supranational, transnational and intergovernmental principles and institutions' (2001: 15). Similarly to Antonsich, Fossum advocates a supranational identity that does not have to compete with the national identities, but it clearly has to be based on Europe's normative values, in particular human rights and democracy, and it has to promote cultural and a host of other diversities through the politics of recognition (2001: 22–3).

As a new European identity is inextricably linked to the legitimacy of the European project, the ongoing federalist agenda therefore needs to be legitimised through the active political participation of Europe's civil society at the supranational level (Kohler-Koch, 2010; Finke, 2007; Charrad and Eisele, 2004). Enthusiasm for EU politics, however, is preconditioned with the sense of being European, and this particular issue presents a challenge to European enthusiasts to transform the EU from a politico-economic construction into an entity that engages people's hearts as well. As a unique post-Westphalian and secular construct, the EU rejects the traditional tenets of identity normally associated with a nation state, but has failed so far to offer anything compelling enough to European citizens that could move them beyond well-established national identities. Given the lack of demos (a collective sense of European citizens) that prevents a successful integration process, to a large degree it seems that an all-encompassing European identity does not necessarily have to rely on common language, traditions, politics and history, as Antonsich claims, and therefore the pursuit of that demos should be based on syncretism of national and post-national sentiments (2008: 506; also Carey, 2002).

The dichotomous division on national and post-national is not surprising given a substantial intellectual input into the construction of the European identity: '[P]ost-national Europe', Antonsich explains, 'is rather popular among intellectuals' (2008: 509), even though the national and post-national identities are somewhat intertwined at the level of the masses. At the same time the bureaucratically determined EU political culture oversaw the EU's steady territorial and economic expansion, a process from which European citizens were largely excluded. This consequently became labelled as the EU's democratic deficit problem, which had to be recognised at the EU's institutional level two decades ago, and continues to generate debates among scholars, politicians, and ordinary people across the EU. Because the institutions of the EU are 'frequently accused of a lack of accountability', explains Carey (2002: 388), the Maastricht Treaty in 1992 attempted to create a closer union between European citizens by establishing the framework of European citizenship, and in 2001 called for a reduction in the democratic deficit by issuing the White Paper on European Governance. Acknowledging that European citizens perceive the EU as both remote and intrusive, the paper stated the following: 'Providing more information and more effective communication are a pre-condition for generating a sense of belonging to Europe. The aim should be to create a transnational "space".... This should help policy makers to stay in touch with European public opinion' (European Commission, 2001: 3.1). This transnational space is meant to create a conducive environment, not only for the fully functioning democratic principles, but also for facilitating the supranational/post-national European identity. The rejection of cultural/national identity should correspond to democratic deficit reduction, and consequently result in a Europe-wide identity, which is conveniently summed up in a set of normative values that underpin European political culture.

Europe and religion

Arguably a degree of convergence between ordinary European citizens on the one hand, and the EU institutions and the intellectual class on the other, is taking place regarding the attitude towards, and the formation of, common Europeanness. This convergence, according to Antonsich and McCormick, tends to find its focus in resentment against certain characteristics in American values and the conduct of its foreign policy, which for all its purposes might be short-lived and even misleading. A more substantial objection to the conclusions brought by Antonsich and McCormick (as well as to those of Manners, Sjursen, Mitzen, Fossum and Diez) relates to the fact that the EU is essentially an economic club that gradually expanded into the areas of social policy, but has no competence in the religious affairs of member states. As such it can offer political identity, based on secular values, to European citizens, which, good though it may be, nevertheless holds limited attraction for a continent that has not only a rich religious heritage, but is also a dynamic and diverse religious actor in current social and political spheres.

The argument here is that the commonly held perception that the EU functions as a secular construct is somewhat inaccurate. On closer inspection it is undeniable that religion, in its various forms, expressions and intensity, is a substantial part of the contemporary politics of its member states and the EU's integration process (Madeley et al., 2009; Foret, 2009; Willaime, 2009; Doe, 2009; Bull, 2009).

This is a development that some of in the academic community in EU studies are willing to admit to and engage with, a problem aptly addressed by Jytte Klausen, who maintains that '[t]he resurgence of combative religion in European politics has put social scientists in a quandary' (2009: 290). This point is even more salient in view of the fact that the EU institutions have recognised the link between the democratic deficit reduction and European identity on the one hand, and religious political mobilisation on the other. Religious political mobilisation is active among many in European civil society and, as such, it is a credible factor in the legitimisation process of the EU. The Vatican may perhaps serve as the supreme example of this, because it 'encouraged a federalist vision of Europe, becoming extremely active during the pontificate of John Paul II' (Madeley and Leustean, 2009: 12; also Kratochvil and Dolezal, 2010; also Chelini-Pont, 2009).

The constructivist framework assumes that the image of a supranational and cosmopolitan Europe (Manners, 2006a: 38–41) that is projected to a global society is a sufficient European identity indicator. However, this framework needs to enlarge and allow a more substantial debate about the reasons why religion was persistently marginalised, or rendered a superfluous actor, in the EU's evolution. Outside of dominant discourse (of the secularised political and academic establishment of the EU) it is quite clear that religion is reasserting itself as a major factor in the construction of contemporary European identity (Laudrup, 2009), which is, arguably, going to impact on the EU's political and social dynamics, as well as on its foreign policy. The resistance to recognising that religion has a substantial normative and political input into the national politics, as well as into the politics of the EU, will weaken as more scholarly attention is afforded to this particular normative strand of EU studies. Even Manners, who argues the case for internal sufficiency and external applicability of the EU's normative values and principles, concedes that they are not immutable (2007: 187 and 2006: 129). Given that those values, good though they may be in themselves, do not hold much attraction for a section of the European population that anchors its identity in religious beliefs, hence the EU's cosmopolitanism might prove inadequate in building a unified European identity.

Cosmopolitanism rejects the existence of the 'Other' as the basis for its identity. National or cultural identities, on the other hand, are always characterised by comparison to, protection from, and disagreement with the 'Other'. In the light of the EU's commitment to the protection of religious diversity (Carrera and Parkin, 2010: 7), two issues seem to arise: firstly, whether Europe's secular mindset cares to acknowledge that the existence of the 'Other' is almost all of the time conceived in a religious context; and secondly, how will the EU deal with the contradictions stemming from full commitment to both free speech and religious expression, as well as the potential tensions arising from competing national rights given to religion and the EU Human Rights Charter? The protection of religious diversity, which is a part and parcel of the western multicultural paradigm (Blake, 2006), reflects very much a desire for a Europe that is defined by multiple identities (Challand, 2009: 66). This in itself presents no problem since Europeans are free to choose one or more identities. The dilemma is rather to what extent religion in general, and which faith in particular, is going to challenge, and even change, some of Europe's normative secular assumptions. In particular the interplay of the religious demands from Christianity, Catholicism and Islam within the EU's political sphere that is guided and driven by secular principles is an issue that scholars only recently deemed important enough to debate (Dolezal and Kratochvil, 2010; Dolezal et al., 2010; Klausen, 2009; Laurence, 2009; Silvestri, 2009, 2007 and 2005; Van der Brug et al., 2009; Hill, 2009; Minkenberg, 2009; Chelini-Pont, 2009).

Laudrup (2009) and Foret (2009) both have a highly pragmatic view of religion in relation to the construction of Europe's identity within the normative secular values. Laudrup in particular argues the case for a 'civil' religion based on Rousseau's concept of the good citizen and Durkheim's concept of religion as a unifying factor (2009: 51). Even though at the risk of her dual conceptualisation of a civil religion being perceived as contradictory, since Rousseau's top-down and Durkheim's bottom-up approaches are at opposite ends, she claims nevertheless that both are ideal in terms of the quality of their propositions, as well as their applicability in creating a successful framework for the purpose of building a European civil religion (2009: 56). Ideally, Laudrup argues, the post-national civil religion that should be promoted in the classrooms throughout Europe would eventually incorporate and promote tolerance as the highest religious virtue in a religiously diverse Europe, and it would be firmly embedded in the European citizenship that holds human rights as the supreme component (2009: 60). Given the complexities of Europe's religious history and contemporary developments, one could argue that Laudrup's argument for a European consensus is possibly over-rated given that people's perceptions and identities are equally formed in the private sphere. From the secular worldview, the temptation to view religion in a Durkheimian perspective as a moral education, as Laudrup does, is logical since its worth could be graded purely in a functional way, but it remains to be seen whether such marginalisation of culturally defined religion can preserve Europe's secular character. Foret and Schlesinger hold a very similar view, questioning whether religion can play a constructive role in 'the legitimation of the EU by shaping a public sphere and a collective identity and constituting "Europeanness" at a supranational level' (2006: 60). This is another challenge for the EU since the union does not have explicit legal competence in the sphere of religion and faith communities in member states, so it has to rely on both formal and informal policy initiatives in the fields of citizenship and fundamental rights, non-discrimination, immigration and integration, and social cohesion in order to engage and understand religion at the policy level of the Commission (Carrera and Parkin, 2010: 4–30). Norman Doe similarly lists eight key principles that the EU could use as a legislative instrument in dealing with religious issues, which could potentially become a 'Common Law' on religion (2009: 148–57).

Christianity in a multireligious Europe

Part of the problem, Foret and Schlesinger maintain, stems directly from the ascribed place of religion in the constitutional process. If this process – being highly symbolic and powerful in imagery – tries to relegate the religious role purely as functional, it will be misguided, since religion through its engagement with the supernatural offers meaning to life (2006: 62–4). In a sense, Foret argues, the problem that the EU faces with regard to religion is a familiar pattern that presents 'a structural difficulty in combining its functionalist requirements with traditional normative allegiances' (2009: 37). Given this fact and the decline of religious traditional function, Foret and Schlesinger argue that Christianity should be acknowledged as an essential part of the collective European memory (2009: 63–4). In addition to the collective memory, the moral consensus that derived from the past horrors of the European experience should constitute also the basis of the European identity, despite the problems associated with such reasoning, such as, for example, the Holocaust denial that is being voiced more brazenly in this decade than ever before (2009: 69; also Butt, 2009).

Within this context, Foret and Schlesinger assess the role of the Catholic Church and its attempt to become a substantial actor in the political decision-making in the EU. By pointing out de-institutionalisation of the religious field and privatisation of religion in the secular European context, they claim that Christianity is asserting its specific role in decision making as a power that sustains European political order from within. Such functional re-orientation, Foret maintains, is not perceived as Christian pragmatism since the constitutive values of democracy and human rights are inherently Christian conceptions of humanity (2009: 73–4). However, given that pluralism is the essence of democracy, the Catholic approach to this challenge is twofold – while the bishops lobby the European institutions and engage in inter-faith/ ecumenical dialogues, they are at the same time maintaining its confessional specificity (sole possessor of the truth) vigorously through the Vatican's inter-governmental approach (ibid.).

The Catholic assertion of the (multifaith) religious leadership in Europe, which incorporates its monopoly of the historical interpretation of Christianity in Europe, is not accepted uniformly, particularly from the ranks of Protestant hierarchy and clergy. Apart from a rapid rise in Pentecostalism (Clark, 2007), Evangelicalism in particular is reasserting itself in Europe, most surprisingly in France, a country where secularism is thought to be 'safe' from religion (Marquand, 2012; Fath, 2005), and it is not willing to give up the political space solely to the Catholic Church. Likewise in Britain 'the lukewarm are falling away, leaving the pews to the more fervent', claims *The Economist*, indicating the corresponding steady rise of Evangelicalism (in all its varieties) and the loss of traditional Anglican authority among its adherents (2012). Moreover, the European Evangelical Alliance (EEA) office in Brussels represents 15 million Evangelicals from 35 countries, whose activism is not confined purely to the spiritual/missionary issue, but involves advocacy regarding humanitarian and political issues, such as human trafficking and freedom of speech respectively (EEA, About).

Given the fact that religious memory is defined by tradition, it has the potential, as Foret and Schlesinger rightly observe, to be an obstacle in constructing a European identity (2006: 76). In addition to the collective memories of Protestant and Catholic masses that stand in the way of a single Christian identity, it is also the contested relationship between Church and State, formed in distinct Protestant and Catholic theological and historical frameworks, that could prove problematic for the institutionalisation of Christianity in the EU. Fraser et al. explain how the Protestant belief of the separation of Church and State determines a fragmented and disunited attitude to European integration (2001: 207). To this end it is rather interesting that Denmark, Britain and Sweden, countries thought of traditionally as Protestant, still retain their national currencies. Minkenberg, similarly to Frazer et al., claims that Protestant churches tend to be rather Euro-sceptic, while Catholic citizens, who, under a coherent spiritual leadership with a clear political agenda, strongly support integration, and are more willing to hold onto a single European cultural identity (2009: 1200–5). However, Minkenberg's conclusions are not quite as polarised, but they rather minimise the Euro-scepticism of countries defined largely by Protestantism, while singling out 'fundamentalist groups [that] stray from the big group of pro-integrationists' (2007: 1207). That factor alone explains why the secular European elites have good working relations with the Catholic Church, but to what extent the Catholic Church will exert its political leverage in years to come is a matter for close observation.

Given the internal-denominational competing interests with regards to historical narrative and contemporary spiritual and political space, it seems that Christianity in Europe is relegated largely to Europe's symbolic politics, particularly when religion is utilised as one among other paradigms 'in the reformulation of national identities in order to incorporate a supranational dimension' (Foret, 2009: 47). Foret illustrates how such a pragmatic inclusion of Christianity could potentially influence the normative discourse on public issues by drawing attention to the stance of the Polish Catholic Church regarding its role in European integration, where the 'exchange of gifts' theory works both ways as

'Europe brings modernity and technical progress to Poland [while] Poland is able to rejuvenate a materialist and disenchanted Europe...' (2009: 40). He argues that the strictly consultative role of the churches allocated by the Commission corresponds to the realities in European societies. One of the consequences of the de-institutionalisation of religion across Europe is that social factors are more decisive than spiritual in forming public opinion, and as such, Foret concludes, it influences greater convergence of religious and secular normative discourses (2009: 44–5 and 47).

There is certainly no objection to the analysis made by Laudrup, Foret and Schlesinger that religion could be utilised to weaken national identity and foster the construction of a supranational/post-national identity. For the EU's policy makers, who search for ways which would effectively facilitate Europe-wide public participation in the public sphere and give much needed legitimacy to the continually evolving European project, it is imperative that they recognise religion as a constitutive element of that legitimacy. The objection is rather directed at the assumption that faith, and in this case Christianity (with all the shades of its denominational spectrum), will willingly remain in a subordinate normative position to Europe's secular foundation. The very claims of the secular foundations to the EU are challenged not only by Catholic scholars, politicians and clergy, but by the range of other scholars who object to a selective academic memory of Europe's integration. Fraser et al. are surprised by such neglect since religion, as one of the most vital cultural elements, has 'shaped modern European politics in crucial ways' (2001: 192; also Sutherland, 2008). Leustean and Madeley explain the indispensable role of the Christian Democratic network, formed in the late 1940s, in the launch of the European integration project (2009: 4), while Casanova explains sanctioning of the Christian Democratic project by the Vatican (2006: 66). Likewise, Luxmore argues for the recognition of Christianity in the EU, given the influence of Christian concepts, such as subsidiarity, popular sovereignty, and the common good, that was evident in the founding of the ECSC in 1952 and in the Treaty of Rome in 1957 (2005: 6).

As a matter of history, Christian Democratic parties were certainly not internally homogenous, since their members often quarrelled over the national priorities and policies, but on a broader level they perpetuated the cross-national support for Europe's unification (Riso,

2009). In political terms, this meant that Christian Democrats had to combine their staunch anticommunism with greater economic interdependence (Riso, 2009: 110), while spiritually they could claim that their support for a supranational Europe is a Christian virtue, since the nation state at its core is essentially a rejection of the heart of Christianity (Sutherland, 2008: 3). The Vatican's support for the Christian Democrat political network and its federalist doctrine was essential in many ways and it was not premised exclusively on moral reasoning (as perceived from the Catholic socio-theological criteria). It also incorporated the Vatican's political goals. Good examples date back to the 1920s when rival nationalisms preconditioned Europe for a war, as well as after the war when the virulent atheism of a communist dogma swept through Eastern Europe (Chelini-Pont, 2009: 132–7). 'Catholicism', argues Frazer, 'drawing on the experience of the High Middle Ages, has sought the unity of Christendom under the Pope's spiritual (and, in the past, temporal) leadership' (2001: 193). Quite clearly, the Catholic Church's inherent distaste of the Westphalian nation state, which effectively ended its stronghold on political power, is at the heart of the Vatican's endorsement and active support for the EU's unification strategy.

It is highly unlikely that the Catholic Church will ever return to its political monopoly of the Middle Ages, and it is debatable whether it entertains such aspirations. However, what is increasingly clear is the aspiration of the Catholic Church, as expressed in the opinion of John Paul II, that Europe must return to its pre-modern culture and cultivate its democracy 'under the guardianship of Christian definitions which have been authenticated by the Roman moral authority' (Chelini-Pont, 2009: 142). Given the political clout of the Vatican, a high level of theological and missional uniformity among its clergy, centralised power base, and centuries of diplomatic experience, it is not difficult to comprehend why the Catholic Church remains the greatest contender for moral leadership in Europe, even though such aspirations will always be resisted by other religious communities in Europe at some level, not only Christian Orthodox or Protestant, but Islamic too.

Islam in a multireligious Europe

While European Muslims have different issues regarding the inclusion of their faith in the political process, they too insist that their religion gives Europe its soul, and they too share memories with Christians of Europe and contend for their European past (Al-Azmeh and Fokas, 2007; Massignon, 2007: 144–5). Aside from the debates relating to the Crusades and the Ottoman Empire, the often debated issue tends to revolve around 'the golden age' of an Islamic rule in Europe between 711 and 1492 AD in al-Andalus (what constitutes today parts of Spain, Portugal and France). The debate ranges from historical interpretations of a benign and tolerant treatment of religious minorities under Islamic rule (Rauf, 2004), to a firm denial that such tolerance existed due to the superiority complex that is inherent in Islam (Fernandez-Morera, 2006; Carson, 2005).

Debates such as these illustrate the diverse attitudes towards Islam, not least because freedom of religion and expression ensures that all versions of Islam are visible in Europe's societies. At one end of the spectrum there is a Sufi version, whose followers, and some academics, claim it is a peaceful and mystical strand of Islam that rejects violence (Mirbagheri, 2012), but at the other end there is a radical Islam that presents a violent face of Islam, so much so that many Muslims describe it as a gross distortion of their faith. The radicalisation that took hold in European societies, particularly in Britain (Phillips, 2006: 1–18), and periodic terrorist activities, which were exacerbated at the time of the Bosnian civil war in the early 1990s (Kohlman, 2004: 15–98), provoke different responses in politics, media and intelligentsia. It is difficult to draw precise and correct conclusions regarding the perceptions about Muslims and their faith in Europe, but there seems to be a polarised opinion about exactly what is to be done with an increasingly assertive and confident Islam in European societies. There exists, according to Laquer 'a curious dichotomy between attitudes of the intelligentsia on the one hand and the political class as well as the majority of the population on the other' (2004: 167; also Pipes, 2005). Shepherd asserts that Muslim political culture is hardwired into the Islamist and globalised discourse where 'a large proportion of Muslims in Europe is being pump-primed with prejudices about Western villainy and Muslim victimhood which at the fringes can then lead to violent outcomes' (2009: 186). Roberson holds a different view and claims that part of the problem lies in the fact that the perception of the virulently anti-Western Islamism and its terrorism is projected onto the Muslim societies in Europe (1998: 117). Consequently it generalises the Islamic

threat (ibid.), just as the assumptions about the Muslim homogeneity
and identity are overstated given the fact that Muslim immigration into
Europe happens from a variety of culturally distinct Muslim countries
(1998: 119).

In view of the issue raised earlier about the necessity of 'Other' in the
formation of a unifying identity, the debate about the spiritual and
political equivalence of Christianity and Islam in Europe is inevitable.
The issue of tolerance, or the rejection of the necessity of 'Other' as the
foundational value of the 'unity in diversity' in Europe's commitment to
multiculturalism, is often disputed by scholars and ordinary people
alike. Luxmoore argues that Europe's Christianity 'combines strong
moral values and spiritual aspirations with a concern for the poor and
excluded. It is also the kind of Christianity that can be, and is being,
defended by Jews and Muslims too, who rightly see in the Christian
churches an ally and source of support' (2005: 8). Likewise, Aggestam
and Hill argue the case for a cultural plurality and maintain that,
although the Islamic idea of a symbiosis between religion and politics
presents a challenge to a European identity, it is nevertheless possible to
project a 'European identity ready to listen and treat[ing] others as a
source of insights from which Europe might learn' (2009: 102).
Challand argues for a cosmopolitan approach and claims that
'multireligious Europe ought to be taken seriously' (2009: 76), while
Silvestri emphasises the positive contribution of interfaith initiatives to
European social cohesion and Euro-Med inter-cultural dialogue (2005:
390–9). Massignon likewise adopts the same attitude and endorses the
EU's institutional approach as a useful framework in which 'it is possible
to have alliances in favour of the common good between the major
religious traditions' (2007: 135).

Others question the wisdom of such commitment, often referring to
it as 'Europe's cultural suicide' (Bynum, 2011; Rubenstein, 2009;
Shepherd, 2009; Phillips, 2006; Ye'or, 2005; Trifkovic, 2002). Ye'or
addresses the issue of Europe's Muslim minorities in a wider context of
the EU's Euro-Med inter-cultural dialogue, and documents extensively
the political, economic and cultural agreements between European states
and Islamic countries that are, in her view, nothing short of a betrayal of
European people by their self-hating, guilt-ridden elites, who are
politically naïve and intimidated by Islam (2011 and 2006). Trifkovic
asserts: 'Islam is "non-white", non-European, and non-Christian, which

makes it a natural ally of the ruling Western elites. At the same time, it has an inherent advantage over the tepid ideology of multicultural mediocrity in that it offers Allah in the place of nothing' (2002: 297). Tibi, in the same manner, bemoans Europe's repudiation of its traditional civilisational identity, and claims that European decision makers are incapable of dealing with challenges of an ethno-cultural nature because they refuse to acknowledge the Islamisation of Europe (2009). Similarly, Rubenstein's bleak prediction that the results of a European secular 'social contract' state could ironically lead to 'a European Muslim caliphate in which the fate of the Cathedral of Notre Dame in Paris and St. Paul's in London recapitulates that of Hagia Sophia' (2009: 5), illustrates that European Muslims are still perceived to a degree as the 'Other'.

The overriding reason for such a deeply suspicious attitude towards Islam stems from its relationship to the State. While sovereignty in Ummah[1] is derived from Allah, in western societies it is, of course, upheld by the popular will. In the words of Trifkovic: 'There is Christianity, and there used to be Christendom, but in Islam such a distinction is impossible' (2002: 7). Such a fundamental difference regarding the separation of religion and state inevitably raises the question about the place of Sharia law[2] and democracy in European societies, most importantly the interpretation and implementation of human rights, such as religious apostasy and women's rights. As a matter of history, contends Michael Nazir-Ali, democracy has flourished in countries with a Christian background, whereas many spiritual leaders of Islamic societies 'tend to regard democracy as leading to moral and spiritual laxity – which they also see as being the main cause of social dysfunction in the West' (2006: 132–3; also Lewis, 2004: 3–24).

Other scholars disagree with such deep distrust of Islam and firm delineation of religion and state. '[S]eparation of religious and political systems does not prohibit the formation of partnerships and cooperative arrangements between public agencies and religious organisations', maintains Willaime (2009: 27), while Madeley asserts that European states were never divorced from religion to the same extent as in the America, which incidentally invented the secular state (2009: 286). What some perceive as an insurmountable contradiction between new Europe (whose values are built on the West-centric definition of human rights) and Islam (whose definition of human rights derives from the

teachings of the Sharia law), presents in fact for many in politics and
academia a negligible normative difference when juxtaposed against the
positive functional purpose of the concepts of Islamic Ummah, Catholic
universalism and the post-Westphalian Europe.

On a functional level, it is arguably the confluence of process that
redefines traditional sovereignty – an inherent feature of all Islamist
groups and the EU itself – that conditions the pragmatic stance towards
the growing multifaceted demands of Islam. Normatively, it tends to be
a positive historical interpretation of the relationship between Europe
and Islam that provides an optimistic framework in which to assess
Islam and its role in a multireligious Europe. Given that the Islamic
contribution to Europe's scientific, cultural and social domain was quite
significant, as Tariq Ramadan claims, then the notion about the
Christian past of Europe is false: 'Europe must learn to reconcile itself
with the diversity of its past in order to master the imperative pluralism
of its future' (2006). A number of academics, such as John Esposito, John
Voll, Scott Thomas, Colin Chapman, Stephen Haseler, etc., would find it
difficult to disagree with Ramadan. The Western world, argue Esposito
and Voll, should seize the opportunity and engage with the Muslim
voices of inter-civilisational dialogue in view of the fact that 'an
important type of Muslim leader-intellectual became prominent, laying
a significant role in Muslim reconceptualisations of religion and
international relations' (2000: 638).

Arguably, being a contender for political influence does not necessarily
reflect a strategy for supremacy, but rather a power-sharing position in a
Europe whose political culture is embedded in a secular framework, but it
seeks nonetheless to accommodate and integrate into its political
participatory system a large segment of the European populace that
rejects secular tenets. The past history is a testament that neither Islam
nor Christianity taught that religion should remain private, but actively
sought to influence the political processes in favour of their own
worldview, and it is unlikely that in current European politics either
religion will concede that space to secular elites. Regarding specifically
European integration, it is likely that the fight for the preservation and
continuation of the nation state will come from Protestant denominations
(specifically the fundamentalist strand), but Catholic understanding of the
universal catholic faith and its yearning for a pre-Westphalian Europe will
no doubt continue to be a positive contribution to a Euro-federalist

agenda. In this regard, the Islamic Ummah, which affirms the redundancy of territorial borders, is also compatible to a Catholic position. Therefore it is not surprising that the Catholic Church is keen on inter-faith dialogue that fosters greater understanding and tolerance between Christianity and Islam. Luxmoore illustrates this by quoting from an 'Open Letter to Dutch Society' written by the Roman Catholic bishops: 'Far from feeling opposed to Islam, the Catholic Church shares the experience of being religious in a secularising society and the conviction that everything is given us by God' (2005: 8). Undoubtedly, the inter-faith agenda of Muslim and Catholic clerical authorities will determine internal European cohesion to a large degree. Whether this agenda has its motives in noble principles and a genuine love of God and neighbour, or whether it stems from the competition to assert moral leadership, will arguably provide a defining framework of a new European identity in a multicultural and multifaith Europe.

Religious lobby groups in Brussels

Of course, the cohesion issue is not solely confined to the relationship between traditional denominations, and/or between traditional churches and Islam. Aside from the fact that secularisation has greatly undermined the role of the churches in European societies, and demography consistently indicates a rise in Muslim population through immigration, it is also the process of globalisation in the media and commercialisation of spirituality that has facilitated the rapid growth in alternative belief systems. Kenneth Houston comments on the EU's proactive approach regarding religion and explains that

> [t]he initial praxis of the provision for structured dialogue with the EU has symbolically concentrated on 'world' faiths, namely Judaism, Christianity, Islam and Buddhism. . . A significant number of Europeans do not subscribe to an authoritative interpretation of transcendence, as exemplified by the monotheistic or dharmic religions, and instead embrace various spiritualities and personal creeds (2009: 215).

Houston's objections to the Commission's relationship with conventional religious representations illuminates an area where a lot more research needs to be done in order to draw a more accurate picture about the religious kaleidoscope in Europe. From both structural and normative grading criteria an important question relates to the status of religious interest representations, i.e. whether some NRMs constitute a conventional fringe, a cult, a sect, or whether they are even religious. The conundrum that sociologists are faced with is very well explained by Silvio Ferrari, whose work on the NRMs highlights the diverse state policies across the EU towards the NRMs, with France being the most stringent, and Germany relatively relaxed (2006: 13–19). This in turn raises the issue of the political participation of (and demands on the authorities by) the NRMs in Europe if definition of the NRMs and legal entitlement varies so greatly from country to country. Likewise Liliana Mihut explains the challenge for the EU given the various forms of church–state relationship in member states: '[I]n France the separation is clear, based on the constitutional provisions, in Germany tax is collected by the public authorities, and in Belgium the churches, as well as the humanist organisations are financially supported by the state' (2011: 76), while Effie Focas elaborates on the divergent attitudes towards Islam at the national levels (2011: 7–10).

Martin Steven's (2009) enquiry is focused on the functional capacity and adaptability of religious interests, rather than their normative significance, whereby the religious institutions, which traditionally operate and seek influence in a national setting, organise themselves competently into faith-based lobbying groups that have to operate increasingly on a supranational level. As a consequence of the supranational character of the EU, Steven claims, a pattern is emerging that is

> eclipsing the older European model of a group of homogenous nation states where one official religion or church is dominant in each autonomous territory. Brussels is increasingly providing a focus for churches to lobby decision makers for their own ends, becoming one interest group among many, albeit one with potentially substantial influence (2009: 190).

An interesting fact, however, is that the main religious organisations have not registered themselves in the Commission's Register of Interest Representatives due to the fact that most have an invitation from the Commission to dialogue about political and social issues, while the EP has a strict accreditation system. 'No doubt', maintains Mihut, 'new developments could occur if the Commission and Parliament will succeed in their work towards a common register and code of conduct for lobbyists' (2011: 79).

Aside from the fact that there remains substantial ambiguity about exactly how religious lobby groups fit into the EU's fluid institutional set up, there is also an objection to the lack of normative clarity of religious lobby groups, which is related to the debate about religious interest representations and European identity/the EU's democratic deficit. In view of the complexities resulting from the impact that religion makes on social, moral, legal and political aspects in Europe, Houston is sceptical about the EU's approach to the religious communities: 'The potential of religious groups to become torchbearers of integration, and their potential to "Europeanise" broader public opinion, is dubious' (2009: 217). Sabrina Pastorelli on the other hand takes a different view due to the research done on the criteria that qualify a religious movement to be represented at the EU level. She explains how the Bureau of European Policy Advisors (BEPA) was given the authority in the early 1990s to oversee the dialogue between the religious groups and the Commission. The fact that BEPA does not make distinctions between religion, sect or cult does not undermine, she argues, the legitimacy of that process, which was formalised in the White Paper on European Governance (2009: 196). On the contrary, the notion of the EU governance in the paper is precisely designed to allow for a significant contribution from all religions and NRMs; it is meant to operate as a pluralist system in which cohesion is upheld through the equality of opportunity and as such it could provide a unified policy towards NRMs if implemented in all member states (2009: 201).

Pastorelli's remark about the significant contribution of all religions to the European governance raises the question of how precisely do the religious lobby groups make positive contributions towards the EU's democratic character. While the increased legislative role of the EP caused a massive expansion in lobby activity in Brussels between 1994 and 2005 and provided legitimacy for European integration, 'it also has put a strain on the openness and transparency of EU policy-making, and pressure for the creation of rules and regulation of interest representation' (Coen, 2007: 4). This was particularly salient in the beginning of the 2000s when the gradual closing down of direct access to the Commission (a result of the 'interest overload') affected some firms and groups negatively, while others obtained the status of 'insiders' through their self-styled role of European identity-builders (Coen, 2007: 7; also Greenwood, 1998). Consequently, even though a level of accountability was set through the Commission's Green Paper 'European Transparency Initiative' in 2006, the most significant development in Brussels over the last two decades has been the emergence of what Coen calls elite pluralism (2007: 9; also Coen and Richardson, 2009: 347; also Woll, 2006: 459). Houston likewise argues that special provision for a structured dialogue between the EU institutions and Conference of European Churches (CEC) and the Commission of the Bishops' Conferences of the European Community (COMECE) is in essence an example of 'elite-driven interaction' (2009: 218).

Such critical appraisal is understandable in view of the fact that these religious representations have ambitious aims, clearly outlined in the Commission's document:

> The work of COMECE follows three main objectives: to monitor and analyse the political process of the European Union, to inform and raise awareness in both the Church and society of the development of EU policy and legislation, and to promote reflection based on the Church's social teaching on the challenges facing a united Europe. The Church and Society Commission (CSC) is one of the commissions of the Conference of European Churches (CEC). The CSC links CEC's some 125 member churches from all over Europe and its associated organisations with the European Union's institutions, the Council of Europe, the OSCE, NATO and the UN (on European matters). Its task is to help the churches study church and society questions from a theological social-ethical perspective, especially those with a European dimension, and to represent the member churches of CEC in their relations with political institutions working in Europe (European Commission, 2006).

In 2003 CEC and COMECE strongly supported the inclusion of a statement in the Preamble of Europe's Constitution that Europe's values were rooted in Christianity, which was, unsurprisingly, resisted by the European Humanist Federation (EHF). According to Mihut, 'there were sustained lobbying campaigns developed by both parts... [N]umerous memorandums, statements, papers, as well as petitions, letters and press releases were issued, addressed to the EU institutions, to the member state governments or to the general public' (2010: 78). The eventual compromise was reflected in Article 17 that contains affirmation of both the religious and humanist roots of European values, signifying that to this end the EU seeks to have informal and structured dialogue with churches, but also with humanists, atheists, agnostics and freemasons (Massignon, 2003; also Massignon, 2010).

The Commission's task of incorporating religious concerns into the EU's political process, and particularly to address social cohesion in Europe, is not only exemplified by its formalised dialogue with COMECE and CEC, but also by its protracted dialogue with the key leaders from Muslim communities across Europe. The inter-cultural dialogue, which was defined initially by the Barcelona Declaration, affected also the internal relationship between the EU and the Muslim communities. One of the EU's concerns about European Muslims was how successful their integration was into European societies, an issue that was placed under the domain of the Forward Studies Unit (FSU), established in 1992 by the then President of the Commission Jacques Delors (Silvestri, 2009: 1217–9). The FSU initiated a range of dialogues with the faith communities, of which the 'Soul for Europe' in 1994 was the most significant programme that provided a forum for faith communities (including Muslim representatives), the Commission and the EP to reflect on religious and philosophical convictions that could impact Europe's future (Silvestri, 2009: 1218; Massignon, 2007: 133–5). Clearly, in view of the fact that the EU is a self-proclaimed normative power and that its institutional progression is embedded in the principle of consensus, it is only logical that its handling of competing religious interests is designed in a framework that rejects a 'clash of civilisations' paradigm. In the words of Massignon:

[T]he European Union is functioning as a cognitive and normative constraint for member states. Access to these forums entails an opportunity for Muslims to place their local and national endeavors in a wider environment. The variety of Muslim actors who are invited to attend these forums can lead to confrontations between the champions of the various Islamic trends, who otherwise would not have the opportunity to meet. Therefore, more than a role of legal regulation, the European Commission is playing, for the time being, the role of a mediator which facilitates interfaith and inter-religious meetings (Massignon, 2007: 146).

Massignon discusses at length the process of mobilisation of Muslim organisations, specifically the communication with the Muslim Council of Cooperation in Europe (CMCE), which was created in 1996 and was considered by the Commission to be an umbrella of moderate groups (Massignon, 2007: 129). However, Massignon goes on, the Commission also closely works with the Forum of European Muslim Youth and Student Organisations (FEMYSO), the European Council for Fatwa and Research (ECFR), the Federation of Islamic Organisations in Europe (FIOE), known also as the Union of Islamic Organisations in Europe (UIOE) which 'represent an Islam often closer to the Muslim Brotherhood' (2007: 130–1). Silvestri also provides a detailed account of the evolution of Muslim mobilisation at the level of the Commission and in the EP (2009: 1221–9), which is a complex process given the anti-hierarchical nature of, and diversity of groups within, Islam (2007: 21). Nonetheless, she claims, the work of the Muslim lobby groups at the EU level has so far been very effective, so much so that Islamic movements, as well as countries that have not put in place appropriate structures for the accommodation of Islam, could benefit from the EU's approach (2009: 1229; also Parker, 2007: 31).

In her more recent work Silvestri details the organisation and lobbying of what she describes as moderate Islamist groups in Europe: 'Most Islamist movements that are present in Europe began as diaspora groups organised by exiles and political refugees concerned with reforming their home countries, or from regions of the world that are experiencing autocracy, corruption and lack of freedoms' (2010: 167). In this respect, perhaps surprisingly, the ECI has more in common with these groups since it is not part of any denominational organisations, i.e. COMECE, CEC or EEA (even though it has its own network), which is similar to an organisational mode in Muslim representations that is defined by the absence of clear hierarchical structure. Secondly, given the contentious narratives about the Israeli–Palestinian conflict among Christian Zionists and Islamists, it becomes clear why Israel would occupy a prominent place in both groups' lobby activity, unlike other

Christian lobby groups. An area where the ECI clearly opposes Islamist groups relates to the common ground of inter-faith compromise and dialogue between Islamist groups and Christian organisations, based on a concern about the linkage between the agenda of Islamist lobby groups in Brussels and the effects upon European societies. The well-organised networks of Muslim lobby groups are best illustrated by FIOE, which manages to coordinate with high efficiency national Islamist movements in Europe since 2003 (Silvestri, 2010: 172). On a general level FIOE promotes a positive image of Islam, strives for recognition of Islam as an official religion in Europe, and encourages political participation of Muslims in all member states, but on a specific level it advocates on issues that relate to Muslim communities on a national level, such as the controversy surrounding the 'Hijab issue' in France (Silvestri, 2010: 172–6).

Conclusion

This chapter elaborated on the normative significance and political implications of the rise of religion in Europe. The initial section discussed the challenges that the EU has to deal with in its foreign policy due to its high functional institutional segmentation and frequent inconsistency in its dealings in the Middle East due to the divergent national foreign policies. Related to the CFSP is the applicability of the EU's values and principles since some foreign policy issues, particularly those in the Middle East, often require 'hard power' solutions, hence the debate about the contradictions in a self-proclaimed normative power EU that rejects the militarisation of union. The problems of the 'domestic' dimension of the EU's normative values – how they are utilised in a constructivist framework for a new European identity, but are failing largely to Europeanise Europe's people – was developed in the third section of the chapter. Even the outbreak of anti-American sentiments in 2003, which curiously provided a platform from which the Euro-federalists could claim that the EU has become a part of Europe's multiple identities, is failing to generate a long-lasting feeling of belonging to Europe.

The objection to the EU's normative values, the argument stated, is in their limited attraction. They provide only a political identity, which for a secular European mindset that rejects militarism and affirms a new multidimensional European identity in a post-Wesphalian framework, is sufficient in its substance and aims. However, for a large section of the European population, which affirms the Divine as a basic pillar of its identity, and believes that spirituality is both private and public, the values on which the EU is built will fail to inspire a sense of belonging, connection, loyalty and duty. Also, the objection to scholars who allow a certain amount of religious normative inclusion into Europe's identity construction is directed at the assumption that faith, mostly Christian (with all the shades of its denominational spectrum), will willingly remain in a subordinate normative position within Europe's secular framework. Not only are the claims to the secular foundations of the EU challenged by Catholic scholars, politicians and clergy, but an additional challenge that Europe's secular establishment has to contend with is a Muslim argument for Europe's Islamic past and Europe's present need of an 'Islamic soul'. Islam's active presence in Europe's politics, developed in section 6 of the chapter, is undeniable, and debates about Islam's role in the construction of Europe's contemporary identity runs parallel to the 'Christian' argument, which is essentially that religion, i.e. Islam, is a constitutive element of that process.

The last section of this chapter discussed the presence of religious lobby groups in Brussels in order to exemplify how the religious actor carves its political space in a new Europe, but also to point out the limited research that has been conducted so far into the religious interest representations at the supranational level. By recognising potentially a constructive role of religious representations in reducing the democratic deficit, the EU has claimed a degree of legitimacy for itself, but in the process it has also created an institutionally favourable environment for religious lobby groups to pursue their agenda more effectively than in a national setting. This could certainly be argued for Catholic and Muslim lobby groups, since Catholic and Islamic dislike of the nation state is compatible with the European integrationist agenda. For European Christian Zionists, as will be shown in Chapters 4 and 5 the issue is not as straightforward since all argue for Israel's absolute right to exist as a nation state, but on the issue of European integration, some find the Brussels scene an unwanted necessity, while others are not so averse. In addition, while Catholic and Islamic groups might, arguably, seek ways to further the inter-faith agenda, Christian Zionists are, for theological reasons, opposed to such endeavours, especially in view of the fact that

Christian Zionist lobbying competes against the Muslim narrative of the Israeli–Palestinian conflict.

Although the research into the religious lobby groups conducted so far certainly reveals an additional insight into the lobby culture in Brussels, it is nevertheless still very modest compared to the extensive research that has been done on the non-religious NGOs and especially business interests. Perhaps this is generally reflective of the fact that NGOs arrived late on the Brussels scene, lacking organisational competence and with limited funds (Karr, 2006: 152), but to what extent this assessment is applicable specifically to religious interest representations is a matter for further research. Research on Christian traditional denominational representation and the Islamic lobby groups currently available contains credible findings from which firm conclusions can be drawn regarding the beneficial dynamics between religious lobby groups and the EU institutions in terms of the concessions to demands and political legitimacy respectively. The literature on religious lobby groups however can be substantiated further with an in-depth research on other denominational groups that are not under the umbrella of the already researched Christian and Islamic organisations, as well as on groups from other conventional religions and on the NRMs.

As a phenomenon that is embedded in a wider normative shift, the proliferation of religious lobby groups in Brussels is bound to have far-reaching political implications. Arguably, the religious lobby groups that are agitating for the policies that could have either direct or indirect impact on the Middle East generally, and the Israeli–Palestinian conflict specifically, should be of considerable interest to scholars of the EU's foreign policy, since the EU's cultural, economic and political ties with the Middle East are more profound than with any other region.

CHAPTER 2

EU–ISRAEL RELATIONS IN CONTEXT

Whenever religious organisations cause a stir in the media or make specific political demands, it is merely an indication that religion has always been, and remains, an important actor in international politics. Like so many other religious movements Christian Zionism too is a modern phenomenon that is on the margins of politics, but at times it occupies the centre of the political process long enough to make an impact, and contemporary European Christian Zionism, for that matter, aims for nothing less. In terms of its character and functioning, European Christian Zionism is a movement that is defined by its own core beliefs and the political, social and religious context in which it exists. Therefore in order to understand current Christian Zionist advocacy in the EU this chapter is structured in a way that explains the wider normative and political context in which it operates, as well as its specific religious beliefs and political activism.

Initially the chapter explains the EU's European Neighbourhood Policy (ENP) as its foreign policy instrument in the Middle East. This is important, firstly, because Christian Zionists in Europe conduct advocacy on a national as well as on the supranational level, and aim to provide an input into the existing good bilateral relations with Israel, as well as to establish a pro-Israel lobby in countries that are less friendly to the Jewish state. Secondly, the ENP is interpreted (and criticised) by European Christian Zionists from the standpoint of the EU's normative values and principles, with the issue of Islamism deemed particularly important, as Christian Zionists do not distinguish it from political Islam, and see it inevitably as a threat to Europe and Israel. Given the EU's inconsistent attitude towards the Islamist groups in the Middle East, particularly Hamas and Hezbollah, and the Christian Zionists' uncompromising stance towards Islamists, the section also discusses a dilemma that the issue of Islamism poses to the EU's policy makers.

The chapter goes on to address the EU's normative dimension of its relationship with Israel, which includes the issue of Islamism, the principle of conditionality, and the persistent problem of antisemitism. The issue of antisemitism needs to be discussed because the fight against antisemitism is one of the key defining features of European Christian Zionism, and it is a crucial part of the ECI's offensive lobby strategy that is discussed later in Chapter 5. The third section in this chapter provides an overview of the peace process and the role of the Quartet, which is also important to understand as the Christian Zionist offensive strategy is mostly focused on issues relating to the peace process. Section 4 of the chapter explains a more positive dimension of the EU-Israel relations, namely economic cooperation, since this too is an area which the Christian Zionist lobby uses in its defensive strategy – in Brussels to promote un upgrade in the association agreement, and in Britain to fight against the Boycott, Divestment and Sanctions (BDS) Campaign.

Current German and British relations with Israel are included in this chapter since the two countries affect the EU's attitude and policy towards Israel to a large degree. Correspondingly, German and British Christian pro-Israel advocacy constitute the two most effective strands of the ECI, which is in some ways a continuation of the attitudes from the past, where, as a matter of history, Christian Zionism in both countries preceded American Christian Zionism, and, arguably, contributed to the re-establishment of the Jewish state. The differences in British and German political culture, their unique relationship with Israel, different lobbying strategies and normative contexts, are (among other national Christian Zionist expressions) indispensable elements that make up the ECI, whose overall effectiveness depends heavily on a national input. The chapter therefore ends with a section that introduces the ECI – it explains the normative (spiritual, political and moral) framework of European Christian Zionism, followed by an explanation of the ECI's

internal structure, and a brief description of the ECI's lobby strategy.
As such it is an overview of Chapters 3, 4 and 5.

The European Neighbourhood Policy (ENP) and the challenge of Islamism

From the time of its inception, the European Mediterranean Policy
(EMP), an instrument consisting of the political and security (peace and
stability), economic (shared prosperity), and social/cultural (civil society
interaction) aspects, was assumed to be sufficient in projecting the EU's
foreign policy in the region (Miller and Mishrif, 2005; Intercultural
Dialogue, 1999). However, in the aftermath of 11 September 2001 it
became apparent that the weaknesses of the EMP demanded further
changes in the CFSP, which consequently took place in the form of the
ENP. As an instrument that essentially complemented the comprehensive structure of the EMP, the ENP was designed to operate on an
individual basis for each country in the Mediterranean, and as such
generate more effectively greater and faster reforms towards building
democracy and combating terrorism. In addition, it was meant to
reassure Mediterranean countries that European enlargement through
the inclusion of CEEC in the EU did not in any way impede the progress
of the EMP (Ye'or, 2006: 140–2). The results of such deeper
engagement in the Mediterranean region are often criticised for various
reasons, usually emphasising the EU's lack of political leverage to
facilitate a democratic change within the political culture in the region
generally (Asseburg, 2009: 1–7; Youngs, 2006), and the direction of the
peace process specifically (Miller, 2011; Ottolenghi, 2010: 27–35;
Asseburg, 2009: 32–7).

Recent regime changes brought about by the Arab Spring have
significantly altered discourse on the Middle East and have further
polarised political and academic debates about Western attitudes towards
the region. The true extent of the institutional reforms may take years to
emerge across Arab societies, but it may also take a considerable time for
scholars in international politics to evaluate what the Arab Spring means
for academia, particularly how it is likely to impact future normative
discourse, such as that in the studies of the EU and its neighbourhood
policy in the region. In terms of the theoretical implications, Gregory
Gause admits that traditional assumptions that Middle East stability is

attributed to the military-security complex and state control over the economy were wrong, and contends that incompetent implementation of liberal economic policies is a factor that destabilised Arab regimes (Grant, 2011: 2–4). Gause's point about the economic policies is significant in view of the fact that several years before the Arab Spring Miller and Mishrif presented an elaborate discussion related to this particular problem, and maintained that the association agreements between Europe and Arab states, the EU enlargement in 2004, and a fragmented Arab economic system were and are an obstacle to a more equal and beneficial economic relationship (2005: 101–6).

Gause also identifies an emergence of a new pan-Arabism and points out the challenge to academics for current and future explanations of the Middle East (2011: 4–5). Although his analysis is helpful in terms of challenging the traditional realist paradigm that has always sought to explain the Middle East, nonetheless his choice of using a concept of new pan-Arabism fails to identify sufficiently the Islamic element, both religious and political, that played a crucial part in the Arab Spring. Michael Tottem (2012) bemoans that Western policy makers failed to anticipate the Islamist hijacking of the Arab Spring: 'Almost all secular Arab governments have failed spectacularly in the modern era. Radical Islam, as a consequence, looks good on paper to millions', while Reza Aslan explains: 'It was only natural that political Islam would rise to prominence in places like Egypt, Tunisia, and so on, because the Islamists were the most well organized and allegedly incorruptible opposition forces out there' (2012: 1; also Matesan, 2012).

A wide spectrum of reaction to the Arab Spring in European media and academia seems to be dominated by a mix of optimism about the changing political landscape in the Mediterranean region and the concern that European countries, as well as rest of the world, were unprepared for such monumental changes (Matesan, 2012: 27–8). Christian Koch is sceptical of an expected speedy resolution to the Arab Spring and warns cautiously that 'the relationship between religion and politics and the structure of future governance will doubtless remain unanswered' (2011). Helene Pfeil, curiously, does not even address the issue of a religiously motivated fervour in the uprisings, but limits the call for a significant change of paradigm in the EU's foreign policy to an economic dimension (2011: 1–3). The EU approach, Pfeil maintains, should include funding democratic institution building and facilitating social and economic reforms through deeper engagement with the civil societies in nascent Arab democracies (2011: ibid.). Likewise Nathalie Tocci warns that the Arab Spring created multiple new political actors in the region, which is a factor that will inevitably cause the restructuring of the ENP if the EU is to remain a relevant player in the region (2011: 3–4). Ayadi and Sessa also criticise the lack of a decisive EU response to the Arab Spring 'while the region is moving towards further polarisation and the involvement of other external players' and outline four possible scenarios for a future EU-MED arrangement (2011: 2–4).

The EU's failed attempts in democratising the region over the years provoked criticisms from scholars and policy makers alike who argue for a substantial and influential EU foreign policy. Certain scholarship focuses on the positive aspects, as well as limitations of, the EU's economic instruments (Miller and Mishrif, 2005), but the overall majority of academic publications tend to focus on the relative level of success of Europe's normative influence in the democratisation process. With a number of contentious issues that are rooted in complex history and politics it is therefore not surprising that debate on the EU's role in the Middle East often produces polarising discourse about, and conflicting proposals for, the EU's foreign policy in the region (Ottolenghi, 2009: 33–6; Assenburg, 2009: 44–51). Alain Dieckoff takes a balanced approach, and while he evaluates the EU's foreign policy with an attitude of constructive criticism, he nevertheless expresses an optimistic view about the EU's institutional capacity, contending that even though the EU is lacking the capacity to act as a state, it nonetheless has 'the means for setting out and acting upon a common policy towards the Middle East' (2004: 57).

Apart from the debate that surrounds Islamism and the Arab Spring, the most contentious debate regarding the EU's role in democratising the Middle East has for some time also centred on the question of the Islamist parties and movements. A typical uncompromising stance that finds the demarcation of Islamism and political Islam as problematic (in its aims, if not in practice) considers the EU's potential political engagement with Islamists as morally outrageous and politically detrimental to Europe's interests in the long run (Ye'or, 2011: 154–83; Guitta, 2010: 4–6). 'Thanks to generous foreign funding, meticulous organisation, and the naivete of European elites', argues Lorenzo Vidino, 'Muslim Brotherhood-linked organisations have gained prominent positions throughout Europe' (2005: 69; also Vidino, 2010). Such deep suspicions are nurtured in the context of a historically antagonistic relationship between Islam and the West (Bynum, 2011; Spencer, 2005; Lewis, 2004; Huntington, 2002) and in the fact that Islam is not only a religion, but is a comprehensive system of inter-related political, religious, cultural, economic and social aspects, which, according to a particular stream of scholarship, is incompatible with Western democratic, as well as Christian, values (Bynum, 2011; Spencer, 2005a; Warraq, 2005; Littman, 2005; Gabriel, 2004; Lewis, 2003; Warraq, 2003; Trifkovic, 2002). In this context some scholars also argue that issues such as post-colonial guilt, post-nationalism and moral relativism have moulded European political culture into a skewed pacifism that refuses to acknowledge the failure of multiculturalism, directly affecting its attitude towards Israel (Shepherd, 2009: 144–6).

A dominant academic discourse, on the other hand, is more pragmatic and optimistic when engaging in the analysis of the EU's cooperation with Islamist parties and tends to refer to it as political Islam. It affirms the EU's promotion of multilateralism and use of soft power through economic instruments, but bemoans the EU's excessively secular character and its reluctance to engage more with civil societies that include such movements (Burgat, 2009: 628–31). Lack of any tangible progress in the ENP, it is argued, is due to the inherent problems with the ENP's methods, which operate as a 'scaled down version of Enlargement' (Youngs, 2006: 3) and as such tends to marginalise the fact that the historical background of the Mediterranean and Middle Eastern region is unique in itself. By using the CEE countries as a template while withholding the greatest incentive, i.e. membership of the union, it is inevitable that the ENP will end in failure. Youngs adds that financial aid for democracy building, allocated annually through the MEDA programme, is not nearly enough to facilitate democratic change. He points out that since 11 September and up to 2006, 800 million euros have been spent on controlling illegal immigration and information sharing with existing Arab governments, while democracy projects received only 10 million. This highlights the need to finance democratic civil societies, reformist groups and NGOs, rather than trying to facilitate democratic change through regimes that could use financial aid to consolidate their hold on power. In addition to calling for a consistency on the part of the EU, Youngs also believes that financial funding to civil societies should specifically include the moderate Islamist organisations, as they stand in opposition to corrupt regimes and often provide valuable social welfare (2006: 5).

Given the steady rise in popularity of Islamist movements since the 1960s throughout the Middle East, brought about by a vacuum left by the failure of the Western ideology of the secular nation state, it is not surprising that calls for the integration of political Islam into the political dialogue between Europe and the Middle East is currently dominating the debates about the Israeli–Palestinian peace process and the democratisation of the region (Behr, 2008: 82–3). In defending the claim that the EU needs to negotiate with the Islamic opposition in the Arab countries, Burgat reinforces the argument that existing Arab governments solidified their authoritarian position through the Barcelona Process 'to the detriment of the quality of Europe's relations with oppositional forces' (2009: 624). Furthermore, he rejects the category of Islamism as an abstract term unable to pinpoint the exact meaning (2009: 618), therefore rejecting the claim of the Islamist threat, so readily voiced by the corrupt Arab governments. For Burgat, a claim that the opposition within Arab civil society is of a religious nature is a myth, used by the existing regimes to deflect from the fact that the opposition is in reality a political protest (2009: 624). The prevailing notion of Europe's secular character among the interlocutors that represent the EU prevents any meaningful progress, he maintains, as such a position leads to misconceptions where the EU cannot recognise the competent partners, i.e. representatives of moderate political Islam, as facilitators of political liberalisation and democratisation (2009: 626–8).

The EU and Israel – normative values and antisemitism

As already discussed in the previous chapter, the EU's commitment to its values and principles, such as democracy and human rights, is both commended for its positive impact on Europe's culture, but also criticised for its inconsistent application as a foreign policy instrument. Nonetheless, that commitment is the normative vehicle with which the union aims to continue to drive the integration process internally, and to achieve an effective and influential role externally (Littman, 2010; Manners, 2008, 2008a and 2006; Smith, 2008: 111–200; Bretherton and Vogler, 2006; 20–35). These values and principles are established through various treaties and upheld through numerous laws, and as such they determine to a significant degree current economic and political dynamics in the EU–Israel relationship. The most important development in the EU–Israel relationship, which culminated in the Association Agreement (explained further below) and entered into force in 2000, clearly states in its preamble that human rights and democratic principles, whose existence and practice are defined through the United Nations Charter, are essential values that determine the EU–Israel political dialogue and economic cooperation (*Official Journal of the European Communities*, 2000). Much debated is the conditionality principle that the EU holds as a major benchmark. Given the EU's resistance to militarisation this principle tends to be regarded as an instrument that exemplifies the EU as a soft power. Although after 11 September the EU decided to make the ESDP 'operational at the earliest opportunity' (Council of the EU, 2001), the ESDP operations are meant to operate within the European normative power paradigm in foreign policy. This, according to critics, is a concept and practice that has little chance of success, given the divergent national military policies, as well as potential military threats to European countries, and different cultural and political values outside of Europe (Hyde-Price, 2008: 31–2). Proponents however argue that there is no contradiction in terms, since the EU binds itself firmly to international laws (McCormick, 2007: 15–17 and 70; Diez and Manners, 2007). This view is compatible with Kirchner's theory of security governance, which emphasises the influence of institutions and the competence of Europe's soft power, which aims to protect its borders through regional economic cooperation while promoting democracy and sustainable peace (2006: 945–9).

On the other hand, the principle could be interpreted as a hard power exercise designed to foster compliance from the EU partners. Just as military power could be used as a soft instrument through aiding and training militaries in other countries, so too economic instruments could promise both a rewarding trade and/or stringent sanctions, proposes Smith (2008: 21). No doubt the EU has found the conditionality an indispensable instrument in its enlargement policy, but whether it will constitute an effective pillar of the EU's foreign policy in the Middle East remains to be seen. Indeed a number of scholars argue that the level of success of such an approach in the Middle East so far is arguably low when assessed against the criteria of Europe's normative values and its economic and political aims (Asseburg, 2009; Stavridis, 2008; Pace, 2007; Smith, 2008: 86–9). This means that the EU will inevitably have to consider, and may have to choose, which path it will pursue in the coming years and decades – whether it will project its values into the Middle East through economic aid, i.e. facilitate a state-building process with Palestinians, or insist on being a political power (though ineffective), as suggested by Miller (2011: 9–12).

Of course the conditionality which both defines the EU's approach in the Mediterranean and/or Middle East regions, and shapes in particular a debate about Europe's relationship with Islamist parties, is predictably understood, interpreted and applied from contrasting views. As an example, Lady Ashton's comment in 2011 that an upgrade in EU–Israel relations depended on Israel's compliance with the EU normative standards has no doubt pleased a number of scholars and policy makers who hold Israel responsible for a lack of a peace agreement. In 2006 O'Donnell claimed that the EU should apply 'tough love' to Israel by insisting that Israel opens the Gaza borders, ends settlement activities, stops having a preferential access to EU markets for products from the settlements and, of course, fully recommits to the peace process, regardless of the fact that, she admits, such demands would prove difficult in practice, because it is the bilateral dimension of the EU–Israel relationship that is in reality the most influential source of leverage (O'Donnell, 2006). Ottolenghi, on the other hand, who affirms the necessity for implementing the principle of conditionality, but disagrees substantially on its partial application, argued shortly before Gaddaffi's death: 'EU insistence on conditionality is remarkable, especially given that it comes at a time when Europe is negotiating an Association Agreement with Libya – a dictatorship whose human rights' record is one of the worst in the region' (2009: 13). Likewise Dieckhof maintains that isolating and suspending the EU–Israel agreements is illogical since '[t]he Arab countries involved in the EMP also have dubious records in human rights' (2004: 60).

Perhaps calls for 'tough love' towards Israel reflect the fact that the EU on the whole regards the Israeli–Palestinian conflict, in the words of Romano Prodi, as 'the mother of all problems',[1] which undermines not only the EU's economic investment in the region, but also radicalises European Muslims (Miller, 2011: 9). Consequently, the resolution of the

Israeli–Palestinian conflict is the issue that takes priority over all the other problems that the region is beset with. As commendable as that might seem, Ottolenghi claims the understanding and analysis of the Middle East through the prism of the peace process is fundamentally wrong for numerous reasons. Firstly, he claims, there is a contradiction at the core of the EU's policies, which stems from European desire to ensure Israel's security (as a result of the legacy of the Holocaust) while adopting the Palestinian narrative of the conflict (2010: 21). Secondly, Ottolenghi maintains, the number one problem of the Middle East that the EU should prioritise is the threat to Israel from Iran, and potentially to Europe, and it is a problem that is most definitely not rooted in the Israeli–Palestinian conflict, but in radical Islamic ideology (2010: 19; also Shepherd, 2009: 154–9). As already discussed in the previous section, the radical Islamist agenda undoubtedly constitutes a problem and a dilemma for the EU, and a clear strategy with which the EU chooses to engage with the Islamist parties that emerged victorious in popular elections is yet to be seen. However it is important to draw attention to the fact that the EU Council adopted a common position in 2001 regarding terrorist activities (*Europa*, 2001), and accordingly in 2002 added Izzedin al-Kassam (the military wing of Hamas) to its list of terrorist organisations in spite of the fact that 'Ireland, Spain, France, and senior European Commission officials were among those more sceptical of the move' (Miller, 2007: 1).

The inconsistency in dealing with Hamas in particular (Miller, 2006: 653–4) clearly contributes to a difficult relationship between Israel and the EU, which, according to a distinct view from Israel, has two major components. On one level, the relationship exists within the context of the sympathy that is afforded to Palestinians, largely as a result of the European view that the Israeli–Palestinian conflict is 'basically a de-colonization process' (Kney-Tal, 2006: 57). On another level, it is, according to Wistrich, the desire of a multicultural and supranational Europe to rid itself of the guilt of the Holocaust, by promoting the discourse of Zionist Nazi Jews and the Palestinian underdog (2005: 37–43). This is, in his view, nothing less than a re-invented antisemitism, which the European secular political left uses to deny '[the] Jewish people a fundamental human and political right that they would militantly defend for nonwhite peoples – above all, the Palestinians – namely, the right to national self-determination' (2005: 12).

Decoupling anti-Zionism and anti-Israelism from antisemitism is a major contentious issue between critics of Israel and its apologists. Norman Finkelstein, perhaps because he is a Jew, affords himself the luxury of being one of the most vociferous critics of Israel, and a passionate promoter of a Palestinian-centric narrative of the conflict (2003a), as well as a relentless critic of both Jews and non-Jews who equate anti-Zionism with antisemitism. His possibly most controversial work, *The Holocaust Industry* (2003), contends not only that the new antisemitism is non-existent (2003: 33–8), but that memories of the Holocaust themselves have been falsified, distorted and used for Israel's ulterior motives – namely financial extortion from Europe.

To what degree this and other similar claims are justified is a polemical topic, which often fails to generate a measured discussion and an appropriate response. Criticism of Israel should, and indeed must, form a legitimate aspect to any debate about the solution of the Israeli–Palestinian conflict. Equally so, the rise of antisemitism, both old and new, that is rooted in secular ideologies as well as in Christian and Islamic theologies (Barnes, 2014; Bostom and Warraq, 2008; Littman and Wadlow, 2005: 342–6; Prager and Telushkin, 2003: 74–154), is an undeniable reality in the Middle East and in Europe, that must be addressed by academia and discussed openly by the EU policy makers. Gerstenfeld believes that at the root of current European attitude and the policies of the EU is a long-lived traditional defamation that 'has shifted from the individual Jew to Israel, the Jewish state' (2005: 2). He elaborates on ways in which the EU's attitudes against the Jewish state fuel European antisemitism, from the voting pattern of some of the member states in various UN institutions and the International Court of Justice to the anti-Israel pronouncements of some of the European Socialist parties that are uncritical of Palestinian terrorism (2005: 3–17). Following Arafat's death 'Chirac and many other European leaders', Gerstenfeld claims, 'paid homage to the man who festered international terrorism more than anybody else in the last decade of the twentieth century' (2006; also Miller, 2006: 647–8).

Although the resurgence of antisemitism in Europe is clearly a problem to a varying degree in the EU's member states, the EU nonetheless does have the instruments that can effectively address the issue, most notably the Organisation for Security and Cooperation in Europe (OSCE) and its instruments that deal with human and minority rights. In addition, the 1997 European Monitoring Centre on Racism and Xenophobia (EUMC) was succeeded by the Fundamental Rights Agency (FRA) in 2007, which regularly collects data of antisemitic crimes and provides appropriate analysis (Whine, 2009: 1–3). Interestingly the FRA report concedes that antisemitism is indeed at a problematic level in the EU, but it states also that nearly all member states have sufficient institutional ability, as well as the commitment, to combat antisemitism, which should serve as an incentive to the Jewish communities to co-ordinate their data gathering with the EU organisations (2009: 7). In 2011 FRA issued a working paper on antisemitism in 17 European countries, which proves that the level of antisemitic incidents has indeed increased, but it also states the following:

> In the course of recent years, there has been a shift in media and NGO reports and in the public perception of the 'typical' antisemitic offender from the 'extreme right skinhead' to the 'disaffected young Muslim', 'person of North African origin', or 'immigrant' and member of the 'anti-globalisation' left. However, this shift, although widely reported, is difficult to substantiate on the basis of the currently available evidence (2011: 32).

Such a conclusion does not inspire confidence among the Jewish communities in Europe, but it also contributes to a perception of the EU in Israel that is informed with 'the problematic, historic dimension of Jewish–European and Israeli–European relations, and with the negative aspects of normative Europe' (Harpaz, 2007: 106). In Europe alone 'Jew-hatred has existed for thousands of years, from Hellenic and Roman society to the leaders of Enlightenment, throughout Christendom and Islam, in Communist and Fascist societies, from ancient times until today' (Prager and Telushkin, 2003: 179), so perhaps on a popular level such deeply ingrained sentiments among Europeans will take much longer to dissipate or be eradicated. On an institutional level however the available instruments in dealing with antisemitism are arguably used very little, or ineffectively, particularly by the EU, whose reluctance to seriously challenge antisemitism in the Middle East countries is puzzling to say the least (Shepherd, 2009: 76–88). Concerning specifically the continuous antisemitic propaganda in Palestinian society, media and education by both Hamas and the PA[2] (Marcus, 2007), critics argue that the EU does not challenge Palestinians effectively for using Europe's taxpayers' money to perpetuate hate rather than build democratic institutions.

Undoubtedly the sheer complexity of European involvement with the Middle East generally, and with Israel specifically, is formulated by different historical, moral and political factors in the relationships between Israel and member states. The admirable fact that the European continent has lived in prosperity for over 60 years due to its values and commitment to peace, projects a realistic scenario, in the view of many scholars and policy makers, in which Europe is capable of extending 'its pacific norm to a region of active conflict and deep-rooted hostilities', and yet somehow 'the Middle East also represents a traditional case study in EU foreign and security policy failure' (Cavatorta and Tonra, 2007: 350). Regarding its involvement in resolving the Israeli–Palestinian conflict, the EU's diplomatic leverage is arguably preconditioned by Israel's insistence to be endorsed as 'a nation state of the Jewish people' (Ottolenghi, 2010: 34). On the other hand this is precisely what the EU finds problematic. Given that Israel is a fully-functioning democracy, and yet insists on upholding human rights within the context of security, its attitude and policies are interpreted as inherently contradictory and contributing, according to Kney-Tal, to Europe's negative perception of Israel as a militaristic state (2006: 54). Steven Beller, likewise, argues that even Israel's security as a nation state must be subordinated to the security of the worldwide Jewry, which is achievable only through the supranational model of a new Europe that sets universal normative values, provides an economic prosperity, and allows its citizens to nurture multiple loyalties (2008: 7–10).

From Israel's perspective such demands are unrealistic. As a traditional nation state that functions within the realist security paradigm, Israel prefers, and enjoys relative success in, bilateral relations, which is an additional factor in Israel's refusal to prioritise relations with the EU, or to emulate the EU's normative framework. The paradox of successful bilateral relations while at the same time having problematic relations with the EU often derives from the critical policies towards Israel from a particular state, thereby allowing for 'the lowest common denominator to determine the EU line' (Kney-Tal, 2006: 54). Consequently, Israel will in all probability continue to maintain good bilateral relationships, such as those with the Czech Republic, Germany, Poland and Italy, while trying to improve the troubled ones, particularly with Spain and Ireland, with a view that successful bilateral relationships will, in spite of resurgent antisemitism, eventually generate a good relationship with the EU as a whole. Barry Rubin (2010) shares such an optimistic view and asserts that, based largely on successful economic cooperation between Israel and European countries, there is no reason why the EU and Israel should not enjoy good and friendly relations in future.

The peace process and the Quartet

The degree of assertiveness that the EU may choose to pursue in years to come regarding its Middle East policies will largely depend on whether the CFSP structural constraints become a less of an obstacle. What is clear, however, is that the EU's commitment to establishing a Palestinian state will continue to define its foreign policy with Israel. This was confirmed in March 2009 when Solana warned a new right-wing Israeli government led by Binyamin Netanyahu: 'Let me say very clearly that the way the European Union will relate to an [Israeli] government that is not committed to a two-state solution will be very, very different'.[3] Given this commitment and the reality that the ratification of the Lisbon Treaty has provided the CFSP with a greater chance to streamline its divergent approaches and objectives, it should be expected that the EU will assert a stronger voice in the Quartet (explained further below), as well as expand its influence in the Mediterranean region.

For the EU, the political realities about the peace process, some old, such as the question of Palestinian refugees and the status of Jerusalem, and some of them new, created with the Arab Spring, will no doubt test its normative consistency and political creativity. The challenge for the EU is not related purely to normative and diplomatic discrepancies that exist in individual foreign policies of member states regarding engagement with Islamist movements, but how it will, as a foundational member of the Quartet, present a unified policy approach. The EU's arrival as a crucial peace interlocutor at the current historical point in the Israeli–Palestinian conflict is a progression of decades-long diplomatic, economic and cultural engagement, which occurred obviously in a wider context of the history between Europe and the Mediterranean. No doubt it will continue because the EU's involvement in any peace deal is logical given that political and economic interdependence between the two

regions will increase. Although involved deeply in the region, the low
level of success of the EU's impact in the peace process, which is often
attributed to the ineffectiveness of the EMP (Asseburg, 2003: 174), is a
topic that few commentators would disagree on. The disagreements
themselves however tend to be premised on the opposing, pro-Palestinian
and pro-Israeli, narrative of the conflict, and consequently, all agreements
relating to the political developments in peace negotiations tend to be
interpreted through the lens of the contending viewpoints.

The Madrid conference of 1991 was a significant point for the EU's
deeper involvement in the peace process. Shortly after it was followed by
the historic Oslo negotiations in 1993, after which the EU's commitment
to support the peace process was based solely on financial and economic
measures designed to improve the Palestinian infrastructure, build self-
governing institutions and, at the time, promote Fatah–Hamas
rapprochement (Miller, 2006). The Barcelona Process in 1995 established
greater credibility for the Palestinian Authority (PA) by giving it a status
of an equal Mediterranean partner, while securing Israel's acceptance by
the Arab states as a partner in the process. Subsequently, the Berlin
Declaration in March 1999 confirmed European political involvement by
including a commitment to support the creation of a Palestinian state in
the context of permanent status talks with Israel. The eventual failure of
the European approach is attributed mainly to the continuing Israeli
occupation and the fact that the EU's aid took the form of 'a post-conflict
peace-building – as if there were no continuing conflict, occupation or
mobility restrictions hampering economic development, reconciliation
and institution-building' (Asseburg, 2003: 177). Miller argues however
that the EU 'is unable to transform its trade ties into political influence,
unless it can earn the confidence of Israel' (2006: 660), while Steinberg
singles out the issue regarding Jerusalem, possibly the most contentious
issue in the peace process: '[The] EU's statement on Jerusalem invoking
the 1947 UN partition resolution was particularly damaging, and
reduced the already limited support for an increased European role in the
political process' (1999: 6).

After the second Intifada, launched in September 2000, the EU
assumed an increased political role in the peace process by becoming a
partner in the Quartet alongside Russia, the UN and the US. In 2002 the
first substantial EU contribution to the Quartet's aim was a proposition to
create the Palestinian state by 2005 through the implementation of the

Roadmap. The core principles of the Roadmap – a demand for Palestinian renunciation of violence and democratic reforms, as well as a demand that Israel accepts the Palestinian government and ends settlement activity in the Gaza Strip and West Bank – were a clear signal to both Israelis and Palestinians that the international community is attaching a great deal of importance to the peace process. Significantly, the EU's increased pro-active role was not perceived as a challenge to the American traditionally primary role in mediating between the conflicting parties, but rather as a useful complementary aspect to the hard-power approach (Perthes, 2000; Dieckhof, 2004). Different approaches by the Americans and Europeans towards building peace in the region are often evaluated by the emphasis that the two influencing powers place on different aspects of the conflict. Cavatorta and Tonra maintain that the American emphasis on the security aspect gives it a leadership status naturally, since for actors in the region 'the "real" game is played with the USA and influential member states, not the EU, which is seen as an economic partner in the more traditional "realist" sense' (2007: 360).

For some time a lack of progress with the Roadmap was commonly attributed to the electoral victory of Hamas in 2006 and disagreement between Bush's administration and the EU over the need to pressure Hamas to recognise the Roadmap's principles and, crucially, whether the financial factor should be used as an incentive or as an enforcement (Dunne, 2010). Despite American and Israeli objections, the EU gave 120 million euros to the newly Hamas-led Palestinian authority, which, according to some critics, perpetuated terrorism and ensured that 'Palestinians are trapped in the squalor of dependency' (Hannan, 2006). But for some analysts this was not only the right thing to do, but furthermore, as Emerson and Tocci argued, the EU should assume leadership in the region, replace the Roadmap with the Arab League Peace Initiative and the 2003 Geneva Accord, and 'collect the support of the Arab world and Russia as its Quartet partner' (2006). It is tempting to excuse such strong assertions given the level of frustration with the lack of progress; however, it would most definitely prove to be counterproductive to European interests, in terms of establishing itself as an impartial broker and gaining Israel's cooperation for a lasting stabilisation of the region. The historical record of both Russian and Arab treatment of Jews (AICE, 2002: 150–68) and the exclusion of Americans from the peace process would clearly neither dispel Israel's deep-seated suspicion of the EU, nor would they provide a guarantee that radical Islamist groups would cease their militant, and at times, terrorist, activities.

These suspicions are held by a section of Israeli society whose distrust towards the EU Harpaz and Shamis categorise as Antagonistic approach in terms of the EU dealings with Israel (2010: 591–9). It is an approach found mostly in the Israeli political right that holds to a conviction that the EU's stance on the conflict is pro-Palestinian (Halevy, 2007) and puts an obligation on the EU to improve its 'credibility and legitimacy in the eyes of Israelis' (Harpaz, 2008: 120). Such perception is certainly not uniform in all of Israel, as Harpaz would point out, but the prevailing narrative in wide social, economic and political circles regards most member states in the EU as 'simply unbalanced and anti-Israeli in its approach' (2007: 99). The two other approaches, according to Harpaz and Shamis, which define the response from Israel's society, academia and political establishment to the EU's role in the Middle East, and by extension the peace process, are Ideological-supportive and Pragmatic/Economic (2010: 591–9). As such neither is inherently opposed to the two-state solution to the conflict, which was officially articulated at the US-sponsored Annapolis Conference in 2007. Since it remained along the lines of the Roadmap and it advocated a substantial Israeli concession that involved giving parts of East Jerusalem to Palestinians, it was actively promoted by the EU. However a few years after the conference the official announcement by the Swedish Presidency in 2009 caused further distrust towards the EU. Calling for East Jerusalem to be the capital of the Palestinian state provoked vociferous objections from the Israeli right wing, some foreign Jewish organisations and Christian Zionists, as it sustains a discourse that shared Jerusalem is part of an acceptable formula for a just conflict resolution.

While the EU has a clear goal of creating a viable Palestinian state, its stance towards including Islamists in a political dialogue has been less assertive. In 2003 'the European Security Strategy explicitly named Islamic fundamentalist groups as among the key threats to the European Union' (Martin and Bicchi, 2006: 197), which explains the fact that Hamas remains blacklisted by the EU. However the problem and dilemma regarding Hamas remains unresolved. Since its electoral victory in 2006, and due to a long-standing sympathy in the EU for Hamas (Miller, 2006: 653), the frequent calls from the EU for legitimisation of the group that refuses to renounce its anti-Israel charter pose serious questions about the EU's political competence. On the other hand, some scholars argue that the EU's negative attitude towards Islamists is detrimental to the peace process. Burgat in particular claims that the EU's foreign policy in the Middle Eastern region needs to include the political Islam, including Hamas, and discard its excessive 'pro-Israel bent' (2009: 629) that damages European credibility among the wider population. Likewise O'Donnell (2009), Asseburg (2009) and Youngs (2006) insist that the inclusion of Hamas in peace talks is a necessary prerequisite for a political breakthrough, not only because Hamas was democratically elected, but its rapprochement with Fatah would create a much needed united Palestinian voice. Likewise, Asseburg argues that a conditional approach to Hamas obstructs the formation of a renewed power-sharing agreement between Fatah and Hamas, which is absolutely essential for a legitimate Palestinian leadership (2008: 42).

Michelle Pace also points out the plethora of issues that impede progress in Europe's constructive and effective engagement in the Middle East, beginning with Europe's historical legacy in the region, followed by a range of factors, such as power asymmetries of the external actors (the EU and the USA) and the functioning of the EU institutions that do not have centralised enforcement authority 'which conflict parties take advantage of' (2007: 15). In addition, Pace criticises Europe's (presumably inclusive) normative values and conditions applied in the democratisation process as 'a semantically empty notion' (2007: 17) in view of the exclusion of Hamas from the dialogue. O'Donnell, like Burgat, openly calls for the EU to make Hamas more acceptable to Israel and the US by helping to create a favourable environment in which the organisation could transform itself into 'a more responsible political player' (2008: 3). This should not be too difficult, she argues, because even though the EU officially requires Hamas to respect the three principles set out by the Quartet, unofficially, she claims, a number of member states are not against 'working with a national unity government which only implicitly recognised the three principles' (2009: 3).

EU–Israel economic cooperation

With the pressing need for a lasting solution on the one hand, and all the contentious, and seemingly irreconcilable, issues involved in the peace process on the other hand, it is not surprising that the Pragmatic/Economic approach, as conceptualised by Harpaz and Shamis (2010: 591–9), is seen as the only workable strategy for the Israeli–Palestinian conflict. After all, the EU is a product of the collective pragmatism of Europe's nation states, and nowhere is this more effectively exemplified as in the area of economics, on which not only relatively successful political convergence is based, but it is also an area where the EU finds itself in a position of strength through building partnerships with the Mediterranean countries through economic aid and trade, including Israel. And so, quite paradoxically, while the political dimension of Israel's relationship with the EU remains uneasy at best, economic cooperation between the two is a completely different story – one that started in 1975 with the Cooperation Agreement (Miller, 2006: 655–60). It established a free trade zone with the European Community (EC) leading to a significant increase in exports to Europe from 1975 to 1996 and an even greater increase in imports from the EC. The trade was complemented by the development of close business connections between entrepreneurs and investors, which consequently strengthened Israel's economic ties with the member countries of the European Free Trade Association (EFTA).

The Cooperation Agreement was replaced with the Association Agreement in 1995, and following ratification by national parliaments of 15 member states, the European Parliament and the Knesset, it entered legally into force in 2000. It affirmed the existing arrangements regarding free trade in industrial products, but it expanded into the liberalisation of services, the free movement of capital and competition rules. In 2010 it expanded into the agricultural domain and reciprocal liberalisation on agricultural products, processed agricultural products and fish and fishery products (Delegation of the EU to Israel), but most significantly perhaps, Israel became associated, as the only non-European country, with the European Community's Framework Programme for Research and Technical Development (RTD) due to its high level of technical competence. Crucially for Israel another significant addition to the Association Agreement (Article 2) made a provision for an enhanced political dialogue and cooperation on social issues. It refers specifically to human rights in the framework of the UN Charter and it attaches a great deal of importance to the struggle against xenophobia, antisemitism and racism (EEAS, 2000).

In further consolidation of the agreements, the Country Strategy Paper for Israel, which covers the period 2007–13 and provides a projected figure of the funding levels under the European Neighbourhood and Partnership Instrument (ENPI) of 14 million euros, states:

> The principal objective of EU–Israel cooperation is to develop an increasingly close relationship between the EU and Israel, going beyond previous levels of cooperation, including a significant level of economic integration, and a deepening of political cooperation including in the area of foreign and security policy and in the resolution of the Middle East conflict and on human rights issues, on the basis of the EU–Israel Action Plan (European Commission, 2006).

Although the EU's freeze for several years on an upgrade in the Association Agreement was premised on political reasons with the official position holding that '[D]evelopments on the ground, such as ongoing settlement activity in the West Bank including East Jerusalem, are an obstacle to our peace efforts and threaten to make the two-state solution impossible' (EEAS, 2011), the overall assessment of the economic cooperation, even convergence, tends to be positive (Tovias, 2011: 12–14). Very few academics would argue that EU–Israel economic cooperation is unfavourable to either party. Back in 2006, for instance, despite all the criticism directed at Israel as a result of the war with the Hezbollah, Israel's relationship with the EU was described by the former head of the European Commission Delegation to Israel as 'very good and improving' (Cibrian-Uzal: 1). He summarises the positive aspects of the ENP Action Plan and maintains that as far as the EU is concerned its ultimate aim is to offer Israel 'full participation, or full integration, in the European Union's single market' (2006: 3). Barry Rubin similarly claims that in addition to very good and continually improving economic relations with the EU, the relationship on a political level is quite good too regardless of the fact that European intellectual and cultural elites, particularly those in the UK, France, Norway, Sweden, Belgium and Holland, are anti-Israel (2008).

Although Halevy does not share such enthusiasm and claims that even the RTD was passed in the EP because the agreement was advantageous to Europeans, he seems to confirm a well-known position when referring to Europe's pragmatism: 'When Europeans have a practical material interest, their ideological considerations become secondary. This is normal and natural' (2007: 2). This was confirmed in July 2012 when, after several years of suspension, the EU decided to upgrade the Association Agreement with Israel.

> Among the most controversial is the addition of areas of cooperation in the Agreement on Conformity, Assessment and Acceptance of industrial products, or ACAA – a deal first agreed in principle two years ago. In this agreement, the EU formally accepts for the first time the authority of Israeli ministers over goods produced in West Bank settlements (Greenwood, 2012).

The upgrade in the agreement is undoubtedly welcomed news for most Israelis, particularly for the scholars and experts who call for deeper economic integration between Israel and the EU, such as Tovias (2011) and Herman (2006). Others, who argue against the further development of economic ties, maintain that Israel has no real benefits from the ENP Action Plan. Marcia Don Harpaz singles out the service sector and argues:

> [T]hree main concerns arise regarding the ENP and services: 1) the language of the Action Plan in the service sector, an area of significant interest to Israel, is ambiguous as to what is expected of Israel; 2) Israel, at a different level of structural reform, is still linked to the timetable and rules of the other Med partners; 3)... the service sectors in the EU are not yet open to competition within the EU itself, hence it is not clear when and what Israel can gain in the short run in the framework of the EU/Israel Action Plan even if a more ambitious plan for integration were instituted (2008: 397).

She concludes that due to the risks associated with overdependence on trade with the EU, and the fact that the political dimension in the Action Plan is disadvantageous to Israel, Israel's better option is in diversification of its trade, namely with the BRIC (Brazil, Russia, India and China) countries (2008: 399–410).

Arguably such assertions could be vindicated in view of the current euro crisis, whose long-term consequences for the economic relations between the EU and Israel are yet to be seen. Nonetheless, it is unrealistic at best, and unwise at worst, to expect Israel to distance itself from the most important trade partner in the region. Such expectations are unrealistic not only because the geographic proximity dictates a high level of trade and a high exchange of people, but from the EU's point of view the solution to the political problems that plague the region and the Israeli–Palestinian relations is inherently bound up with the economic dimension. As such it will always have its critics, expressed so elaborately in Don Harpaz' assessment (2008), but it will also have its proponents who will effectively argue the case of Europeanisation of Israel through economic means (Tovias, 2011; Harpaz, 2008). Tovias in particular argues that regardless of the distinction in economic and institutional convergence, Israel is very much European in terms of its 'culture, entertainment, sport and mass media activities' (2011: 21). Furthermore he asserts that it is possible to maintain the EU's and Israel's structural convergence not only due to the fact that Israel is a country that is characterised as 'post-industrial, service-based, with a booming high tech sector and with a shrinking agricultural and manufacturing base' (2011: 27), but the EU itself has changed into a multicultural and multireligious society through the process of globalisation and enlargement, and as such has come closer to the Israeli model (2011: 23–4).

Theoretically economic prosperity should provide a powerful incentive for a peaceful coexistence to any faction or nation involved in a conflict. In the case of the Israelis and Palestinians, however, whose conflict is defined by so many historical, geographical, cultural, ideological and religious factors, the idea that the EU solution to the conflict is based on economic cooperation, is rather naïve, and even ludicrous to its biggest critics. Although a vision for the EU's successful export of its federalist agenda to the Mediterranean region, as Lucio Levi argues, should and could start with 'a hard core made up of Israel, Palestine, Lebanon and Jordan' (2011: 5), that nevertheless does not diminish the other unresolved issues. Presumably this integration process would be premised on the European model where member states are committed to successful economic cooperation, but the critics would argue that the EU has no leverage – political, normative, nor perhaps economic – to define the region in any meaningful measure. Even though as a unique post-Westphalian construct the EU can assert a considerable amount of influence, it can do so only provided it evaluates its strengths with a healthy dose of realism.

The structural inconsistency in the CFSP, which demands a greater degree of harmonisation in EU foreign policy (and that includes the united stance in the Quartet) will not define the EU's level of political and normative success in its engagement with the peace process, but it will undoubtedly reflect the EU's level of political creativity and the commitment to its own normative principles. Both will be enormously affected by the process and the outcome of Arab Spring, which essentially revolves around one single important question – what will the EU do with political Islam? Never has this dilemma been so crucial for Israel as the country continues to deal with the threats from Hamas and, up to now not blacklisted, Hezbollah, as well as the threat from, one might call it, 'the real mother of all problems' – Iranian nuclear armament. In addition, the prospect of newly established hostile Islamist regimes in Egypt, Jordan and Syria are bound to determine the level and nature of the EU's demands on the Jewish state.

British and German input into the CFSP regarding the Middle East and Israel has been so far a significant, and at times an influential factor, such as the British-led campaign (against the French-led position) within the EU in 2003 for a crackdown on Hamas (Miller, 2006: 653). While German or British governments will not be able (or allowed) to impose their national policies on the EU's foreign policy with Israel, their political leverage will undoubtedly continue to determine the EU's attitude and policies to a varying degree. As pointed out in the introduction to this chapter there are several reasons why these two countries were included in this book. Historically Christian Zionist expressions in both countries contributed to the re-establishment of the Jewish state. Their current resurgence in both countries plays an important role in the political landscape, but they are also the two most influential national strands that contribute to, and strengthen the work of, pan-European Christian Zionist advocacy. It is at this level that the difference between American and European Christian Zionism is most apparent since each national Christian Zionist expression in Europe is unique for its own reasons. Both the German and British Christian Zionist strands are defined by biblical eschatology, but they are also political movements that exist and contend for influence in a particular political, and in the German case moral, context.

The most obvious context is that of distinct positions towards the unification of Europe, which also determined to a large degree the bilateral relations between the two countries. In Britain the period between the end of the war until the early 1970s was characterised by great scepticism in contrast to West Germany where the attitude was enthusiastic. This enthusiasm was two-dimensional; on a broader level the integration was perceived as instrumental in preventing another devastating war on the continent, but in terms of German national interest, its membership in the ECSC was meant to re-establish Germany's respectability among the nations (Larres, 2000). In the 1960s Britain's attitude shifted in favour of an economic integration, largely as a result of British realisation that the loss of the Empire also meant that cooperation among the Commonwealth countries was not an adequate substitute for the growing significance of the European Economic Community (EEC). Under Edward Heath's premiership in the early 1970s Britain became genuinely more in favour of being integrated into Europe, but such sentiments were greatly undermined under Margaret Thatcher's government where the concept of the nation state sovereignty, as well as the Anglo-American 'special relationship', was revived. Meanwhile the Franco-German alliance solidified throughout the Cold War and post-Cold War, as did the progression of European integration, most effectively under the joint leadership of President Francois Mitterrand and Chancellor Helmut Kohl. By the 1990s, during which British attitude became more constructive under Tony Blair's premiership, Germany became known as the EU's economic powerhouse and the main source of the euro currency.

Although British attitude towards the EU ranged from extreme scepticism to healthy pragmatism, it is still largely defined by scepticism, and remains so, an attitude that, according to Thomas Risse, is rooted in a very strong British nation state identity (2011). Germany, on the other hand, remained steadily the supporter and active facilitator for integration because the new European values resonated very well with its new nation state identity that rejected traditional German nationalism (Risse, 2011).

Israel's relations with Germany

Germany's relationship with the Jewish state has always been unique because it was defined by the memories of the Holocaust, although Germany's interaction with its past did not occur until the late 1950s.

It was the recognition of its moral debt, which was most effectively presented to the German nation during Eichmann's trial in 1961 (Hornstra, 2006: 32; Rapaport, 1997: 32) that conditioned the favourable treatment of Israel that was enshrined in the Luxemburg Agreement in 1952 (Balabkins, 1971: 138–54). The cornerstone of all subsequent policies towards the Israeli state was Germany's long-term commitment to financial reparations, as well as compensation to individuals who suffered under Nazi crimes, with the initially agreed sum of $715 million and $110 million respectively (Belkin, 2007: 2). This policy was enhanced after German unification, when the compensation laws were expanded in 1992 in order to include individuals who were for decades denied restitution from East Germany. However, as much as moral debt conditioned the good relationship between Germans and their post-war Jews in general terms, it also created a great deal of uneasiness due to the inadequate denazification process and persistence of antisemitism (Rapaport, 1997: 30–8).

The debate about the extent to which the issue of moral debt will continue, or should continue, to define German–Jewish, and by extension German–Israeli, relations is preconditioned by acknowledgement of new realities in twenty-first century Germany. A largely optimistic analysis of Jewish existence in Germany, free from its painful past, is offered by Jeffrey Peck: '[T]he Shoah generation is dying out... Jews form an important, though not singular, segment of a society increasingly composed of immigrants' (2007: 84), '[and] a new Jewish identity and even an evolving future German identity would find common ground in the global migration of peoples that transcend borders of state and demarcated regions' (2007: 162). Other voices, which included Israeli Foreign Ministry officials in 2008, are less optimistic, bemoaning the lack of Germany's moral leadership in Europe in the face of Iran's virulent antisemitism: 'The outrageous thing is that Germany of all countries, with its unusual moral history, is the weakest link among the three largest European countries (Germany, France and Britain) in terms of toughening the sanctions on Iran' (Sofer, 2008).

It is relatively easy to understand German pragmatism and its ability to compartmentalise domestic and foreign policy issues into moral and non-moral. Arguably, its status of an economic powerhouse of the EU allowed Germany to maintain its dominant trading links with Iran (Ottolenghi, 2009: 184), as well as ensuring that its good relations with

Israel particularly excels in the area of economic cooperation. Germany is, after the USA, Israel's largest trading partner, as well as the strongest advocate of preferential trade agreements between the EU and Israel. Drawing on the arguments of the former Israeli Ambassador Avi Primor, Belkin likewise maintains that it is the bilateral trade, which is worth 3.7 billion euros, and the increase of German investment, that are of primary importance to the German relationship with Israel (2007: 4).

Besides stable economic cooperation, Germany and Israel maintain close military and defence cooperation, which initially started as a clandestine affair in 1957 through Germany's arms shipment to Israel, but got suspended once a German newspaper exposed the deals and generated a crisis with the Arab world. Nevertheless, the historical accounts reveal, claims Belkin, that since the late 1960s 'successive German leaders have remained committed to far-reaching defence cooperation with Israel and Israel continues to be a top recipient of German military technology' (2007: 5). Belkin also emphasises that the German government in 1999 and in 2000, despite opposition from Left and Green parties, financed 50 per cent of the costs for three Israeli submarines, with an additional commitment to pay 1 billion euros by 2010 for two more submarines (2007: 6). In addition to defence cooperation, Israel and Germany committed also to substantial intelligence sharing in combating terrorism, which started in 1972 after the Munich Olympics terrorist attack.

A significant factor that influences German–Israeli relations derives from the Jewish community in Germany. The Jewish population, according to Susanne Urban, numbered no more than 15,000 after World War II up until the late 1980s, but currently stands at 300,000 as a result of migration from the former Soviet republics (2009: 32) 'Due to the influx of Soviet Jews', the EJC points out, 'Germany has the third largest and fastest growing Jewish population in Western Europe' (EJC, Germany – History and Demography), which is a welcomed trend as it provides evidence that the socio-political process in post-war Germany has developed towards normality (Urban, 2009: 36). An important aspect of this influx relates to the fact that, although the percentage of a Jewish minority has substantially increased, the re-invigorated Jewish expression in German society is certainly not a monolith, but demonstrates that 'new German Jews have become the quintessential hybrid diaspora people' (Peck, 2007: 157; also Urban, 2009: 34–7). Though challenging perhaps for the existing Jewish community in

Germany, the formation of the Jewish pluralism was nevertheless successfully met by the Central Council of Jews in Germany, an umbrella organisation that represents the German Jewry and provides a religious instruction to the immigrants about their Jewish faith while facilitating the process of integration (EJC). How precisely this substantive influx impacted specifically on the Israel lobby in Germany (in terms of its efficiency and success) has not been researched yet, but the available evidence points to the strong lobby activity of the Jewish groups and their cooperation with pro-Israel Christian organisations (discussed in Chapter 5).

The integration and Jewish identity issues are of course inextricable from the issues relating to a Turkish minority in Germany and Turkish accession to the EU. While Jews account for a very small percentage compared to Turks, who number 2.3 million, and while the Jews were German nationals for centuries compared to the Turks whose acquisition of German citizenship is a recent phenomenon, nonetheless they both share, according to Peck, the status of the 'other' in German society (2007: 86–96). Peck's analysis of intercultural relations carries certain merit, particularly when he discusses the discrimination against both minorities and concludes that '[i]t remains to be seen how Jews and Turks will work together in the future, be it in political lobbying against discrimination or through multicultural events that demonstrate that there are different ways of being German' (Peck, 2007: 108). However, this analysis is rather superficial as it fails to address the issue of Islam and how it relates to both the 'Turkish and Jewish questions'. Sara Silvestri places Turkey's accession to the EU in the wider context of the twenty-first century relations between Europe and political Islam and outlines the dilemma:

> [I]ntercultural dialogue seems to work so long as Turkey is part of the "outside" Muslim world with which the EU is so keen to establish social and cultural exchanges. But when there is a prospect that Turkey might become part of the EU, the logic of intercultural dialogue does not seem to work' (2007a: 64).

The place of Islam in Germany is important not only because of the role that it performs on a general level in re-defining European identity, as discussed in the previous chapter, but specifically how is the level of accommodated Islam going to affect the multicultural fabric of German society, particularly relations between the Muslims and the Jews. Although some scholars, such as Peck (2007), have an optimistic outlook on the prospects for the Jewish minority in Germany, and others claim that Muslims (mostly Turks) are victimised to a degree because of the right-wing populism (Dolezal et al., 2010: 174 and 186), there are influential voices in politics and academia who question the compatibility of Muslim demands with a German political culture. Angela Merkel's announcement in 2010 that German multiculturalism has 'utterly failed' (Weaver, 2010: 17) followed Thilo Sarrazin's highly controversial book about the negative impact of the Muslim population in Germany (*Der Spiegel*, 2010b). The ignited debate included also Muslim scholars, such as Rauf Ceylan, who argue that some imams in Germany do indeed preach hatred (*Der Spiegel,* 2010a), and Hamed Abdel-Samad, who went as far as to say that debate about violence in Islam has been stifled for too long and even the term 'Islamophobia' is misleading because 'the dangers posed by Islamists are real, and many Muslims' unwillingness to integrate in Germany is a serious problem' (*Der Spiegel,* 2010c).

While integrating Islam into German society as an equal component in all areas is an unfolding process that varies from länder to länder, particularly in the educational system (Hofhansel, 2010), there is no doubt that its religious and political influence is already affecting the Jewish community in Germany. Given that 51 per cent of the German population believes that Jews are representatives of Israel and that they are more loyal to Israel than to their own country, writes Urban, it is no surprise that traditional antisemitism in Germany has morphed into a twenty-first century form that incorporates Islamic and left-wing variants (2009: 42–9; also Urban, 2005). She also explains that the scholars who reject the notion that antisemitism and Islamophobia are identical on multiple levels argue also that such comparison minimises the threat of Islamism and the devastation of the Holocaust (Urban, 2009: 46–7). Matthias Kuntzel takes the argument further and asserts that in view of the fact that antisemitism is inherent in the Islamist ideology, antisemitism has increasingly become a part of Muslim identity in some circles in Germany (2005). Likewise Wistrich lists various examples from the German media and political circles between 2002 and 2005 in order to illustrate the prevailing Palestinian narrative of the Israeli–Palestinian conflict and to demonstrate the convergence of a left anti-Zionist sentiment with the Islamic antisemitism that reflects what is generally true for most of Europe (2005: 24–31). Particularly loathsome is a comparison of Israel with Nazi Germany, which is arguably an extension of the argument that draws moral equivalence between antisemitism and Islamophobia. Zvi Rex, an Israeli psychiatrist, is adamant that Nazification of Israel is an expression of German (and for that matter European) self-rehabilitation that effectively nullifies any remaining moral debt to the Jews (Gerstenfeld, 2006: 4; also Kuntzel, 2007 and Wistrich, 2005: 28–9).

When critics of Israel present the case that the charge of antisemitism in Germany is used by the Israel lobby as a moral weapon in order to silence the academic dissent (Fathollah-Nejad, 2010), such argument should not be dismissed outright since a legitimate criticism of Israel does not necessarily conceal antisemitic tendencies. However, it is undeniable that the current antisemitism in Germany (regardless of whether it is conflated with anti-Israelism) is a problem that never completely ceased to exist in Germany and is taken with utmost seriousness by German Christian Zionists (demonstrated in the last section), and also by the 'Anti-German' pro-Israel splinter left group. Simon Erlanger (2009) provides a history of the movement, its challenge to Islamic antisemitism and the post 1967 anti-Zionist consensus on the left, and concludes that '[o]ne may hope that the tide is now turning and that, due to the work of the Anti-Germans, the German left has become more sympathetic to Israel than it was in the past' (2009: 5).

On a governmental level it is questionable whether Germany remains one of the friendliest countries towards Israel. Possibly with the exception of Schroeder's government in the years between 1998 and 2005, who never visited Israel during his time in office, all German Chancellors have been keen to retain a positive relationship with Israel, even when displaying what Israel supporters would label as a pro-Arab stance. For instance, during the German EU presidency in 2007 Angela Merkel was supportive of the formation of a national PA–Hamas unity government and even suggested the broadening of the Quartet partners by including Syria and Egypt in peace talks, while at the same time insisting that Hamas must meet the Quartet conditions for peace if it wants diplomatic recognition. Sceptics however would point out that German behaviour at times causes concern in Israel, exemplified clearly in 2010 when the Bundestag passed a resolution, an action that evidenced, arguably, a prominent departure from a traditionally pro-Israel stance. The resolution, which was passed unanimously by all German parties, called for an immediate lifting of the Gaza blockade and, significantly, blamed Israel for the outbreak of violence on *Mavi Marmara*. Less than a year later 'Germany did something unthinkable. It voted in favour of a UN Security Council Resolution calling the Israeli settlements in occupied Palestinian territory illegal and demanding the immediate halt of all settlement activity' (Dempsey, 2011). Likewise two years later, an abstention vote at the UN General Assembly regarding the Palestinian request for 'a non-member observer state' status added to the growing scepticism about the supposed German–Israeli friendship. Such changes could be attributed to what Patrick Muller conceptualises as the steady process of Europeanisation of German foreign policy and Germany's interest in improving relations with rich Arab countries (2011: 398–9). Since the establishment of EPC in 1970, Muller contends, 'Germany found it easier to shift from its one-sidedly pro-Israel policy that had emerged since the 1950s to a more even-handed diplomacy' (2011: 398). For the Israel lobby in particular the Bundestag 2010 vote is conceivably a cause for deep concern since it demonstrates that traditional German support for Israel cannot be taken for granted, but it is also an added motivational factor in stepping up the efforts in pro-Israel advocacy.

Israel's relations with Britain

Although Germany's moral debt is as unique as the crime of the Holocaust, Britain too, in some ways, has an issue of moral debt regarding the abuse of the Jewish people prior to and during World War II. Its debt however is of a far lesser magnitude than that of Germany, and depending on whether the British role in the re-establishment of the Jewish state is viewed favourably or critically, that debt is owed not only to the Jews, but to the Palestinian people also. Aside from the role of the British establishment in creating the Jewish state in 1947, and the Balfour Declaration specifically – an event that is recalled with delight in Christian Zionist circles and with mourning among pro-Palestinian supporters – it is the 1939 White Paper that is viewed by Israel supporters as the most shameful document (and policy) produced during the British Mandate in Palestine. Even Winston Churchill, the then Secretary of State for the Colonies, who was considered by most historians as friendly to the Zionist cause (Mandel, 2009), caused distress among Zionists when he called in 1938 for a ten-year plan to restrict Jewish immigration (Gilbert, 2007: 153). The restriction continued into the war with tragic consequences:

> The gates of Palestine remained closed for the duration of the war, stranding hundreds of thousands of Jews in Europe, many of whom became victims of Hitler's Final Solution. After the war, the British refused to allow the survivors of the Nazi nightmare to find sanctuary in Palestine. On June 6, 1946, President Truman urged the British government to relieve the suffering of the Jews confined to displaced persons camps in Europe by immediately accepting 100,000 Jewish immigrants. Britain's Foreign Minister, Ernest Bevin, replied sarcastically that the United States wanted displaced Jews to emigrate to Palestine 'because they did not want too many of them in New York' (Bard, n.d.).

A documentary produced by a British Christian Zionist company details the tragic events and callousness of the British government, and maintains that its double standards and hypocrisy caused not only the demise of the British Empire (as a divine punishment), but also set the pattern for all subsequent British policies towards the Jewish state (*The Forsaken Promise*, 2006). Undeniably, the British inability to resolve the Jewish–Arab conflict was a self-inflicted malady due to its inconsistency in dealing with both Jews and Arabs, and it relegated Britain to the margins of political influence in the Middle East. While such power restructuring was confirmed with the Suez Crisis, during which the US Eisenhower administration forced a ceasefire on France, Britain and Israel, and used financial pressure (a threat to withdraw Marshall Plan aid) on Britain in order to end the invasion of Egypt, the relationship between Britain and Israel nevertheless continued to form an important aspect for both foreign policies. Saidel and Joffe (2011) sum up several decades of bilateral dealings as such:

> Although Britain delayed recognition of Israel for eight months after its independence, relations warmed again during the 1950s and 1960s. Britain was a chief weapons supplier to Israel, and even joined forces with both France and Israel against Egypt during the

1956 Suez War. This ebb and flow continued throughout the rest of the 20th century. Britain declared an arms embargo on Israel and the entire region during the 1973 Yom Kippur War, and again, on Israel specifically, during the 1982 Lebanon War – only to see Margaret Thatcher, in 1986, become the first sitting British Prime Minister to visit Israel.

In assessing the outcome of the Yom Kippur War, or the Arab oil weapon as Roy Licklider puts it, British involvement in the Middle East and its policy, he argues, was driven by the necessity to keep on good terms with Arab states, and by the conviction that Israel has been 'a diversion from Britain's real interests in the area' (1988: 212), concluding that the oil weapon accelerated pro-Arab direction in British foreign policy (1988: 213). Jonathan Rynhold disagrees somewhat and takes the view that British foreign policy was consistently both diplomatic and strategic, and concludes that

> only Britain has played any serious diplomatic role in the Israeli–Palestinian arena, due to its consistent support for the US and its acceptability to Israel, which in turn is due to both the American factor and to the fact that it has generally adopted a more balanced approach to the conflict than the EU as a whole' (2006: 28).

In the area of economic and commercial matters also, Rynhold comments that Britain uses a diplomatic approach (2006: 27), which is clearly evidenced by the fact that '[a]nnual bilateral trade regularly exceeds the US$3 billion mark. Commercial, industrial and academic missions cross over on a weekly basis. There are over 300 known Israeli companies that have set up operations in Britain, creating wealth and encouraging growth', according to the Israel–Britain Chamber of Commerce (IBCC, n.d.). However such relations do not extend necessarily to political issues. Leaving aside the successful amendment to the universal jurisdiction laws in 2011[4] the political domain of Britain–Israel relations is viewed increasingly as problematic by Israel. The official British stance about the peace process that endorses the Arab initiative is viewed by most Israelis as anti-Israel because of its calls for readmission of the Palestinian refugees to the Jewish state. Furthermore, the British government's commitment to establish Jerusalem as the capital of both Israel and a future Palestinian state, as well as its attitude towards the settlements in the West Bank, all of which is perceived as unfriendly towards Israel, are described on the Foreign and Commonwealth Office (FCO) website as such: 'Settlements as well as the evictions and demolitions of Palestinian homes in East Jerusalem are illegal and deeply unhelpful to efforts to bring a lasting peace to the Middle East conflict' (FCO, Middle East Peace Process).

Whether the FCO's stance is evaluated as traditional British pragmatism, or as a typical stance of an institution that is influenced by the Arab lobby, depends largely on whether the British historically pragmatic attitude towards Israel is viewed as a prudent foreign policy. According to the Institute of Jewish Policy Research, a survey in 2010 revealed that 53 per cent of the British Jews consider Israel important, and 29 per cent assert that Israel is central, to their Jewish identity (Boyd and Graham, 2010: 16). For these British Jews British foreign policy might be somewhat problematic, although the same survey reveals that 74 per cent of respondents disagree that settlement expansion in the West Bank is justified (Boyd and Graham, 2010: 28). The authors of the report conclude:

> Israel resonates in the thoughts, feelings and identities of a wide cross-section of the Jewish population in Britain. Jews in Britain are both worried about, and protective of Israel. Yet, notwithstanding these concerns and the significant mobilisation of material and human resources on Israel's behalf, they hold a wide range of opinions about Israel's politics, civil society and conduct. As a consequence, the topic of Israel has the potential to both unite and divide Jews. As monolithic as Jews in Britain are in their caring and concern for Israel and its long-term survival, respondents have highly divergent views on the controversial issues (Boyd and Graham, 2010: 36).

One of the findings of the survey relates to the question of conflicts of loyalty, where 83 per cent assert their British identity and two-thirds of respondents answered that there is no conflict, but respondents who live in the most densely Jewish areas feel more comfortable as Jewish persons than those who live in peripheral regions (Boyd and Graham, 2010: 32–3). 'Feeling comfortable' is of course related to the question of the extent of antisemitism in Britain and future demographics of the Jewish population. Unlike in Germany, which experienced a rapid expansion in its Jewish population in the late 1980s, the British Jewish population steadily contracted between the mid 1950s and 2001 by 28 per cent and currently stands at around 300,000 (Abramson et al., 2011: 5). However, according to the Board of Deputies of the British Jews, the latest survey reveals that '[i]t is becoming increasingly clear that the community's demographic profile has turned a corner and, in every year since 2005, the number of inferred births has exceeded the number of recorded deaths' (Vulkan, 2012: 17).

With regards to antisemitism, much like in the rest of Europe, in Britain too the traditional strand that is rooted in Christian supersessionism has morphed into a more comprehensive expression of antisemitism that includes now the Islamist and the far left strands (Rosen, 2010; Phillips, 2007; All-Party Parliamentary Inquiry Into Antisemitism, 2006). From a more comprehensive analysis that takes into account the cultural shift in Britain, where aggressive promotion of the multicultural agenda has led to tolerance of radical Islam (Phillips, 2006: 101–15; Cohen, 2005: 7), to a more specific singling out of media institutions, such as the BBC, that often contain an anti-Israel bias (Rosen, 2010: 42), the common conclusion among some academics is that resurgent antisemitism in Britain is powered mostly by the alliance between the far Left and Islamists. This is particularly problematic because of the extreme anti-Zionist expression (Klaff, 2010), as well as overt Islamist influence and active recruitment at British universities (Whine, 2006), which when combined with the BDS movement[5] amounts to a campaign that seeks to delegitimise Israel, and, according to some analysts, to normalise antisemitism.

The European Coalition for Israel (ECI)

While German and British Christian Zionists abhor equally all forms of antisemitism, they nonetheless single out the Islamic form as particularly problematic given the inherent antisemitic dimension in Hamas, Hezbollah, Islamic Jihad etc. ideology, but also a threat that comes from an Islamic Iranian regime. In addition, the line that distinguishes anti-Israelism and antisemitism from demands for stronger Islamic political clout in European societies is a very fine one indeed as far as Christian Zionists are concerned. The interpretation of Islam's increasing presence in Europe's political sphere, i.e. does Islam have expansionist goals or is it a religion that is on the receiving end of Europe's 'fortress mode', will be largely determined by the type of political, ideological and religious prism through which Islam itself is being examined. The prism through which Christian Zionists view Islam renders it a rival religion, as well as a political ideology, that seeks to establish its primacy in Europe, and consequently make a decisive impact upon contemporary European religious identity.

The contentious nature about identity, and religion in particular, was aptly demonstrated during the discussions about the drafting of the European Constitution and the Treaty of Lisbon. The ECI was one among many voices that objected to the omission of God in the EU Constitution. This objection was not merely confined to the notion that the refusal to acknowledge Christianity in the Constitution as an undisputed spiritual, ethical and cultural framework of the contemporary European identity is a de facto recognition that Christianity in Europe is a religion in decline. Its objection went, and it still does, beyond essential issues regarding the level of compromise between religious and secular aspects of a collective European identity. Europe's identity itself, as far as Christian Zionists in Europe are concerned, is inseparable from Hebrew scriptures and Jewish suffering, and so, by extension, Europe's Christian Zionists are actively seeking to ensure that Israel, as a Jewish state, forms an important part that defines Europe's identity.

European Christian Zionism, although not as influential as the American variant, is currently experiencing a renewal in European churches, some Evangelical, but mostly Pentecostal and Charismatic. Although there are variations in intensity and degree within the normative framework of European Christian Zionism, it consists generally of three aspects: spiritual, political and moral. In terms of its spiritual values, European Christian Zionism tends to be, like the American variant, based on Protestant hermeneutics and pre-millennial eschatology. The obvious difference between American and European Christian Zionism, however, relates to the fact that, as a pro-Israel lobby that has to operate in a distinctly secular context, European Christian Zionist advocacy rarely draws attention to eschatology; rather it emphasises the normative values upon which the EU is built. Also, whereas American Christian Zionism tends to be exclusively right-wing, the ECI could be characterised as centrist since it has members whose political affiliations range from centre left to the right.

Although the ECI endorses the values upon which the EU is built (the rule of law, democracy, human rights, equality etc.), and actively supports the implementation of the same values in the Middle East, the organisation also insists that Europe's political culture can relatively easily co-exist with Christianity, and that Europe's reassertion of its Judeo-Christian foundations is the only way to effectively prevent the Islamisation of Europe. The ECI admires Israel as a country that has the political culture of a fully functioning democracy, and as such should be supported by the EU through maintaining political, economic and cultural cooperation, and most certainly by challenging any form of antisemitism. It is at this particular point that European Christian Zionism differs substantially from the American variant, since the history of European and American Christianity in relation to its Jewish population is very different. Resurgence of antisemitism is for Christian Zionists in Europe a powerful, if ugly, statement that the old hatred towards Europe's Jews never really went away, but also another chance for European Christians to do what they failed to do prior to, and during, the Holocaust. Therefore, this sense of special responsibility is as equally a strong motivating factor in the ECI's advocacy as its religious convictions.

The ECI is the only pan-European Christian Zionist organisation that had to learn how to lobby in a unique political setting, and that learning process included certain structural changes in its internal configuration over the last eight years. The ECI started its journey with five founding organisations (British, Dutch and American), whose several common ministries could be divided into three spheres: spiritual (contending against supersessionism in churches), political (encouraging Christian political activism and facilitating Aliyah) and charitable (supporting charities in Israel and the Jewish communities abroad). Regarding the evangelistic outreach, none of the groups states explicitly that they aim to proselytise the Jews, and the emphasis on particular ministries vary from group to group, but in terms of 'serving' the Jewish people, the groups network very well and organise many joint events and campaigns, a reflection of the experience they gained over the last 30 years. Even so, of the original five founding Christian Zionist organisations, only two remain currently within the ECI structure, interestingly both European in origin.

With regard to the hierarchical nature of the organisation and the networking, the ECI's organisational capability can be described as a mixture of a numerically small, but firmly established, leadership team in Brussels (with a semi-permanent representative), and a loose network that extends throughout Europe into which any association, church or individual is welcome. The leadership team, which consists of the Founding Director, Chairman and board members, makes and executes decisions for which they are responsible to an extended leadership team that is composed of members from most of Europe's countries. This is also a reflection of the unique lobbying culture in Brussels where most lobby groups (and that includes Christian Zionists) tend to have a well-established and more elaborate and extensive structure in their national capitals, whereas in Brussels they have smaller representations and a more focused approach. As such the ECI's network is a pragmatic combination of a Christian core and a wider network that consists of various non-Christian organisations and individuals with different normative and political backgrounds.

The ECI functions largely through an access mode that includes meetings with MEPs and Commissioners, as well as officials from national governments, but it also aims to establish its credibility and raise the level of its effectiveness by organising campaigns, conferences and petitions. On occasions the ECI also participates in public protests, like in Rome in 2010, where government ministers and parliamentarians demanded an end to the delegitimisation campaign of Israel. Perhaps most significantly however, the ECI's use of social media, Facebook in particular, exemplifies its savvy when using voice mode in its strategy. Given that the organisation lobbies within the EU's normative premise and in a unique political setting, its strategy is accordingly a mixture of both defensive and offensive-style advocacy, depending on the issue that it deems to be important, or at times, urgent. Both styles aim to promote the pro-Israeli narrative of the conflict, as well as to improve Israel's image, in the EU institutions and media during the periodic crises. The ECI's unique achievement within the context of offensive lobbying is most definitely the annual Holocaust Remembrance Day in the EP, which the ECI co-hosts with the European Jewish Congress (EJC). Offensive lobbying seeks also to influence EU policy in a pro-Israel direction, and it is focused most of the time on issues related to the peace process. For example since 2010 the ECI has been conducting the San Remo Initiative, a campaign taken not only to the EU institutions and to several European capitals, but to Japan and the UN also, in order to educate the policy makers that the division of Jerusalem would constitute an illegal act according to international law. Eight years after its inception the ECI has remained a small and autonomous, but relatively successful, organisation that has not only solidified its strategy, and secured a level of respectability, in Brussels, but has also earned recognition from the Jewish state for its efforts in pro-Israel advocacy.

Conclusion

This chapter initially focused on the multifaceted challenges that the EU is faced with in its role in the Middle East, specifically how the ENP, an instrument that is meant to project the EU policies in the Middle East according to the EU's values and principles, is criticised from different ideological perspectives. Islamism was singled out since it is a particular contentious issue for Europe's Christian Zionists. To understand the EU's dilemma whether to engage with Islamist parties, it is worth remembering that it is not only the discrepancy in foreign policies regarding this issue between member states, but it is the institutional make-up of the EU itself also that adds to the complexity of Europe's pragmatism and normative premise. A neat categorisation of the traditional foreign and security policy functioning was certainly something that the European integration process challenged with relative success with each successive treaty, but it nonetheless created a dichotomy on the institutional level by dissecting foreign policy into various spheres and delegating the decision making to both national and supranational authorities. Any nation state that needs to engage diplomatically with such a complex institution would find it challenging, but Israel particularly so for two reasons. Firstly, the EU's approach to, and policies for, the Middle East tend to be conditioned by its perception of the ongoing Arab–Israeli conflict (European Commission, 2009; EU Committee, 2007: 92–111); and, secondly, Israel's security concerns (which include Islamist parties) are better addressed in a bilateral context with European countries rather than on the EU level where divergent national attitudes determine an exceptionally high degree of pragmatism on the part of the EU regarding Islamism.

The ECI understands this, and although it too has a degree of pragmatism and flexibility in its membership policy and lobby strategy, on the issue of Islamism the ECI is uncompromising, because, aside from the argument that it poses a continuous threat to Israel, the ECI also links Islamism with the rising influence of Islam in Europe, as well as with the spread of antisemitism. These themes were important to address since the ECI never uses its spiritual and theological beliefs to pursue its aims and goals in the EP and with the Commissioners, but appeals to the EU's normative values, especially the principle of conditionality, in order to call the EU to account if it perceives that certain attitudes and policies directed at Israel are anti-democratic and/or even foment antisemitism. The author discussed the peace process and the role of the Quartet, as well as the economic cooperation between the EU and Israel as these constitute areas where the ECI strives to influence policies in a pro-Israel direction (elaborated in Chapter 5). While the ECI may not view the Quartet role as impartial, especially since the Obama administration moved its position closer to the EU's and adopted a more compatible view with the EU's understanding of, and policy recommendations for, the conflict (Eran, 2009; Dunne, 2010), the ECI nonetheless recognises that the Quartet has a political leverage. As far as trade and commerce goes, the ECI always appeals to Europe's pragmatism and argues, in contrast to proponents of 'tough love' towards Israel, that the mutual benefits of trade agreements should never be undermined by the political issues in the region.

Although the focus of this book is the Brussels-based lobbying, it is important to bear in mind that an integral part of the ECI's strategy is Christian Zionist lobbying in member states, which is one of the reasons why German and British Christian pro-Israel advocacy have been included in the book. Since both countries are among the most influential member states, whose leverage over the EU policies towards Israel and the peace process is presumably high, Christian Zionist lobbying is correspondingly dynamic in both countries. Therefore in sections 5 and 6 the author presented general information about the most pertinent political and social issues currently in Germany and Britain respectively, as well as their relations with Israel, all of which constitute a context in which Christian Zionists conduct their advocacy. At the end of the eighteenth and throughout the nineteenth century both German and British philosemitism played an important role in the re-establishment of the Jewish state, and given that the Christian Zionist movement in both countries is experiencing a revival in the twenty-first century, it could be argued therefore that this trend is a continuation of pre-American Christian Zionism, which, of course, is taking place in a considerably different political context that is mostly shaped by their shared status as the strongest pillars of the ECI.

CHAPTER 3

THE ECI STRUCTURE

One of the questions that the author addresses relates to the level of the ECI's organisational capacity in its quest for influence over the EU's agenda shaping and decision making. In light of the fact that studies on lobby groups in Brussels, including the religious representations, do not offer detailed research on their internal structure and how those structures determine lobbying success, this particular chapter therefore reduces the literature gap by focusing exclusively on the internal configuration of the ECI. As evidenced in the first chapter, the majority of scholarship on lobbying in the EU holds the view that the success of lobbying is determined by the knowledge of which institution should be approached with the information and at what specific stage of the policy cycle – usually the policy formulation stage. Heike Kluver's findings of lobbying success in the EC, however, were contrary to the majority of the scholarship. These findings were shaped by the empirical analysis of a wide variety of interest groups in Brussels, and the analysis itself was based on two defining standards – the nature of the interest groups (those with a cause and sectional) and organisational form (the quality and the stage of information supply) (Kluver, 2011), as well as the organisational ability of the lobby groups and their relationship with the decision makers (Kluver, 2012).

While Kluver's study could potentially be more authoritative if identical research is conducted into the interest representations in the EP, her work nonetheless is significant for two reasons. Firstly, her findings challenge the commonly held assumptions that lobby groups with strong normative foundations have less success in lobbying, which is a clear indicator of the EU's transition from a purely economic actor into a political entity where a host of (competing) normative actors can affect or even shape its identity. Secondly, and relevant to this chapter, Kluver's findings about the lobbying success that is determined by organisational form, where, incidentally, she identifies a gap in the literature (2011: 2), challenge also the assumption that interest groups have to have an access in the initial stages of policy making in order to exert an influence in the legislative process.

Kluver, however, admits that her own study contains a weakness related generally to the lack of literature on the internal organisational structure of the lobby groups: 'Further research needs to investigate the determinants of the organisational structures and how they relate to lobbying activities and success of interest groups' (2012: 505). Questions that she raised, such as '[H]ow organisational structures vary across different types of interest groups, [and] do NGOs have more decentralised decision-making structures than business associations' (2012: 506), demonstrate the need for further empirical research into the organisational capabilities of various interest representations. While this chapter does not provide definitive and comprehensive answers regarding the gap in the literature about the internal structures of all lobby groups, it nonetheless narrows that gap, especially in view of the fact that some recent insights into Muslim lobby groups across Europe and in Brussels (Massignon, 2010; Silvestri, 2009a; Parker, 2007) and Christian denominational mobilisation in Brussels (Massignon, 2010 and 2003) have already introduced a particular stream of research into the EU interest representation. Furthermore, this chapter (as well as subsequent chapters on the ECI's values and lobby strategy) could generate some discussion within the comparative studies about the internal structures of pan-European religious lobby groups, where organisational capabilities are possibly quite similar or even identical, even though the normative premise and aims are vastly different.

To provide as clear a picture as possible about the ECI's internal structure, this chapter is divided into seven sections, starting with the leadership of the ECI: who comprises the leadership, what are the professional backgrounds of those individuals, what role do they perform in the ECI and what is their contribution to the organisation (especially in the political domain), who are they accountable to, and how hierarchically structured is the ECI leadership. The second section looks at the founding Christian Zionist organisations at the time when the ECI was launched in 2004 and more recently in 2012 and aims to explain to what extent the structure of the ECI has changed and whether it has strengthened the organisation or impeded its progress. Such changes are inextricably linked to the extent and quality of the network in Brussels and in member states (Britain and Germany), which is dealt with in the following two sections. The chapter proceeds to present the ECI's communication skills, which is particularly important as the ECI, in addition to its several years of using Facebook and Twitter, recently also took steps to include the media more effectively in its strategy by partnering with Revelation TV. The following section evaluates how the ECI manages its financial resources in view of the fact that it is a small organisation that needs to balance its funding against the frequency of conferences, summits and working visits to national capitals. The last section of the chapter raises the issue of the process of professionalisation of the ECI during its eight years by specifically evaluating whether the organisation has established itself as a credible voice, with an office and a permanent representative in Brussels.

The leadership

Kluver's (2012) work on the link between the organisational characteristics of the lobby groups and the quality of the supply of information to the decision makers concludes that the material resources of the lobby groups, i.e. money and staff, and their internal configuration, i.e. professionalism and decentralised decision making, tend to determine a higher level of success in lobbying the Commission. Although she does not provide any insights into the effect of the leadership in the interest representations, there is, nonetheless, some available literature on charismatic leadership, which is useful and relevant to this chapter. 'While the management of trade associations is clear and statute-based', explains Gueguen, 'identifying the "power source" is very difficult in terms of the NGOs' (2007: 56), which implies the prominence of a charismatic leader in NGOs. Ensher and Murphy (2008) also provide findings into charismatic leadership that manages creative teams, while Cox et al. (2003) explain the ability of charismatic leadership to operate as an individualised or a group level type, depending on the organisational context. In addition, the work on 'socially close', as opposed to 'socially distant', leaders demonstrates the importance of interpersonal characteristics on a small group level (Shamir, 1995), while Varella's et al. (2012) similarly in their research about social networks demonstrate the link between a low level of sanctioning and leader inspiration and integrity.

All the above is relevant in view of the fact that '[i]n the late 1990s Tomas Sandell, then an accredited journalist to the European Commission in Brussels, discovered that Israel had few friends in the European Union'.[1] Sandell is a committed Christian philosemite whose vision for, and tireless work in, pro-Israel advocacy on a pan-European level has come to fruition in a relatively short time. The combined elements of Sandell's academic background in political science and his Christian faith led him to seek Christian Israel ministries that would be willing to provide a 'united Christian voice on behalf of Israel in the EU capital'.[2] During seven years of work in a unique institutional setting, there was, according to him 'almost a monopoly of opinions being articulated in Brussels and when it... came to Israel, those opinions would be very negative'.[3]

Sandell's official title in the ECI is that of the Founding Director, but his role and responsibilities encompass also informal aspects of exercised authority. Sandell is the 'face' of the ECI wherever the delegation happens to travel and represent Israel's interests, whether that be 'at home' in Brussels during annual policy conferences in the EP, or visiting the capitals of the member states and lobbying the upcoming EU presidencies, or contending at the UN against the unilateral declaration of the Palestinian state, or alerting the Japanese parliament about the Japanese government's role in the League of Nations in 1920 regarding the legality of the Jewish state.[4] Naturally, being the most visible and most vocal personality in the ECI leadership, Sandell's credibility among the political establishment in Brussels grew alongside the official recognition of the ECI as a respectable lobby organisation in the EU.

Sandell's informal authority is exercised mostly through social media, where ECI's Facebook page, at the time of writing this book, listed over 10 000 members. For example, although it was Sandell's prerogative to act as the 'gatekeeper' of the information that members could post on the ECI's Facebook page, nonetheless the diversity of political and spiritual posts appearing daily tended to be largely tolerated by the

ECI administrative team. That however changed in April 2012. Given the number of members that also includes non-Christians, mainly Jews, the nature of some of the spiritual links posted caused some friction, which led Sandell to be more stringent with the selection of posts that appear on the page. Members were asked to e-mail links to Sandell for approval, and since then the posts that appear on the page are almost exclusively of a political nature, which, interestingly, reflects the fact that ECI's public concern for Israel is primarily in the political domain.

Another level of (informal) authority that Sandell assumes is of a spiritual nature, clearly exemplified at the ECI Prayer Summits. The combination of Sandell's assertive attitude about the ECI's political goals and his personal charisma when addressing the Christian audience, while coming across as a genuinely humble and at times an emotional man, has endeared him over the years to Christians from across Europe who endorse his spiritual leadership. As a leader who is rarely seen in person by the members of the ECI, Sandell belongs to a category of what Samir conceptualised as 'distant charismatic leaders', who are 'more frequently characterised as having rhetorical skills, having an ideological orientation and a sense of a mission, being persistent and consistent with respect to their mission, being courageous, and having social courage in the sense of expressing their opinions without fearing criticism or conforming to social pressures' (1995: 31). According to Sandell's personal assistant, his role in establishing the ECI and doing pretty much everything in its early days was indispensable[5] and as expressed in his own words: 'I think it's correct to say that the vision was mine... so it's fair to say that I was instrumental.'[6] Nevertheless, Sandell is accountable to the ECI board that currently consists of Christian leaders from several European countries and its Chairman Harald Eckert, who started his work in this capacity in April 2010. In this sense Sandell could be described as the first among equals, where 'shared leadership involves mutual influence... depending on the nature of the specific tasks of the team and the knowledge, skills, and abilities of team members' (Cox et al., 2003: 171).

Harald Eckert is a German Christian, trained in business administration (Dipl. FH) and theology. He is currently involved with four different pro-Israel ministries, of which the Chairmanship of the Board of Christians for Israel (C4I) in Germany for over four years,[7] as well as of Initative 27 Januar, are perhaps the most significant for the ECI, as he brings with him the necessary expertise acquired during several years of establishing networks in Germany. Morally, the most powerful aspects of Initiative 27 Januar are its contribution to coordinating public relations efforts from various organisations in Germany to make known the plight of Holocaust survivors in Israel, and also in Diaspora, which brought to the organisation not only an official recognition from Israel as a major partner in humanitarian efforts, but also an accreditation in the Bundestag. In the same way the ECI is recognised by the European Commission as a credible partner in fighting antisemitism, because, as Eckert points out, Initiative 27 Januar 'is very much working in the same spirit and towards the same goals as European Coalition for Israel does on an international, European level'.[8]

Just as Eckert brings the know-how from Initiative 27 Januar and the German branch of C4I into the ECI, so does Andrew Tucker from the Dutch branch of C4I, where he serves as the Executive Director. At the time of interviewing Tucker in 2010 his participation in the work of the ECI was defined by extending the support for Israel in European churches, rather than being concerned primarily with the political issues that affect Israel. Political lobbying, as he explained, 'is really a secondary, or even a tertiary aim with us... our first and foremost target group are the churches'.[9] Hence Tucker's extensive worldwide travels with the aim of educating, and making an impact upon the churches regarding the role of Israel according to divine purposes, promote not only the work of C4I (such as assisting Aliyah), but they also introduce the work of the ECI as the only Christian organisation that tries to make a political impact in the institutions that are regarded as largely anti-Israel by Israel supporters. In the past few years however, Tucker's involvement with the ECI, determined largely by two factors, has increased considerably. The combination of his own professional background in international energy law and advocacy against delegitimisation of Israel convinced Tucker that he needed to assume more responsibility within the ECI: 'My role is to assist the ECI to further develop its presence in the EU institutions, and to advise generally on international law related issues. I travel regularly to Brussels to represent the ECI.'[10]

David Adeola is another member of the ECI board, who joined the ECI in 2007 and whose role encompasses two different aspects of ministry. He, like Tucker, is responsible for expanding an ECI network beyond Europe, namely to Africa as well as strengthening the links between the politically active Christian Zionist groups in the UK and the ECI.[11] Occasionally, he is a part of the ECI delegation when it travels outside of the EU, mostly to the UN. The other dimension of his involvement with the ECI revolves around the ministry of prayer, which, as observed by the writer during the Prayer Summits in 2010 and 2012, seems to be an area where Adeola holds a great amount of authority among fellow believers. This is usually exercised by leading a charismatic-style corporate prayer, as well as supporting and encouraging Tomas Sandell in his work by privately praying for him. The importance that he (and other members of the ECI) attaches to prayer is perhaps best summed up in his own words: 'I attended the Prayer Summit for that year [2007], and ever since the Lord has asked me to continuously lift up his [Sandell's] hands.'[12]

As a native Nigerian who came to live permanently in the UK in 1999 and became very soon involved in the leadership of Kensington Temple,[13] Adeola exemplifies one of the twenty-first century trends within European Christianity, namely a process of reinvigorating influence among mainly Protestant Evangelical churches by an influx of African Christians (Asamoah-Gyadu, 2008; Jenkins, 2002). Adeola himself puts it succinctly: 'England brought the Gospel to us in Africa, and it's more like payback time in a good way now where God is bringing us back to hold the hands of our Fathers. It has been prophesied that most of the Revival coming into Europe will be through Africans.'[14] In addition, the European Christian Zionists consider the black congregations in both Europe and Africa a ground that needs to be won fairly quickly for pro-Israel causes. To this end Adeola, among other 400 Christian leaders, attended the 'Africa lifts up Europe' conference in Brussels in 2008, of which the ECI members were informed that the ECI aims to 'inspire the African leaders to start their own Coalition for Israel'.[15]

Lennart Fjell is another board member whom the author interviewed in 2010. Although his interview does not shed much light on British and German Christian Zionism, his connections to the ECI are particularly interesting given that he represents a country that is singled out as one of the most hostile to Israel on the European continent. Fjell is a member of an evangelical Word of Life church in Sweden that numbers over 2,500 members, and has a fourfold focus in its ministry: propagating the Christian faith in Sweden, contending for an Evangelical Christianity abroad, affirming God's role for Israel and, lastly, training Swedish Christian youth into future ministry. Fjell claims enthusiastically that since 1993 he heads 'everything we are doing with Israel, including the Aliyah, including all the Israel tours which we are doing every year',[16] and perhaps because of his intense involvement with issues relating to Israel, Fjell, unlike Eckert and Tucker, wears the Christian Zionist badge with pride. While Fjell's (and Christian Zionist) political impact in Sweden in terms of pro-Israel advocacy is modest, which he puts down to a general anti-Israel attitude in the political and media establishment since the late 1960s, he nonetheless brings a network of churches to the ECI and in turn takes his experience back home. His relationship and involvement with the ECI he describes as such:

> [F]or me it has been like school being here... being around the Board of the ECI and seeing how they are having their context into the political arena, and see how they are working there, because that I can implant back home in Sweden together with other friends in the political arena there... Encouraging the politicians who, who really want to stand up, but maybe not always have the facts... But we can support them with that...[17]

Another person who is not involved in decision making in the ECI, but is indispensable to the organisation, is Katariina Salmi, a personal assistant to Tomas Sandell and in her own words 'an all-round woman'.[18] Salmi's job entails day-to-day running of the office, of which arranging the meetings, sending the newsletters to the ECI members in several languages and taking care of the ECI website are the most common tasks. Most of the time Salmi's working days are spent in the office in Helsinki (for she is Finnish like Sandell), but she also travels to Brussels for conferences and important meetings. Although Salmi is not a decision maker as such, her authority derives out of a well-earned respect from fellow believers who acknowledge that she works very hard for Israel's causes. This in particular was observed on several occasions by the author, both in the EP and prayer summits. Her work ranges from overseeing minute details in meetings between the ECI leaders, MEPs and guests who contribute to the ECI events, to taking care of diverse practical concerns, such as arranging accommodation for often over 300 participants at prayer summits, as well as organising various schedules. There is no doubt that this is often done under considerable pressure, but with great efficiency, positive attitude and professionalism nonetheless.

From the inception of the ECI to its current composition, regarding the core leadership team, both Sandell and Eckert were, and still remain, two pillars of the ECI. For several years this core remained very few in number, but the first significant change in leadership occurred in 2008 when it coincided with Israel's 60th anniversary as an independent state. Having come to the conclusion that the ECI performed well in its first five years, but bemoaning the fact that churches in Europe withdraw mistakenly from the political process in modern times, the ECI made a decision to change its network organisation to make it more conducive for pro-Israel individuals and ministries to get involved in activism.[19] This decision also affected the leadership structure: '[T]he ECI leadership team was expanded to include David Noakes and Michael Fenton-Jones from the United Kingdom and Perrine Dufoix from France',[20] which was seen as a positive development because it ensured an added level of accountability within the organisation, as well as better co-ordination between newly included groups into the Coalition. Nonetheless, the expanded team, as Sandell explained, does not hold any executive power:

> [W]e decided to make ECI structurally, legally, very lean and mean, you know, very small. On a networking level we are very open and inclusive, but still to this day on the legal side of things, on the decision-making things, we have decided to keep it very, I would say, operational. So as to make sure that we are not stuck in a huge bureaucratic, you know, monster.[21]

One could argue that this is perhaps inevitable given that, generally, lobby groups in Brussels have to operate in a political environment of elite pluralism where access strategy is a more productive mode of lobbying (Coen, 2007: 4) and where, according to Berengere Massignon, effective Christian mobilisation is harder to achieve due to differences in denominational ecclesiology (2003: 6). Since Massignon's conclusions are based on the Catholic, Orthodox and Protestant lobby groups, where traditionally well-entrenched positions are difficult to shift, it is therefore probably a correct assumption that the ECI, as a lobby organisation that is comprised of a variety of national churches and individuals that are Evangelical in their theology, worship and practice, does not have such deep disagreements among its members and leadership as other interdenominational organisations do. Nonetheless, as with all religious groups, so too with the ECI, the prospect of internal divisions over spiritual and political matters remains real, and that in itself presents a strong factor behind the ECI's decision to simplify its approach regarding the leadership as much as possible in order to keep the focus on complex issues.

It is important at this point to refer to Kluver's work where she identifies areas that require further research about the democratic principles within the lobby groups in the EU (2011: 18). Her specific question as to whether the members have any input into decision making in the lobby groups needs to be answered, in the case of the ECI, on two levels. Firstly, both the leadership and the Christian members of the ECI have firmly agreed theological foundations and moral convictions, which allows for a considerable amount of trust in the way the organisation is led. Secondly, members of the group are well aware that the ECI is the only Christian Zionist lobby group that operates in a political environment that is far more complex than the national ones, and as such the ECI leadership needs a focused strategy pursued through pragmatic means.[22] Finally, Sandell is perceived as a visionary by the ECI members, as he single-handedly started the organisation, and had sufficient faith[23] that it would succeed in some measure in achieving its aims. This confirms Shamir's assessment that 'distant charismatic leaders' are invariably respected for their commitment and perseverance, as well as for their 'belief in the moral righteousness of the cause' (1995: 37).

The founding organisations

Part of the statement on an official ECI website reads the 'European Coalition for Israel is a joint initiative by major international Christian pro-Israel organisations with activities in Europe to address the issue of growing antisemitism and anti-Zionism in Europe'. These founding five member organisations, Christians for Israel (C4I), Christian Friends of Israel (CFI), Bridges for Peace, Ebenezer Operation Exodus and International Christian Embassy Jerusalem (ICEJ) are listed in the

15 August 2006 ECI press release. As far as the common ground is concerned there seem to be several elements on which these groups hold an identical position (explained below). This is important to emphasise in view of the fact that Christian Zionism, as a philosemitic umbrella of numerous groups, tends to have, like all other religious organisations and lobby groups with a strong normative base, more than a few points on which to disagree. Nonetheless, while Christian Zionists may disagree among themselves on some minor theological issues that relate to eschatology, and at times to pneumatology,[24] they find it relatively easy to unite in their zeal for Israel and defence of Christianity, as long as those disagreements do not challenge any of the fundamentals of Christian faith. An issue that does tend to cause tension within the movement, and at times acrimony, very often leading to divisions that split the groups, is that of proselytising Jews.

This is perhaps best illustrated by the case of the best-known American Christian Zionist pastor and pro-Israel activist John Hagee, who published a book in 2008 *In Defence of Israel*, which generated severe criticism from various Christian Zionist ministries. Among other claims that earned him the label of a heretic from fellow Christian Zionists (and considered most offensive) was a contention that Jews do not need Jesus for salvation since they already have a relationship with God the Father, and therefore there is no need to proselytise them. An interesting outcome of his theological position, which became identified as Dual Covenant Theology, was a polarisation within the movement into Christian Zionists who, as already mentioned, regarded him as a heretic from that time on and Christian Zionists who continue to laud him as one of the greatest friends of the Jews and Israel. Although all Christian Zionists believe that Jesus is the Jewish Messiah and that He will return as the reigning King over the whole Earth, some ministries, including those who tolerate Hagee's theology, refuse to proselytise Jews for the simple reason that the prophetic texts in the Bible are absolutely clear about the spiritual condition of the Jews when they return to the Land, i.e. they will return in unbelief,[25] but will recognise Jesus as their long-awaited Messiah only when He personally returns to Jerusalem. As a result of such a dichotomous view on the 'relationship' between Jesus and Jews, two interesting trends developed within the Christian Zionist movement over the last several decades – for and against proselytising of the Jews.

Christians and ministries who are actively involved in, and who are arguing for, giving the Gospel to the Jews tend to stay clear of any political involvement on behalf of the state of Israel. The best example of one such organisation, which in its essence is firmly philosemitic and contends for the Jewish state, and is yet uncompromising in its missionary zeal to the Jewish people, is the Anglican Church's Ministry Among Jewish People (CMJ) founded in 1809. Although it has since changed its original name (London Society for Promoting Christianity Amongst the Jews), the continuing missionary focus that defines CMJ attracts criticism from the Jewish community. Rabbi Shmuel Arkush, for example, who heads Operation Judaism, an organisation dedicated to opposing missionaries, has called for CMJ to be disbanded, and Jonathan Sacks, the Chief Rabbi of the United Hebrew Congregations of the Commonwealth, praised the then Archbishop of Canterbury George Carey for declining to be the Patron of CMJ in 1992.

In view of such strong reactions from Israel and the Jewish communities, as well as the theological debates and arguments that the issue of proselytising Jews provokes, the anti-missionary, or at times ambiguous, stance taken by some Christian Zionist groups is not surprising. The ECI, which fights first and foremost against antisemitism, is among those organisations that tend to steer clear of this particular issue, which is perhaps best expressed in the words of its Founding Director: 'If people start bringing up a particular theological point of view, I would go back to say, well, do you think the righteous gentiles, during the Second World War, who were saving Jews... do you think they had the time to discuss theological nitty-gritty? I don't think so.'[26] Hence, in contrast to the groups that do not get involved politically, the ECI and all other Christian Zionist groups that have an ambiguous or negative attitude regarding the issue of evangelising the Jews, find it perfectly acceptable to be politically active on behalf of Israel precisely because of the level of pragmatism involved regarding the issue.

Of all the organisations that initially comprised the ECI, it is C4I that is perhaps most keen not to be accused by the Jews of having an ulterior motive. Andrew Tucker, its Executive Director, explains in his interview the aims of the organisation: 'It [the organisation] was started by... Christians who wanted to do two things. First of all, raise a voice in the Church about God's promises and purposes for Israel... secondly, to support the Jewish people and their re-establishment in Israel in a practical way',[27] but does not mention giving the Gospel to the Jews, which is also specified on the C4I International website (About Us). The absence of an ulterior motive was affirmed by Michael Freund, a journalist for *The Jerusalem Post*, who writes that C4I are primarily 'missionaries to the church, attempting to convince their fellow Christians that they have a biblical responsibility to stand with Israel and the Jewish people' (2011). Recognition and appreciation was officially confirmed at the Knesset session in November 2011, where, among other Christian Zionist organisations, C4I was singled out and commended for its fight against antisemitism in addition to the extent of its established network activity. Although C4I has its offices and activists in numerous European countries, its concerted effort to generate support from Christians in non-Western countries is perhaps its most unique feature.[28]

Christian Friends of Israel (CFI) International was established in 1985 by an American couple Ray and Sharon Sanders (Ray is also a charter member of the Knesset Christian Allies Caucus), and since then they have successfully overseen the organisation grow and branch out into over 20 countries with varying degrees of political influence. Of all the countries that have an established CFI branch it is perhaps the CFI UK that is most successful in terms of political advocacy (more below). The CFI position on giving the Gospel to the Jews is not explicitly a negative one, which means that the support that the organisation receives is generated from the whole of the spectrum of Christian Zionism, at least in the UK anyway. In terms of CFI's most significant contribution to the ECI during its initial years (at the leadership level), it was undoubtedly the role that Ray Sanders played when he served as a board member of the ECI.

Bridges for Peace does not prioritise pro-Israel political activism over other issues that affect Jewish–Christian relations. Indeed its specific purpose to 'encourage meaningful and supportive relationships between Christians and Jews in Israel and around the world' (Bridges for Peace, About) clearly reflects the organisation's emphasis on overcoming some of the deeply held suspicions and at times hostilities between the two faith groups rather than the overt concern for the eternal destiny of the Jews. In this way, the organisation holds the same view as C4I regarding the issue of conversion of the Jews to the Christian faith, which is hardly surprising given that the organisation branched out of Christians United for Israel in the USA, whose current Chairman happens to be the controversial pastor John Hagee.

Ebenezer Operation Exodus (known also as Ebenezer Fund) as implied in the name of the organisation, gives priority to Aliyah. Its website page illustrates how its twin ministries of training churches through teaching and building up worldwide networks serve to accomplish a goal of helping Jewish people make Aliyah (Ebenezer, n.d.). With its head office in Bournemouth, UK and with active networking since its establishment in 1991, Ebenezer Operation Exodus now has representatives in over 40 countries worldwide. Although the extent of its political advocacy on behalf of Israel is not as prominent, and probably not as effective as that of CFI, nonetheless its active financial participation in assisting Jewish people and families from around the world (especially from the former USSR) to make a new life in the Jewish state has had considerable political implications. This was most notably among the Israeli political right, whose cooperation with Ebenezer Fund (and other Christian Zionist organisations) saw the establishment of the Knesset Christian Allies Caucus in 2004, although recently the recognition of Christian humanitarian and political activism went beyond the political right. The *YNET* news agency thought it worthy of reporting in 2012 that the Knesset Christian Allies Caucus held its sixth annual 'Night to Honour Our Christian Allies' in conjunction with the World Jewish Congress (WJC), where Knesset members from across the political spectrum and government leaders honoured Christians who have been steadfast in their commitment to Israel.

Of all the organisations, ICEJ (the fifth founding member of the ECI) is, without question, the best known Christian Zionist organisation that has over the years generated a great deal of controversy relating to the Israel lobby in American foreign policy and the Israeli–Palestinian conflict (Clark, 2007: 201–55; Cohn-Sherbok, 2006: 167–70; Sizer, 2004; Wagner, 2003). As far as conceptualisation of European Christian Zionism is concerned, the ICEJ does not add as much to understanding the dynamics, norms and values of European Christian philosemitism as it undoubtedly does in the case of America. Its significance in general terms is most probably in the fact that as an organisation that has embedded itself to a degree, albeit a modest one, in Israeli politics, culture and society, it has given an active endorsement to a pan-European Christian Zionist lobby group. As an integral part of the American Christian Zionist lobby that is heavily modelled on AIPAC, according to Donald Wagner (2003), ICEJ has undoubtedly shared a lot of know-how about influencing political circles in the pro-Israel cause, most notably its successes during the presidency of George W. Bush (Rammy, 2006). Specifically, however, it is the connection between the ICEJ and German Christian Zionists that has benefitted the ECI. Dr Jurgen Buehler, who was a board member of the ECI and a founding member of the Christian Forum for Israel (a German umbrella group of Christian Zionist organisations), joined the ICEJ staff in 1999 and was appointed its Executive Director in 2011. It was his paper on the alternative European funding model for the Palestinian Authority (Buhler, 2005) that was presented at the ECI 2006 annual policy conference in the EP in Brussels, which, in combination with the ECI policy paper, was influential in the suspension of aid to the Palestinians in 2006, according to the ECI (elaborated in the last chapter).

With the brief review of the ECI's five founding organisations, and with ample evidence available on their official websites, it is clear that there are four firmly embedded common features in their ministries. Firstly they are all committed to educating churches through various means against supersessionism; secondly they are all active supporters of Aliyah; thirdly they are the initiators of various charities that benefit needy Israeli citizens; and fourthly they are politically active on behalf of the state of Israel. All have their offices in Jerusalem, with ICEJ, CFI and Bridges for Peace headquartering there, and all have good working relations with the Israeli governments, and, unsurprisingly, very warm relations with the Israeli political right. The ECI, of course, is a lobby group that operates in a considerably different political, cultural and social context and, due to its size and structure, does not spend its energies and resources on all four aspects of pro-Israel activism, but focuses its efforts in creating a political impact. Although the ECI made its start in Brussels as an organisation that contained a substantive American Christian Zionist input, it nevertheless strongly contends for its unique European flavour. This is based mostly on its normative framework that it seeks to harmonise with the EU's normative values, but also on its strategy model, which is discussed in the next two chapters.

Membership and network

An interesting development that took place regarding the ECI structure since its launch in 2004 is that currently only two of the original member organisations remain within the Coalition – C4I and Ebenezer Fund – both founded outside the USA. Salmi refers to the changes that have taken place as a transitional time where the ECI was considering new partners 'who are kind of supporters without... voting rights'.[29] The information about what precisely took place between, on the one hand the leadership of the ECI, and on the other hand ICEJ, CFI and Bridges for Peace, has not been disclosed to the researcher, but it seems that the withdrawing of the original three founding members could have contributed to the ECI's pragmatism and its development of a more inclusivist ethos. It is pertinent at this point to raise two points: firstly, in view of Salmi's reference in the above quote to potential supporters not having voting rights, it is tempting to speculate that there may have been disagreements at the leadership level in terms of executive decision making in the ECI. As already mentioned, the information about the reasons and nature of the withdrawing of American Christian Zionist groups from the Coalition was not available, which is to be regretted since it could potentially shed further light on the differences between American and European Christian Zionism. Secondly, all speculation should be set aside given that all original member organisations continue to cooperate and retain links, particularly the British branch of CFI and the ECI.

How precisely these changes will impact upon the future of the ECI's structure is still not clear. What is apparent is that the starting point of restructuring the organisation, the transition that Salmi refers to, dates back to 2008 when the new changes were announced to its members and a press statement was also released:

> [T]he Coalition will start inviting new groups and churches to partner with them in order to build an ever stronger base of support for Israel in the European Union. The Coalition has recently changed its structure from being a closed membership based organisation to becoming an open and inclusive network which seeks to actively partner with national and local churches as well as with associations and private individuals.[30]

This announcement was immediately followed by the ECI's presentation of its work to the leaders of Pentecostal European Fellowship (PEF), a loose network of about 12 million Christian Charismatic believers,[31] and less than a year later to the leaders of Aglow International, a global women's ministry of more than 200,000 members and with affiliations in all European countries.[32] According to the monthly reports numerous national leaders from both ministries were enthusiastic about the prospect of supporting the ECI. Given this response it is fairly certain that the ECI's numerical expansion as a network will continue due to new partnerships, which may or may not include some non-Christian organisations without voting rights. Both Tucker and Eckert contend that the ECI has grown significantly since its inception in 2004, but also since the restructuring in 2008.[33] Sandell too provides more concrete figures of the ECI's numerical expansion:

> We started obviously from scratch but have now some 13,000 people on our mailing list who receive all of our regular updates. On Facebook we have our 8,000[34] members, many who are not on our mailing list. Given that we have still a few members, like Christians for Israel and Ebenezer, who have together over 100,000 people on their mailing list, we reach also these constituencies.[35]

In its work towards securing a numerical expansion and a more influential coalition the ECI endorses ecumenical efforts,[36] demonstrated in 2008 when the leadership of the organisation attempted to involve leaders from all mainline denominations in its campaigns against antisemitism, including the Roman Catholic church, the Orthodox churches, Protestant, Messianic and free churches.[37] In addition, Eckert's reference to the Jewish community is particularly revealing since from its launch in 2004 the ECI's non-Christian partner organisations were, and remain up to this date, Jewish,[38] all of which confirms Massignon's conclusion that '[i]n order to influence the European decision-making process, Church structures and secular humanists have to integrate or gather wider coalitions of interests' (2010: 4). This Christian–Jewish cooperation ranges from an ongoing partnership with the European Jewish Congress (EJC) to ad hoc partnerships when the ECI issues invitations to the Jewish organisations to participate in the ECI campaigns and conferences, such as the Jerusalem Institute for Justice (JIJ) in 2012, the Simon Wiesenthal

Centre (SWC) in 2009 and the Palestinian Media Watch (PMW) in 2005, to name but a few. Likewise in 2008 the ECI was welcomed, as the only non-Jewish organisation, to participate at a strategic meeting in Geneva on the issues regarding the Durban II conference in 2009.[39] Following this meeting the Director of the SWC attended the 2008 ECI annual conference in Brussels and presented a message that defamation and condemnation of Israel at the Durban I and (forthcoming) Durban II is in its essence the globalisation of antisemitism (ECI, Documentation). In retrospect it was the partnership with the EJC in particular, formed in the beginning of the ECI's advocacy in 2005, that established the ECI as a trusted ally among Jewish communities and organisations, and this was confirmed several years later in the ECI's letter to its members where the ECI's cooperation with the SWC was described as a 'significant indicator to a growing trust and cooperation between Christian and Jewish groups in Europe'.[40]

German and British groups

Without extensive research into Christian Zionism in all 28 member states, accurate conclusions regarding the level of efficiency and success of national Christian Zionist advocacy, and how much exactly they contribute to the ECI's lobbying (i.e. membership, financial contribution, and sharing best practices), would be impossible. Having attended, however, several ECI conferences and prayer summits in Brussels, as well as events organised by pro-Israel British and German groups, the author came to the conclusion that British and German Christian Zionist networks are the two strongest pillars of the ECI. While German advocacy brings a strong normative dimension, formed by the Holocaust, the British input into the ECI network seems to revolve around tangible factors. Numerically the British contingent tends to be strongest at the ECI gatherings,[41] but in terms of lobby strategy also the ECI does not seem to discourage other national leaders and members from emulating the British mode of lobbying,[42] which generally tends to be pluralist and competitive, as opposed to a corporatist and mostly consensus-based German style (Saurugger, 2009; Eising, 2008: 7; Eising, 2004: 217–18; Kohler-Koch and Quittkat, 1999; Zimmer, 2000). It needs to be pointed out that both German and British Christian Zionist networks consist of numerous groups, some of which are involved in the political domain and others that are apolitical, but in the light of the adopted definition of Christian Zionism in the introduction of the book, this section is therefore focused only on organisations that seek political influence among national policy makers and provide a direct input into the ECI advocacy.

Initiative 27 Januar (mentioned briefly in the first section) explains on its website that it is 'an interdenominational coalition of citizens and organisations who are committed to the Christian–Jewish and German–Israeli relations' (Initiative 27 Januar, Home). Its activities originally started under the auspices of the Bavarian Parliament and its success in Munich led to its accreditation on the federal level in 2010.[43] As an NGO, the Initiative is active in the Bundestag by pursuing three specific goals: to keep the memory of the Holocaust alive, to oppose antisemitism and anti-Israelism, and to strengthen the relationship between Germany and Israel. For example in 2011, in cooperation with other pro-Israel organisations, the Initiative gathered 47,000 signatures in support of Merkel's refusal to recognise a unilaterally declared Palestinian state, and in June of the same year the Initiative organised a symposium at the Bundestag on this issue. More recently, in January 2012, the Initiative's promotion of German–Israeli cooperation, and its expression of concern about the rise of antisemitism in the German public, was demonstrated at a meeting for the 70th Jahrestag der Wannseee-Konferenz statt (Anniversary of Wannseee Conference) with members of the German–Israeli Parliamentary Group, which in the words of Harald Eckert is 'one group that we try to influence more than others'.[44] As the Chairman of the boards of the ECI and the Initiative 27 January, Eckert is the connection between the two organisations that ensures a maximum level of coordination between national and pan-European information supply to policy makers; but Eckert is also one of the most respected pro-Israel activists whose credibility within the EU institutions stems from his role in fighting against antisemitism on a domestic level.

Eckert has also close links to Saxony Friends of Israel (SFofI), which is an organisation whose members are mostly but not exclusively Christian, and was formed specifically to promote strong links between Saxony and Israel (Beck, 2010), but also aims to influence pro-Israel policies on the federal level. Its Chairman, Lothar Klein, a devout Evangelical Christian, explains that the organisation was started by like-minded (pro-Israel) politicians from East Germany, where state Communist policies were, according to Klein, pro-Palestinian and supportive of terrorist activities against Israel.[45] SFofI was launched in 1989 on the 50th anniversary of the foundation of the state of Israel and since then it organises meetings in the Bundestag in order to pursue Israel-friendly policies. The association's influence is maintained, mainly, through regular contacts with the Christian Democrat Union (CDU) politicians, and demonstrated in its annual congress that is attended by the Prime Minister and other ministers.[46] While specific examples of SFofI's influence are discussed in Chapter 5, it suffices to point out here that, as the former CDU deputy and the member of EPP in the EP, Klein established good working relations with Sandell as far back as 1994 and helped to establish the pro-Israel network in the EP, most notably by sharing its work place: '[T]he staff of the parliament didn't give the official observers of Israel in the European Parliament their own office. So I opened my office to them.'[47]

Both SFofI and the Initiative 27 Januar network with other pro-Israel (both Christian and non-Christian) groups, of which the most significant ones are the Jewish. The extent of such cooperation was demonstrated at the second annual 2011 Israel Kongress[48] event where both organisations, as well as the ECI, held a well-attended seminar that placed a particular emphasis on the message that a strong pro-Israel voice and policies should not only be cultivated on a domestic German level, but must be projected onto the EU institutions.

In Britain there is no doubt that an organisation that attracts politically-minded Christian Zionists is the CFI. On the most basic level it targets churches with the anti-supersessionist message and it encourages its members to continue expanding the Christian Zionist network. The CFI Director Jacob Vince is also an elected member of the General Synod of the Church of England where he aims to provide a pro-Israel voice and prevent any anti-Israel resolutions, such as the one passed in 2010 at the annual Methodist conference.[49] Although the CFI UK is one of the numerous branches of the CFI International, its advocacy is not restricted to the national issues regarding Israel and the Jewish minority in Britain, but it works closely with the ECI. According to Tomas Sandell, of all the national groups that are part of the ECI network British Christian Zionists are least enthusiastic about European integration,[50] which is undoubtedly a reflection of general British euroscepticism, yet their zealous support for the ECI's work in the EP is demonstrated by the high numbers (compared to the other national groups) in which they consistently turn up. The fact that most British members of the ECI are also members of the CFI makes the link between the two organisations quite strong, which was further solidified in March 2012 at the ECI's first Youth Symposium.[51] Such strategic strengthening is logical given that the CFI also aims to recruit and educate young Christians in the British churches for pro-Israel work (Hailes, 2010).

Naturally, the CFI's work in Britain is not done in isolation from non-Christian groups. Although Janine Roberts is correct in saying that CFI has 'particularly close ties with the Tory [Conservative] Friends of Israel' (2008: 5), she fails to identify that the CFI's closest lobbying partner is the Zionist Federation (ZF) of Great Britain and Ireland. This strong partnership is most clearly demonstrated at the annual Lobby Day of Parliament,[52] where members of almost all Jewish and Christian communities have meetings with MPs from all parties, and voice their concerns and demands. What CFI seeks to do, explains its Director, is to rectify past Christian treatment of the Jews, be aware of the areas of concern to the Jewish people in Britain, and 'provide a Gentile voice rather than just a Jewish voice'.[53] Clearly just as the Brussels-based lobbying is premised on a sense of special responsibility towards the Jewish people, so too among British Christians the pro-Israel advocacy is interwoven with their acute sense of historical Christian–Jewish relations.

This motivational factor is an integral component of another organisation that has links with the ECI, as well as with the CFI and the ZF, namely Mordecai Voice. The choice of the name for the organisation, based on a prominent biblical character speaks volumes,[54] as does the fact that its founder, Timothy Gutmann, is a Messianic Jew.[55] As a student at Mattersey Hall Bible College in Doncaster he was incensed by, what he describes as, the blatant antisemitism of some fellow students and institutionalised Replacement Theology,[56] to the point that it proved to be a strong motivational factor in founding Mordecai Voice in 2010. What is interesting about Mordecai Voice is that the organisation became very quickly known among the British Christian Zionists, as well as on the blogosphere among the harsh critics of Israel,[57] most probably because it uses public demonstrations in its pro-Israel advocacy. In its short existence so far Mordecai Voice has staged several relatively large demonstrations and counter-demonstrations, which Gutmann attributes to a successful identifying of the strategy gap in British Christian Zionist advocacy: 'I genuinely think that there were hungry people who wanted to be heard... people who wanted to be seen, and they wanted to do something collectively'.[58] In terms of Gutmann's views on the EU-based pro-Israel lobbying, his support for the ECI is based on the fact that the ECI is the only Christian group in Brussels that supports Israel, and that its work is not based purely on theological grounds but on the grounds of international politics and international law. In addition, while Gutmann maintains that public demonstrations are indispensable to the lobby efforts on a national level – a conviction that was shared at the ECI's annual gathering in Brussels in November 2011 – he is also adamant that the ECI's work is crucial for pro-Israel advocacy because it provides much needed lobbying at a supranational level.

Media

Apart from networking on a personal level with political figures in both national and the EU institutions, it is the ECI's use of media as an integral part of its 'soft' lobbying that is very important to its leadership. According to Massignon, developing savvy in religious mobilisation in Brussels lobby culture involves strengthening media resources, particularly during Conventions (2010), and the ECI's progressively greater engagement with media since its establishment is no exception. How precisely, and with what success, do media tools fit into the ECI's strategy is considered in the last chapter; here the author merely aims to outline the main avenues that the ECI uses in order to present its message, which most of the time relates to contending for Israel's positive image, refuting (as the ECI perceives) lies and defamation against Israel in times of crises, and expanding its network.

   As with some other aspects of the ECI's structure and functioning, i.e. the leadership and the network, so too the media outlets, as Sandell explains, have evolved to a degree over the past decade of the ECI's existence: 'Our engagement with the media has grown over the years though we have consistently chosen to be effective rather than visible. Media visibility is not always a recipe for achieving one's goal; on the contrary, many times silent diplomacy is much more effective.'[59] Although the occasional contribution in opinion editorials and columns in media outlets, such as *The Wall Street Journal* (Sandell, 2010), *The Jerusalem Post* (Sandell, 2011) and *The Jerusalem Post* (Gale, 2009), signifies that the ECI is at least acknowledged as an organisation that could contribute to the debate about Israel in the secular media, Sandell nonetheless admits that 'we still have a lot to do to seriously penetrate the secular market'.[60] The ECI's resolution to engage with the media more strategically in its battle for a pro-Israel message was taken up in 2011 with the production of the short documentary *Give Peace a Chance* and talk shows in the EP that started in 2012. How much of an influence these efforts are going to make in the policy-making institutions in the EU and outside the EU, and whether they will make a substantial impact on the general public in Europe and abroad, has yet to be seen. Regardless of the outcome, it is highly likely that the ECI's use of media, which is effectively divided into two distinct modes – regular and irregular media engagement frequency – will continue to play an increasing role in the ECI advocacy.

In terms of regular media engagement the ECI is active in five different outlets. The press releases that started appearing on the ECI webpage in January 2005, very soon after ECI was launched in the EP, represents its first and longest media strategy. Four other regular media engagements were launched subsequently in 2009, largely determined by the rapid expansion in social media in the past decade, hence the ECI Twitter account and the ECI Facebook page, where its message can be diffused in a serious, yet more relaxed and informal manner. Perhaps equally important is the fact that the ECI steadily gains in membership (in terms of numbers anyway), particularly with the Facebook page, as members are encouraged to add new members. The last two of the ECI's regular media engagements were subsequently launched: the monthly video reports (as a part of the press release section on its webpage) with the first one made available in July 2011, and the talk shows produced in the EP, of which the first one was produced in March 2012 during the Youth Symposium in Brussels. Both the video reports and the talk shows are available on the Youtube channel.

The irregular media engagement involves the ECI's ad hoc projects in partnerships with other (so far) Christian professional companies, organised as the particular situations arise, and usually considered very important for Israel. So for example in 2009, as part of its 'Pray and Vote 2009' campaign, the ECI informed its members:

[The] ECI is busy coordinating an ambitious pan-European campaign to inform, inspire and mobilise Christians to pray and vote in the upcoming European Parliament elections on 4–7 June. The campaign is being promoted by Christian broadcasters... With the help of Tudor Petan of Alpha and Omega TV in Romania and Leenard Fieret in the Netherlands, we have produced several video trailers that inform the constituency about the importance of voting.[61]

Alpha and Omega TV is an Evangelical channel that also has programmes broadcast in English through satellite cable and the internet, and in that way reaches thousands of people in Europe and beyond (Alpha Omega TV, n.d.). So too the British-based Christian Zionist Revelation TV has a relatively broad audience, whose Middle East Report broadcast journalist Simon Barrett explained that its pro-Israel messages reach people mainly on Sky, but through the internet and Roku[62] also.[63] In March 2012 Barrett travelled to Brussels in order to attend the ECI's launch of its European Christian youth ministry[64] in the EP and to produce a programme (the first talk show in the EP) that, he believes, gives the channel a European voice and increases European participation, as well as 'educates and informs Christians in Europe of what is happening in Brussels in relation to Israel and the Jewish people'.[65] In view of the fact that back in 2004 the introduction of the ECI to the Revelation TV viewers did not lead to ongoing cooperation between the ECI and the channel, Simon Barrett's involvement with the ECI's Youth Symposium in the EP is understood by both the ECI and the Revelation TV to be a significant step in a positive direction for pro-Israel advocacy and, on a broader level, for the defence of Europe's Judeo-Christian heritage against Islamisation and secularisation.[66]

Financial resources

Other than exposing the work and aims of the ECI to thousands of Christians and encouraging them to participate in the political arena by the use of media, the ECI could potentially ensure faster numerical growth and secure greater funds for its work. According to Kluver, since members of cause groups are more concerned with diffuse ideals and principles rather than material interests, they are therefore 'not willing to provide the same amount of [financial] resources as members of sectional groups' (2011: 4), which consequently lowers the level of lobbying success. Although the validity of her (and previous) research about the correlation between the nature of lobby groups and financial resources is authoritative, these findings nonetheless are not entirely applicable to the ECI. The classification of the ECI as a cause group, as Kluver puts it, is certainly accurate, but the motivational (religious) factor of its members is not comparable to the motivational factor of purely political lobby groups, i.e. environmental interest representations, as the ECI finds its members quite reliable when the issue of funding is brought to their attention.

It is important at this point to stress that the ECI receives no contribution from the Commission, but is funded solely by its members. Unfortunately, some interview questions by the researcher about the ECI's financial resources remained unanswered, which makes it difficult to establish precisely what the reason is behind the lack of funding from the Commission. In light of the fact that the ECI is fully accredited as an NGO in the EP, and that the Commission 'values the expertise which many organisations working to implement human rights possess' (European Commission Delegation to Israel), a lack of generosity towards an organisation that campaigns vigorously against antisemitism is puzzling to say the least. According to a report produced in April 2008 by the NGO Monitor the limited transparency and accountability of EU funding for NGOs is directly responsible for the EU's support 'for the NGOs that are very active in the conflict, and which pursue objectives in direct opposition to the goals proclaimed by EU officials' (Steinberg, 2008: 29). While it would be speculative to attempt to find a link between the ECI's financial resources and an implied pro-Palestinian bias in the NGO Monitor report, the issue about the transparency in NGO funding nonetheless remains, which, of course, raises a host of other questions that are related to a debate about the democratic deficit in the EU.

As already discussed in the first chapter the Commission acknowledged the EU's problem of democratic deficit in 2001 in the White Paper on European Governance. Given the lack of direct participation in EU politics by Europe's citizens, the Commission's pledge to facilitate a greater inclusion of NGOs in its legislative process by providing some funding to NGOs is logical (European Commission, 2001: 18).

Whether, and how much, this financial contribution extends to any religious lobby groups is not known, which clearly demonstrates that financial resources is one aspect of the internal configuration of religious lobby groups that remains unexplored so far. As far as the ECI is concerned its periodic reminders to its members confirm that the organisation is not a recipient of the Commission's generosity: '[P]lease keep in mind that our only source of income is the generosity of friends and supporters like you',[67] and: 'Please note that we are not financed by any government or by large foundations, but simply by friends and supporters like yourself.'[68] In its press releases the only indication of the ECI's readiness to accept gifts from the pro-Israel public (both non-Christian and Christian) is a 'donate' button at the bottom of the text, while its monthly reports for the members contain a standard message regarding voluntary donations to the organisation.

Apart from this standard message there is no fixed pattern to the ECI's appeal to its members for more money. The analysis and comparison of the reminders and appeals in the monthly reports between January 2008 and June 2012 point to a fairly relaxed attitude about the funding on the part of the ECI administration, except on occasions when the ECI is starting or stepping up a campaign, such as the one in the 2010 monthly reports[69] in preparation for the forthcoming San Remo campaign. 'It is now clear', states the December 2010 monthly report 'that there is an urgent need to inform Members of parliaments and governments as well as other opinion shapers about the history and the solid legal foundations of the Jewish state'. Specifically it was the prospect of the Palestinian bid for statehood in 2011 that generated a strong appeal for finances:

> To counter this latest attack against Jerusalem we have decided to make a film documentary which establishes the legal rights of the Jewish people to their ancestral homeland of Israel and to Jerusalem as their undivided and eternal capital... [W]e have already raised 33, 000 euro towards the project and need 'only' another 67,000 euro.[70]

Overall, as with the other aspects of the ECI's internal structure that have changed since its inception, so too its financial resources have grown, largely as a result of the membership restructuring since 2008.

When the author asked Sandell whether the extended membership secured and/or substantially increased the ECI's financial resources, he answered by stating that even though the ECI is small (in comparison to some American Christian Zionist organisations), and whenever the ECI faced a dilemma regarding aggressive marketing, the organisation chose to remain, in his words,

> organic and genuine and a community. But having said all of that, we have grown, and one way of looking at it is of course to see... a clear increase in giving, a clear increase in people who are interested in the work and who want to make a difference.[71]

Professionalism

These findings affirm Kluver's conclusions on the effect that financial resources create in lobbying. Her assertion that greater financial resources determine higher lobbying success (2011: 5) is certainly applicable to the ECI's initial stages of the 'San Remo' campaign (discussed in Chapter 5). The fact that the ECI's delegation travelled across the globe to present its message points to the fact that the ECI as a lobby group is capable of raising a sufficient amount of money in a relatively short time. On the other hand, however, even if a lobby group, and the ECI for that matter, possesses great financial resources, but is short on human resources, the successful outcomes of any given strategy would be highly doubtful. 'Money alone', contends Coen, 'does not equal influence' (2007: 12); and Massignon likewise argues that institutionalisation of religious groups in Brussels, among other structural facets, includes also appointments of their representatives. She demonstrates this by listing the appointments of official representations from the Vatican in 1999, the Orthodox Church of Russia in 2004, and the Greek Orthodox Church in 2004 (2010: 4).

The ECI is no exception in this respect, and although the ECI did not acquire its own office and a representative as early as the above-mentioned religious interest groups, its professionalisation process was relatively successful considering the facts that the ECI's financial resources derive purely from its members, and that its presence in Brussels is autonomous, i.e. not sponsored by any traditional denominational structures from member states. A close look at an interview with the Founding Director of the ECI in 2011 and a monthly report in 2012 identify a few issues that were important in the ECI's journey in the last couple of years. To the author's question as to how he would rate the level of professionalism of the ECI and whether the ECI has its representative in Brussels, Sandell responded: 'We are in a transition where we are looking for... a permanent one. But we are also very aware of the fact that unless you have the right person, or the persons, it doesn't necessarily have the impact that we would like it to have.'[72] A year after the interview took place the ECI members were informed that the Executive Director of C4I (Andrew Tucker) would serve as a semi-permanent representative of the ECI: 'Andrew is a trained lawyer...[and] he will remain based in Holland but will travel to Brussels on a regular basis to meet and dialogue with MEP and EU officials.'[73]

Apart from the fact that the ECI's focus on the San Remo campaign determined the priority and strategy for lobbying, and consequently the allocation of the financial resources, the above statements reveal that the ECI administration understood that in order to exert any amount of influence in the EU institutions, lobby groups need to provide expert knowledge to relevant agenda setters and policy makers on a regular basis. As evidenced in the first chapter, research done on interest representations in Brussels demonstrate that a higher level of professionalisation determines greater potential for lobbying success.

Interest groups which have a large amount of resources at their disposal provide on average more information... Moreover, interest groups that are characterised by a high degree of professionalisation find it much easier to provide information to decision-makers than interest groups that largely rely on untrained volunteers, asserts Kluver (2012: 505).

Hence the ECI's decision to have two people as their representatives in Brussels – Tucker as a successful professional in international law and Sandell as an experienced lobbyist and a political scientist, even though both serve on a part-time basis due to their other existing commitments.

When assessed in general terms, it could be argued that the ECI's speed of professionalisation process was rather slow, given that it took the organisation six years to open its own office and announce in 2010 that it has a representative: 'At long last ECI has a permanent and staffed location in Brussels... In addition to celebrating the opening of the new office we have the pleasure of welcoming Monica Tamagnini from Italy as our new Brussels representative.'[74] The degree of Tamagnini's success in the office, however, was minimal due to her health issues, which forced her to leave the position after only a few months – an insufficient duration for anyone to become part of the lobbying culture in the EP, but possibly also due to her educational background which is in linguistics, rather than politics. Nevertheless, her short time in Brussels was a milestone for the ECI: 'I was the first person to actually represent the organisation in Brussels... and for the first time [the ECI] acquired headquarters in Brussels, and headquarters have got more meaning when somebody is there to represent the organisation.'[75] When the same questions regarding slow professionalisation of the ECI were presented to Eckert, his response included an acknowledgement that the ECI needs a permanent representative, but also an optimistic attitude: 'On the operational side, we got this apartment [office]... around the corner from the European Parliament, which strengthens our presence in Brussels',[76] which does not seem to be misplaced as the ECI managed to come up with a relatively effective solution to its problem. After the initial several years of Sandell's substantial role as a representative (when needed), and a few more years since then of relying on dedicated volunteers, the ECI appointed Andrew Tucker as its representative in 2012, which perhaps may not be evidence of a high level of professionalism, since it is on a part-time basis. Nevertheless, Tucker's expertise and his commitment 'to assist the ECI to further develop its presence in the EU institutions and to advise generally on international law related issues'[77] demonstrates that the professionalisation process of the ECI is progressively improving.

Conclusion

In view of Kluver's objection that 'interest groups have so far been treated as black boxes without any attention to their internal configuration' (2012: 505) this chapter concludes that such criticism is valid given that interest representations (including the religious ones) are included in the EU's policy cycle. Research on the internal structure of lobby groups is therefore important if there is to be a high level of academic precision in terms of the linkage between the internal configuration and lobby success, but crucially the linkage between the internal configuration, transparency and democratic deficit reduction. To that end this chapter offered some valuable insights about the ECI's competence in establishing itself as a professional and influential pro-Israel lobby organisation in Brussels.

It initially explored the leadership of the ECI – the individuals in the core leadership team (who hold the executive power), their professional backgrounds and involvement with national Christian Zionist organisations, and how these involvements and years of experience benefit the ECI. One of the questions that Kluver raised is how meaningful is the impact of the interest groups on the EU's democratic deficit if there is a substantial gap in the knowledge about the normative standards within the interest groups themselves (2011:18). The ECI leadership team is certainly very small (and deliberately so) and responsible for executive decisions regarding the policies, campaigns and strategy, for mainly operational effectiveness. That, however, does not imply that it is not accountable to the extended leadership team, which most definitely has the capability to influence the congregations from their respective member states should the ECI leadership in any way abuse its position. The impression obtained through interviews and by observing the interaction between the ECI leaders and the members during many of the ECI's sponsored gatherings in Brussels confirmed that the ECI leadership team and style are endorsed for two reasons. Firstly the members do not doubt the Christian Zionist normative framework of the ECI and by extension the motivation of the leaders who set the agenda of the organisation. Secondly the members are also aware that the ECI's primary focus is of a political nature that requires an effective carving up of influence within the EU's institutional set-up. This set-up is often perceived by the majority of the members as incredibly complex and at times alien (when compared to national democratic institutional functioning), which serves as a convincing reason to give a free hand to the core leadership team in agenda setting, strategy modelling and resource allocation. Therefore in terms of Kluver's reference to the extent to which members are participating in the interest groups' decision making, it is clear that in the case of the ECI the level of democracy in the organisation corresponds accurately to the wishes of its members.

The chapter proceeded to describe the five Christian Zionist founding organisations of the ECI and their areas of priority regarding pro-Israel advocacy. Although the American Christian Zionist organisations are no longer part of the Coalition, the mutual cooperation continues. The precise reasons for the withdrawing of these organisations from the Coalition is unknown; what is clear nonetheless is that, firstly, this development allowed the ECI to reassert the European identity of the Coalition, and, secondly, it gave the ECI more room for a pragmatic approach in lobbying by defining its priorities in political rather than in spiritual terms. Such an approach is essentially in line with the normative/spiritual characteristic that defines the ECI (discussed in the next chapter). Although true to its Christian Zionist convictions that Jews will recognise eventually the Messiahship of Jesus Christ, the ECI nevertheless does not advocate active proselytising as it seeks to build friendly and productive relations with Israel and the Jewish communities.

The chapter has also demonstrated the link between the individuals in both the core and the extended leadership teams and the network. Here it seems that in quantitative terms the ECI has expanded and that it has forged strong links with numerous Christian Zionist organisations in Europe and beyond, as well as with the Jewish ones in Europe and Israel. This was clearly a result of the restructuring that took place in 2008 when the ECI made a pragmatic and a strategic decision regarding its inclusivist ethos in the ECI membership policy. This conclusion is reinforced by the evaluation of German and British Christian Zionist organisations, the two most significant national constitutive parts of the ECI, which closely cooperate with the national Jewish groups. Clearly Massignon's contention that formation of short- and long-term alliances between interest groups with similar or identical aims predisposes groups for better results on an organisational level, as well as in their repertoire of actions (2010: 5–7), is applicable to the ECI as the organisation's added level of pragmatism increased the ECI's lobby efficiency.

This restructuring and greater efficiency is also reflected in the ECI's extended engagement with the media, frequent appeals for funding, and a heightened level of professionalism. The review of beginnings and changes over the eight years in these three aspects of the ECI's internal structure points to the fact that the ECI has reached a sufficient degree of success in the professionalisation process. Such conclusions are relative to the fact that the organisation is small (regardless of its recent numerical expansion) when compared to most American Christian Zionist organisations, and its financial resources are derived exclusively from its members. On the other hand, the level and quality of networking could be, as admitted by the interviewed individuals, greatly improved, even though it is the issue of the permanent representation that determines considerably, as the ECI leadership is aware, the professional status of the organisation. While the ECI is managing to allocate sufficient financial resources to maintain its office at the heart of Brussels' political institutions, it has yet to employ a full-time representative like other religious interest representations.

Overall the ECI's organisational capacity to influence the EU agenda shaping and decision making has so far proved to be high. Although the capacity does not necessarily translate into success, this chapter has demonstrated nonetheless that the ECI's internal structure has progressively evolved over the period of eight years to the point where the organisation has managed to assert itself as part of the EU policy network where it pursues its agenda with relative success, and its organisational ability to retain that political space is sufficiently competent. That organisational ability, as well as the lobby strategy (discussed in the last chapter), is preconditioned by the ECI's normative standards, which the next chapter conceptualises as a set of spiritual, political and moral values, drawing some distinctions from existing academic analysis that conceptualises Christian pro-Israel advocacy explicitly within the context of American politics and religion.

CHAPTER 4

THE ECI VALUES

Having explained the ECI's internal structure in the previous chapter, the focus of this chapter will be on the fundamental positions that the ECI holds on Israel in terms of its principles and values. As argued in the first chapter the issue of the democratic deficit in the EU has become inextricably linked to the role of the religious lobby groups, which are positioned probably better than any other groups to raise the question about the identity of a new Europe. The politics of the EU, and possibly its foreign policy will, arguably, be determined to a significant degree by the values and principles of religious actors, which is consequently going to challenge the notion that the EU is a secular and soulless economic club. In the case of the ECI, the tenacity of its pro-Israel advocacy is framed within the normative mixture that contains a certain measure of dogmatic spirituality, as well as political pragmatism that enables the organisation to utilise the EU's secular humanist values when advocating for pro-Israel policies.

One of the questions raised regarding the influence of Christian Zionism in Brussels concerns the normative impact that the ECI has sought to achieve in the EU's agenda shaping and policy making. This chapter will therefore explain the values of the organisation, but also demonstrate that it has indeed made a lasting mark at the EU institutional level by embedding some of its values in EU politics. As already mentioned in the introduction to the book, European Christian Zionism is distinguished from the American variant, not so much in terms of the specific components that drive political activism, but rather in terms of the emphasis that is placed on each particular component.

For that reason this chapter initially presents those spiritual distinctions; i.e. the ECI's anti-supersessionism, Christian Zionist eschatology and Judeo-Christian ethics, and how they are occasionally interwoven into its advocacy, before proceeding to explain the Christian Zionist position on the politics of Islam, specifically the ECI's opposition to inclusion of the Islamist parties in the political dialogue with the EU. This strong normative position is classified as both spiritual and political, as the ECI often conflates its spiritual support for Israel and its contention for Judeo-Christian values with its political opposition to Islam.

Section 3 discusses the ECI's political position regarding the EU's normative values and principles, as well as its criticism of the EU's foreign policy performance in the Middle East. Finally, the last section in the chapter explains the moral dimension of European Christian Zionism, and why its fight against resurgent antisemitism is a key defining feature of the movement. This particular principle not only demarcates European Christian Zionism from the American variant as a primary source of pro-Israel advocacy in national parliaments and in Brussels (as opposed to the eschatological element that is prevalent in the American Christian Zionist groups), but it is also used by Christian Zionists to combat the supersessionist stream in European churches. European Christian Zionists maintain that it is Replacement Theology that provided the spiritually, morally, and ideologically conducive environment in which the persecution and murder of Jews continued more or less uninterrupted in European history.

The ECI and Christian Zionist spirituality

It is undeniable that American Christian Zionism has exerted a level of influence on current Christian Zionist fervour in Europe. From pro-Israel Christian conferences, where some invited speakers hold firm pre-millennial eschatological views, to the Christian bookstores that sell books on Christian Zionist themes, one could easily be impressed by the volume of American input into European churches and pro-Israel groups. On a more profound level, however, it becomes apparent that European and American Christian Zionism do not share an identical theological ground, as the American variant tends to be mostly dispensationalist,[1] while in Europe Christian Zionism is much more historically oriented (Pawson, 2008: 23), and it is not so homogenous, as the intensity and degree of its spiritual, political and moral values vary from country to country.

These values are conditioned by several factors, of which domestic political culture and political process, as well as the Jewish experience with national churches in the past, are most significant. Likewise the mode of Christian Zionist lobbying strategy is often determined by the nature of the issues that Christian Zionists agitate about and by the socio-political context in which the issues are being raised. The ECI, for that matter, has managed to achieve a fairly effective balance with regard to conveying its values. Although the religious representations have carved a significant political space for themselves in Brussels and, in the process, affected the debate about the new European identity and democratic political culture, it is important to remember that nearly all religious representations are the outposts of large denominational structures, and as such they present their 'religious' demands relatively successfully in the EU institutions. For the ECI, on the other hand, the context in which it has to contend for influence remains exclusively secular, since the ECI is a network of mainly, but not exclusively, charismatic and Pentecostal groups on the margins of the European Church. Therefore the necessary level of pragmatism, i.e. its spiritual Christian Zionist premise remains confined to its immediate Christian membership and network, while the political values of the ECI, which are embedded in the EU's normative values and principles, form the platform from which the organisation conducts its pro-Israel advocacy. This recognition on the part of the ECI is perhaps best illustrated by the fact that its chosen name omits any adjective that would suggest a Christian organisation (as opposed to all the founding member organisations).

Another important reason why the ECI tends to leave its eschatological element out of its advocacy is related to the fact that Christian Zionism was (and still is) deeply criticised, and often caricatured, because of the hawkish stance by many American Christian pro-Israel organisations. In the words of Andrew Tucker:

I think the term Christian Zionist is a rather misunderstood and misused term, and I think there are difficulties with it. I believe that if you basically believe and follow in God's word you, by definition, are a Christian Zionist. As a Christian you support the Zionist cause... The problem is, I think, the notion of a Christian

Zionist has been very much associated with mainly North American dispensationalism, and that's where I would think that it doesn't fit well in Europe.[2]

Similarly when Harald Eckert was asked whether he would consider himself a Christian Zionist, and whether it is accurate to label European Christian supporters of Israel as Christian Zionists, he explained:

If that's the term I like most I would doubt, but for scientific clarification sake that's probably the box in which people would put us. . . I think the eschatological dimension is not as strong in Germany or Europe as it would be in the United States. We are much more history oriented than the American friends would be.[3]

While both statements demonstrate the ECI's commitment to a global pro-Israel advocacy, which would be impossible without Christian Zionist efforts from America, they at the same time explain that the ECI leadership seeks to build its respectability by retaining its 'European identity'. This was conveyed in 2008 in one of the ECI's updates to its members: 'The US will always be a key ally in the global battle for the survival of Jewish state and as Europeans we need to find ways of joining up in this battle while preserving our European identity.'[4]

Notwithstanding the ECI's need to assume a pragmatic normative position in order to distance itself from American Christian Zionism and to adapt itself to Brussels' political culture, it is important to remember that the ECI shares basic spiritual tenets with all Christian Zionist organisations, of which commitment to prayer takes primacy. 'What makes ECI distinctly different from any secular pro-Israel organisation', the ECI members are told, 'is our faith in prayer'.[5] This, of course, is inextricable from its commitment to a particular hermeneutics since the ECI, as all Christian Zionist groups, interprets both the Hebrew scriptures and the New Testament holistically and firmly endorses and contends for the biblical promises given to the Jews by God Himself. This is exemplified at the ECI's annual prayer summits, held (most times) in Brussels, where Christian Zionists from across Europe participate in corporate worship and encourage one another to persevere in the fight against antisemitism in societies where they come from and to refute supersessionism in their churches, but also to continue tenaciously in pro-Israel advocacy at the national political level. Each prayer summit is defined by a particular issue and agenda, depending on the overall political and spiritual events that affected Israel and the Israel–EU relations that particular year, or by the forthcoming events deemed important by the ECI leadership. A good example would be the comparison between the church service in 2010[6] and the prayer summit in 2012.[7] Apart from the usual reinforcement of Christian Zionist commitment to the Jewish people and the Jewish state, the emphasis in the 2010 church service was more on the need for the European churches to show repentance for their role in the Holocaust. A German pastor Jobst Bittner gave a message about the detrimental effect of the Hellenistic philosophical influence in the Church, most notably how it paved the way for the supersessionism and hatred of Jews among Christians; and Rick Ridings, a leader from the CFI branch in Jerusalem, spoke about Europe's current historic crossroad, and the choice it has to make between Islam, secular humanism and Christianity. In contrast, at the 2012 prayer summit where Eckert exclaimed: 'Our foundation was lifted up from where it started ten years ago', the overall message emphasised the political mandate of the ECI on behalf of Israel, as well as the network expansion of the organisation, which included specific prayers for, and 'laying on of hands'[8] on the Christian youth.

Quite clearly the politics of European Christian Zionism is determined by the spiritual values and history of the Christian–Jewish relationship. However, before proceeding to a discussion about political positions of the ECI, it is pertinent at this point to refer briefly to the spiritual premise and historical background of British and German Christian Zionism, since the pro-Israel advocacy from these two countries constitutes the most substantial input into the ECI pan-European strategy. The author is steering clear of any in-depth discussion on the history of British and German philosemitism and political advocacy for the Jewish state, since the book is concerned with the contemporary politics and advocacy of Christian Zionism in a post-Westphalian context. Nonetheless, should readers wish to understand the historical context of European Christian advocacy for the re-establishment of the Jewish state in more depth, or develop a comparative outlook on Christian Zionist activism before and after World War II, the available literature is more than adequate to serve the intended purpose, or at least to point in the right direction, as in the case of German, or to put it more accurately

Prussian, eighteenth and nineteenth century philosemitism. Likewise, the literature on the development of a pre-millennial eschatology among the British Puritans/Evangelicals, as well as its political influence in the Middle East, conveys to an interested reader that scholars, who understood that Christian Zionist input into the creation of modern Israel was not insignificant, are polarised on the issue (Lewis, 2010; Gribben, 2008; Clark, 2008; Wilkinson, 2007; Cohn-Sherbok, 2005; Sizer, 2004; Merkley, 1998; Tuchman, 1984; Murray, 1971). The 1917 Balfour Declaration in particular continues to be viewed by many Jews and Christians as undoubtedly the most important event because it afforded Zionism credibility and legitimacy despite the fact that the confusing and contradictory politics of the Empire, which tried to accommodate (and use) both Arabs and Jews, also created hostility towards Zionism. Consequently, the impact that the Balfour Declaration made on politics also affected scholarship where the role that British Christian philosemites played in the re-creation of the Jewish state is well documented, whereas research on German Christian philosemitism is comparatively minimal.

While development of British Christian Zionism took place in a socially and politically relatively steady environment, the prevailing attitudes towards the Jews and Jewish homeland among German Christians in modern history could be adequately described as the German spiritual pendulum that swung according to the extreme socio-political changes. The original Pietist influence that interpreted specific biblical texts in the same manner as British Puritans was short-lived due to the political ambitions of the German government in the late nineteenth century (Merkley, 1998: 29–42). In addition, Germany (and indeed the whole of Europe's Christendom) was at that time experiencing an internal conflict regarding the authenticity, authority and applicability of the Bible. This is no small matter since the rise of liberal Christianity in Germany dangerously conflated with the thoroughly documented antisemitism of the great reformer Martin Luther, which, according to a number of scholars, paved the way for the Holocaust (more below).

Islam and Europe's Judeo-Christian identity

An area where the ECI's spiritual values start to blend with its political convictions consists of the issues of Europe's identity and Islam.

Christian Zionists contend that Islam is a comprehensive system whose spirituality is derived from the corrupted Hebrew scriptures and the New Testament, and whose political values, i.e. the Sharia law, diametrically oppose the values that underpin and sustain Western democracies. The ECI's denunciation of Islam as a false religion remains for most of the time a spiritual position, although in January 2010 its annual policy conference[9] in the EP politicised its anti-Islam stance. The conference speakers included a human rights activist, David Littman, and a controversial historian, Bat Ye'or, and raised the issues of human rights abuse in Muslim countries, EU immigration policy, and also the implications of the currently assertive Islam for Europe and Israel. Although the overall message, presented in an alarming tone, urged European policy makers to prevent the Islamisation of Europe, the highlight of the conference was Littman's presentation of human rights abuses in Islamic countries and a call to the EU to uphold universal human rights at the UN (Littman, 2010). Likewise, several years previously, at an ECI 2006 annual conference, the panel discussing the relationship of Europe and Islam included a former French Minister of Health Georgina Dufoix, who proclaimed:

> The caliphate [the rulership of Islam] is incompatible with European values... These values are not only contrary to Judeo-Christian values but are also in contradiction with generally accepted European values such as freedom, brotherhood and equality... This should not lead us to fear or hatred but to a true soul searching in order to rediscover the Judeo-Christian roots which can again make Europe strong and also appeal to those of other faiths.[10]

The European Christian Zionist stance regarding the values that should define Europe and relations with European Muslims are perhaps best summarised in a rhetorical question of the ECI's monthly report: 'What better way is there to integrate [all the minorities] than to cling to sound Judeo-Christian values that in the past made Europe so great.'[11] In light of such an attitude towards Islam, European Christian Zionism could certainly be categorised as a right-wing politico-religious movement. Nonetheless in terms of its involvement in the political process, both nationally and in Brussels, such neat categorisation would be rather simplistic. Whereas American Christian Zionism tends to be overtly biblical and evangelistic due to the fact that the Christian religion is embedded in its political system (regardless of the constitutional separation of Church and State), the ECI's approach is deliberately toned down, because, as already explained, the EU's political context is not so conducive to the Christian Zionist agenda, but also because the ECI's projection of its public image is conditioned by its priority in focusing on the political, rather than the spiritual, agenda. In the words of Sandell: '[I]f we look and say there's a political arena, there's a spiritual arena... and our primary goal is perhaps in the political arena.'[12] In addition, when compared to American Christian Zionism, which is embedded in right-wing politics, it is apparent that European Christian Zionism incorporates a wide variety of political views. This became apparent to the author who over the period of four years held many private conversations with individuals from across Europe, where, to the best of her judgement, European Christian Zionist political affiliations range from the centre-right to the centre-left political spectrum. In light of the fact that the European scene is more complex compared to the American 'two-party' system, it is not surprising to find Israel's fervent supporters in most political parties. When Sandell was asked specifically whether the ECI is a right-wing or a left-wing organisation, and which political parties in Israel it prefers to work with, he claimed emphatically that the ECI is an apolitical organisation and its work is pragmatic:

> [W]e would never allow ourselves to be... defined by anyone as left or right. You know, I think it's fair to say that we are in that respect, more in the centre... [W]e don't mess with domestic policy in Israel, so regardless of who is in power we will work together with that government and support them.[13]

In relation to the above mentioned ECI's stance of Islam, the organisation has also consistently held the position that Islamism and political Islam are indistinguishable facets of the politico-religious system that is inherently hostile to Judaism and Christianity, as well as Israel and Europe. For that reason, for example, the ECI had called on the EU and the upcoming German Presidency in 2006 to add Hezbollah to the list of terrorist organisations: 'According to the Coalition there are no excuses to keep Hezbollah from the terrorist list regardless of the opposition of some European member states governments.'[14] As explained in the first chapter, the CFSP is anything but common as the consensus, or 'common position', in the European Council is extremely difficult to achieve. This is exemplified in the difficulties of defining Hezbollah, where France, as the most vocal opponent of designating Hezbollah to the terrorist list, along with Italy, Belgium, Spain, stands in opposition to Poland, the Netherlands, Germany and Britain. The ECI of course understands that institutional changes in the Council, particularly the extension of the QMV in common strategies, are potentially beneficial to Israel, especially in view of the fact that the EP passed a resolution in 2005 stating that the Council should take appropriate steps to curtail Hezbollah's terrorist activities, for which there was clear and ample evidence. Nonetheless, in June 2012 the EU reiterated its position and resisted the pressure from the US and Israeli governments, for which it was accordingly criticised by the ECI.[15]

The electoral success of Islamist parties in the Arab Spring was a cause for concern for the ECI to the extent that the organisation's annual policy conference in November 2011 was devoted to the negative political implications for Europe and Israel from all the newly established Islamist regimes (elaborated in the next chapter). Affirmation of the EU's active engagement in political dialogue with the emerging Islamist movements/ governments, premised on the argument that they are the legitimate expression of the democratic process and will of the people, and that political Islam is a force and reality that Western policy makers cannot simply ignore (Grant, 2011), is dismissed by the ECI as dangerous advice. The ECI argues that calls for the inclusion of Islamist parties in the current process of democratisation of the Middle East tend to be at the same time critical of Israel and specifically show very little regard for Israel's security concerns '[b]ecause the general attitude of the Western world is to point to appeasement as the answer to world problems'.[16] Its stance would very much reflect the opinion of historian Benny Morris who argues that an essential component of the Arab Spring is hatred of Israel. He asserts that Israel has very little room for optimism given that 'the long-term consequences of the Arab upheaval are unclear [and that] radical Islam may replace authoritarian secular regimes' (2011: 9).

The ECI's uncompromising view on Islamist parties has remained consistent throughout its existence as a pro-Israel advocacy group, and was certainly confirmed with the developments of the Arab Spring.[17] Back in 2006, the ECI reported regarding the election of Hamas to power: 'The European Coalition for Israel deeply deplores the landslide election victory of Hamas... We see this as a direct result of the systematic Islamisation and radicalisation of the Palestinian youth over the past twelve years, since the establishment of Palestinian self-rule.'[18] Likewise towards Fatah, which the ECI holds responsible for 'the Palestinian rejectionist cause' (ibid.), the ECI's attitude is one of distrust, even though the PA is categorised as a secular institution by Western policy makers. Certainly the proponents for the EU inclusivist foreign policy could argue that Islamism itself is a positive challenge to the EU's clear demarcation of secular and sacred (so clearly exemplified by the exclusion of God in its constitution), or even commend the engagement with Islamists as yet another example of a much-needed pragmatism that has so far served Europe very well. The critics, on the other hand, which include Christian Zionists, would view such policy as nothing short of a disastrous appeasement that would cause not only immediate damage to Israel, but inevitably would be a long-term headache for Europe too.

Human rights, good governance and economic cooperation

While such a hawkish attitude could be interpreted as an endorsement of Huntingtonian clash paradigm on the part of European Christian Zionists, they would probably (based on numerous interviews) define it more as a demand for moral and political consistency from the EU policy makers. For the ECI the question of the EU's relationship with Islamist parties is not exclusively confined to the normative framework of, and contention for, the Judeo-Christian values, but extends to the very norms and principles that the EU assumes for itself and seeks to project in its close proximity. The review of an uneasy relationship between the EU and Israel in the second chapter conveyed the reasons for the lack of a unified EU approach to the Israeli–Palestinian conflict. The condition-ality principle in particular is often invoked as an instrument that the EU does not use effectively in its foreign policy, noting specifically its lax attitude regarding the corruption in Fatah-dominated institutions (Miller, 2011: 4). Likewise, the ECI's stance on which side of the conflict the EU conditionality principle should be applied is expressed clearly in its challenge to the Commission in 2005 regarding the funding that the PA receives from the EU (elaborated in the next chapter). Its unwavering support for Israel stems generally from its admiration of all Israel's achievements and a conviction (expressed on a regular basis through several media outlets) that Israel's political culture and economy are very similar, or even identical, to that of Europe. Moreover, the ECI's specific singling out of human rights, good governance and international law is a normative standard with which the ECI holds the EU accountable, and challenges its policies regarding the Israeli–Palestinian conflict.

The ECI certainly endorses the EU's proclamatory nature of its norms and values, but it also tends to highlight the lack of a unified response to events and policies of the member states. It aims periodically to remind and inform its members about the complexities of the EU institutional make-up and political leverage:

> The European Parliament is not a legislative body and it does not have any competence in the area of foreign policy. It is important to note that only the EU member states can decide on foreign policy... The EU does not have, and should not have, a united voice on foreign policy...[19]

The assertion that the EU 'should not have' a unified voice in foreign policy very much reflects the fact that the ECI does not believe in a federalist agenda for Europe even though it identifies itself as a pan-European lobby group. In light of the ECI's view that 'the hypocrisy and naivety of the EU and the Western world is nothing new, [and that] the EU policy in the Middle East has sadly proved to be a complete failure'[20] its insistence that Israel needs an advocate in the EU institutions may seem incoherent. However this is not the case, since the ECI leadership believes that the EP's power and influence in foreign policy is increasing, and relationships forged in the EP are well worth maintaining since 'you may be sitting [and] talking with a future government minister, which has been the case many, many times, in the European Parliament'.[21]

Another reason that the ECI recognises that, however limited the EU's political leverage is, its influence is not negligible because the EU affords credibility to Islamist parties. Although the EU imposed economic sanctions on Hamas following its electoral victory in 2006, Ashton's visit to Gaza in 2010 was interpreted by the ECI as 'a new openness in Brussels towards slowly normalising relations with Hamas, which has been on the EU terrorist list since 2003'.[22] Her position on the *Mavi Marmara*[23] incident a few months later was equally criticised by the organisation: 'ECI regrets that the EU foreign minister now chooses to side with enemies of Israel instead of the only democracy in the Middle East.'[24] Therefore, as the ECI perceives the EU's attitude towards Israel as consistently negative, it also perceives itself as an organisation that has been brought into existence by a divine providence to be specifically a pro-Israel voice and, as such, it must take a principled stance using, as expressed in one of its updates, 'a window of opportunity to impact the views and decisions of governmental leaders and parliamentarians in Europe'.[25]

It is important to stress at this point that, compared to the US, where the majority of Christian Zionists are politically very active, the percentage of European Christian Zionists that are willing to agitate for their agenda (domestic, as well as pro-Israel) is quite small. Based on interviews with prominent individuals and on conversations with many Christian Zionists, the author concluded that such an attitude tends to be a source of frustration for some of the Christian Zionist leaders, such as Simon Barrett:

> [W]e've seen a rise of Islamic extremism across Europe, and this is because of the European experiment to introduce multiculturalism as a means of diluting, if not dismantling, the Judeo-Christian heritage... It's important that Christians get engaged within the political process of Europe, to influence Europe in defence of our Judeo-Christian heritage and in defence of Israel and the Jewish people.[26]

While further research needs to be undertaken in order to determine to what degree Barrett's assertions confirm the assumption that the issue of Christianity informs national Christian Zionist activism in Europe, it is clear that the issue is not considered to be a primary concern in Brussels. The ECI's main objectives, as already pointed out, are in the political domain, which relegates the identity issue and Christian religion in new Europe to the periphery of the ECI's overall objective. 'Though it [Judeo-Christian values] may be the values of most of us who are involved', explains Sandell, 'it is not the stated objective of ECI... our goal is not to promote a Christian Europe, our goal is to promote good relations between Europe and Israel.'[27] This is done on a regular basis in the EP and in the context of promoting Israel as the only fully-functioning democracy in the Middle East, whose values are compatible with those of the European democracies. These campaigns, as discussed in the next chapter, are part of the lobby strategy, where the ECI often partners with the Israeli organisations, and demands that the Commissioners and the MEPs challenge the profligacy of the Palestinian leadership (Buhler, 2005), as well as human rights abuses in Gaza and the West Bank (JIJ, 2012).

In addition, the ECI argues that Europe needs to maintain and deepen economic relations with Israel. In this sense the ECI resonates with the EU's 'economic instruments for political means' and advocates for a stronger economic integration of the Israeli economy with the EU, which is not only mutually beneficial, according to Christian Zionists in Europe, but is logical given that Israel is western in terms of its social values, political culture and economic model. The surprising fact however is that the ECI, since its launch in 2004 until 2011, rarely presented its view on the economic relationship between Israel and the EU; and even when it did appear in its monthly updates or press releases, it tended to focus on the political impact that certain EU positions on economics would have on EU–Israel relations. In 2008 it reported that the EU will upgrade its relations with Israel, despite objections from the PA and other Arab governments over settlement buildings in the West Bank and Jerusalem: 'Israel won three key advances: increased diplomatic cooperation with the 27 state bloc, participation in European agencies and the establishment of a working group to investigate the country's integration into the European single market.'[28]

Several months later the ECI voiced its displeasure with the perceived power of the anti-Israel lobby that is entrenched in the European left: 'Despite Israel's commitment to peace the European Parliament on Wednesday December 3 voted to suspend the vote on Israel's participation in the EU's community programmes.'[29] The same report also included the decision by the EU Presidency to boost ties with Israel, which provided another reminder to the ECI members that the final decision about EU policies does not rest with the EP:

The European Parliament vote was only declarative in nature whereas the decision by the Council will guide EU-policy. The upgrade will make Israeli participation in a wide variety of EU-programmes, covering trade, transportation, energy and culture that were previously closed to it (ibid.).

Perhaps the ECI never explicitly focused on the trade issues between the EU and Israel given that the economic relations, as evidenced in Chapter 2, went from strength to strength despite difficult relations in the political domain. Providing that the EU decisions regarding trade are not politicised, the ECI regards these matters more or less 'safe' from anti-Israel interference. At the end of 2011, however, a year that brought some changes to the ECI's strategy and focus, the ECI also decided to emphasise a positive aspect relating to Israel–EU relations, and perhaps create a more optimistic framework for its advocacy. A monthly report with one of the subheadings[30] describes that

> there are over 500 new start ups every year in Israel (population 7.1 million) whereas Europe (population 500 million) can only account for 700 start ups... As we support Israel, it is important that we also consider aspects other than war and conflict. In the future ECI will focus more attention on presenting these little known facts about the miracle of the modern state of Israel.[31]

In the same way, the letter that the ECI sent to the Secretary General of the UN in December 2011 protested, against what they called, 'UN's campaign to delegitimise the Jewish state through the "Annual Day of Solidarity with the Palestinian People" where all references to Israel were derogatory and hostile.'[32] It also asserted that Israel's accomplishments over the past 65 years should be officially acknowledged: 'Given the extraordinary achievements of Israel and the Jewish people, ECI would like to propose a special UN day to celebrate the creation of the Jewish state, and to recognise its unique contributions to the international community' (ibid.).

Resurgent antisemitism

For the ECI the UN itself or, to put it more precisely, the UN General Assembly, is a platform where discussions and resolutions have nothing to do with an even-handed approach to conflict resolution, but it is a 'platform for an international campaign to brand Israel as a criminal state.'[33] Speaking on the UN Human Rights Council and Durban II the ECI stated: 'Now the Council would want to follow up the disastrous United Nations conference on racism, which was held in September 2001 in Durban, South Africa, and developed into an openly antisemitic hate-fest.'[34] The same update bemoans an Islamic influence in the UN and quotes a UN insider (the name undisclosed) who claimed that 'the Muslims are simply too powerful within the UN' (ibid.). The link that the ECI makes between the Muslim presence in the UN and antisemitism stems, as already explained, from the ECI's firm opposition to any political dialogue with Islamist groups, an area where, according to the ECI, Europe's countries in particular show a great deal of weakness.

When the ECI makes the criticism that '[m]any governments are also pushing for a "watering down" of the conditions for negotiating with Hamas in order to dialogue with the terrorist organisation'[35] the ECI is not only challenging the EU's (perceived) lax attitude towards terrorism, it also aims to raise the issues of Islamic antisemitism, discrimination and human rights abuses. Of course, the issue of antisemitism is not only discussed in relation to the religion of Islam but it goes beyond this. As Sandell explained in an interview:

[Y]es, we are concerned about the rise of Islamism in Europe, we have had a particular conference designated to that topic... But we need to remember that the Holocaust didn't happen in Islamic Europe. If we are to point fingers in any directions, it is just as much to the so-called Christian Europe.[36]

When the ECI in 2009 expressed particularly a concern about the resurgence of antisemitism in the Nordic countries it went far beyond the Islamic element: 'An unholy alliance of anarchists, socialists, Islamists, neo-fascists and Christians in Europe are leading the way in the current hate campaign against Jews and the state of Israel.'[37]

As already explained in the second chapter, the normative dimension of relations between the EU and Israel, largely determined by 2,000 years of history that includes a common Judeo-Christian heritage and culture as well as Europe's past treatment of its Jews, is often relegated to a place that is significant but nevertheless of secondary importance when juxtaposed to contemporary values of the supranational European construct. This is clearly not the case from the Christian Zionist perspective, which is exemplified by the ECI's multifaceted aspects of campaigning against antisemitism. These range from normative, in the Church and in politics, which warns that in addition to traditional antisemitism, it is an Islamist strand that is dangerous to the Jews in Europe, to the practical, which addresses the problem of antisemitism first and foremost on a national level. The traditional refers, of course, to right-wing hostility towards the Jews, which traces its roots to supersessionism of the Church. A particular strand of scholarship tends to lament the fact that, although sixteenth century Reformation challenged the Gnosticism[38] and, to a lesser degree, Scholasticism[39] of the Middle Ages with relative success, it nevertheless did not go far enough in rescuing the scriptures from Hellenistic influence, a major error that consequently solidified Replacement Theology (Maltz, 2013; Diprose, 2004; Wilson, 1989; Prasch, n.d.). Regarding Germany specifically, the failure of the Reformation to re-Judaise the Bible which institutionalised supersessionist hermeneutics, and Luther's antisemitic writings that continued to permeate the German Church and society, tragically led to a moral and spiritual failure of its ecclesiastical leadership in the first half of the twentieth century. 'In terms of responsibility', maintains Diprose,

> the tragedy of Shoah cannot be attributed exclusively to the Third Reich... It is now generally realised that part of what made both the pogroms of Russia and the Shoah played out in Central Europe possible was an attitude of theological contempt towards Israel that had its foundation in replacement theology (2004: 178).

Although current antisemitism has multiple expressions, ranging from neo-Nazi to radical left and Islamic (Prager and Telushkin, 2003), and therefore cannot be laid squarely at the feet of supersessionist Christianity, it is true nonetheless that through the process of de-Judaising the Bible (while at the same time appropriating God's promises given to the Jews), the majority of Christian theologians through the centuries have managed to precondition Christendom to view and treat its Jewry with contempt (Horner, 2013; Maltz, 2010; Dixon, 2006; Diprose, 2004; Wright, 2002; Wilson, 1989). In Germany particularly, Paul contends, the politically pragmatic 1933 Concordat signed by Hitler and the Vatican was possible because of the inherent antisemitism in Catholic history and literature (2004, 2–11). 'Hitler was a Christian', asserts Paul, 'but his Christ was no Jew' (2004: 5). Likewise Susana Heschel (2008) demonstrates how the aggressive process of de-Judaising the scriptures between 1939 and 1945 was relatively easy since it took place in spiritually, politically, and socially fertile ground prepared mainly by the German Protestant Church. Her case study of the Institute for the Study and Eradication of Jewish Influence on German Church Life, which effectively Aryanised Jesus and Nazified the German Church (2008: 26–66), demonstrates the convenient conflation of two aspects of Jew hatred:

> Through the Institute members had the chance to link the theological anti-Judaism that had long pervaded German Protestantism with the racist antisemitism promoted by the Nazis, and to link their historical claims of the allegedly degenerate nature of Jews in antiquity with the alleged degeneracy of contemporary Jews. Arguments about Jesus' relationship to Judaism were suddenly lifted from the narrow world of gospel interpretation and placed at the centre of the third Reich's politics: solving the Jewish problem (2008: 199).

In view of such a pervasive spiritual attitude, the philosemitism of earlier German Moravian Christians and the Pietist movement itself were, arguably, an anomaly within modern German Christianity. The overwhelming tide of antisemitism in the German Church and in thoroughly Nazified German society provoked little resistance during the war, either out of fear or indifference. Moreover, even after the war the Church's complicity with, and silence about, Nazi depravity was downplayed in order to exonerate theologians (Hornstra, 2006: 28–30; Wright, 2002: 90–3). The myth of the Confessing Church, Heschel maintains, 'was carefully maintained by Niemoeller, among others' (2008: 281), and it was as late as 1980 that the first critical examination of Nazi era theologians took place. Logically then, current (twenty-first century) German Christian Zionism constitutes both reassertion of the seventeenth, eighteenth and nineteenth century philosemitism as well as acceptance of special responsibility towards the Jewish people and the Jewish state by a section of the German Church.

Heschel demonstrates how the 40-year long resistance among the academic community against evaluating the role of Nazi era theologians further legitimised the Christian defamation of Judaism, but she also points out that a number of Christian theologians have formulated a new Christology since the 1980s because of the guilt related to the Holocaust (2008: 287–9). Heschel is of course correct in identifying the link between academic re-evaluation of the role of the German Church in the Nazi era and emergence of Christian re-Judaisation of scriptures in the past 30 years in Germany. However, the formation of Christian Zionist groups in post-war Germany, which were based on acknowledgement of, and sorrow for, the guilt of Germany's population at large, took place as early as 1947 with the Evangelical organisation The Sisterhood of Mary. The primary motivation, explains Hornstra, for the Sisterhood's liturgical emphasis on the Jewish roots of Christianity, its charitable deeds performed mainly in Israel, and its political support for the Jewish state, derived from its 'unequivocal confession of German and Christian responsibility for the Holocaust' (2008: 136). It is not surprising therefore that German Christian Zionist groups constitute the most vocal pro-Israel network when compared to other national Christian Zionist movements, and that, as part of the ECI's network, they provide a substantial input into the education about Holocaust-related issues and pro-Israel advocacy that is conducted in the EU institutions. At both national and pan-European level, Harald Eckert argues, Christian Zionists aim to use education about the Holocaust and resurgent antisemitism in order to generate support for Israel that is not derived solely from Christians: '[W]e have to strive to find a much broader base than hardcore Christian Zionists... to include church leaders, political leaders, leaders in professional life for a broad solidarity and a broad alliance with the State of Israel.'[40]

Clearly, the leadership of the ECI is aware that antisemitism in each European country has its own unique characteristics, which require corresponding unique remedies, particular resource allocation, and adaptation of the best strategy on the part of national Christian Zionist networks, where cooperation with non-Christian organisations that fight against antisemitism is of paramount importance. Its advocacy in Brussels, on the other hand, reflects the ECI's recognition that, in general terms, Brussels' growing importance is evidenced in the exponential growth of the interest representations, including anti-Israel lobby groups. This influence is not only evidenced, as far as the ECI is concerned, by the fact that on a general level religious representations have access to the agenda-setting and decision-making institutions, but specifically by the EU's approach to the problem of growing antisemitism. The ECI understands that the EU's leverage in combating antisemitism is quite substantial even though its instruments are not, from a Christian Zionist perspective, used consistently and effectively. The criminalisation of racism and xenophobia in member states by the Council in 2008 (The Council of the EU, 2008) is particularly regarded by the ECI as a powerful vehicle with which to drive the issue and agitate against the parties and governments it considers to be displaying antisemitic attitudes and policies.

Among the ECI, and indeed among philosemitic European Christians in general, the common understanding of the need to fight against Jew-hatred is primarily a duty to God and an opportunity to do the right thing this time around in European history. For that reason the ECI leadership would argue that the Holocaust Remembrance Day, which the ECI initiated in 2005, is one of the greatest achievements in its advocacy so far. This is not only because the repeated remembrance of the Holocaust horrors is used to highlight the current resurgence of the same hatred; but its commitment to the eradication of antisemitism was undoubtedly a decisive strategy that established the ECI as a professional lobby group. The organisation was afforded respectability and credibility on the institutional level by a formal recognition of its campaign, where attendance of dignitaries at the Holocaust Remembrance Day, most notably Catherine Ashton, signifies also the EU's commitment to its normative standards. This formal recognition undoubtedly played a key role in the decision, made by the President of the EP, Martin Schultz, to outlaw Holocaust denial in the EP and to declare the International Holocaust Remembrance Day as an official EP event from 2013.[41] Perhaps equally important is the trust afforded to the ECI by the Jewish groups, and their willingness to work with the ECI if specific campaigns require such cooperation, a development that was reported eight years after the initial commemoration event in one of the ECI's reports: 'The Holocaust Memorial is today co-sponsored by a number of important Jewish associations and is organised under the patronage of the President of the European Parliament.'[42]

While the following chapter demonstrates how the ECI aims to make a political impact with its normative commitment to the issues surrounding antisemitism, it suffices to end this chapter by quoting from the ECI's update sent to its members following the ECI's leaders attendance at the 70th anniversary of the Wannsee conference in 2011. It conveys clearly the way in which the ECI connects the past and present horrors of antisemitism, and how it conflates the issues of Holocaust denial, antisemitism and anti-Israelism:

> Together, we will look at how we can strengthen the Christian voice against antisemitism and Holocaust denial as we defend the legal rights of the Jewish people to live in security in their own ancestral homeland, Israel. The next three years, from the 70th anniversary of the Wannsee conference to the 70th anniversary of the liberation of Auschwitz, will provide us with a unique window of opportunity to speak out about this tragic period in the history of mankind.[43]

Conclusion

This chapter was written with the aim of presenting the values that brought the ECI into existence and that motivate its political activism. This was necessary since this book is conceived within the normative parameters that values, and in this case religious beliefs, have potential to determine substantially the outcomes of the political process. While the ECI's motivational factors behind its advocacy are not purely spiritual, it is true nonetheless that the inner, Christian core, network of churches, groups and individuals that comprise the ECI consider the spiritual element of their Christian Zionist identity as the most important in their pro-Israel stance. To put it simply, the ECI's primary political goals are pursued on the basis of religious Christian Zionist fervour.

The chapter included a brief reference to British and German philosemitism, which the author thought to be helpful since these two countries constitute the two most influential pillars of the ECI network. In addition, it was somewhat important to highlight that the religious zeal of German and British Christian Zionist predecessors demonstrates that current German and British Christian pro-Israel advocacy is not solely a product of American Christian Zionist influence, but is rather a re-assertion of earlier European philosemitism. The chapter also explains why the ECI's spiritual values, although crucial to its establishment as a pro-Israel lobby group in Brussels, are nonetheless secondary in terms of the organisation's goals. European Christian Zionists, like their American counterparts, emphatically reject Replacement Theology and believe that their movement, though it may have been concealed in various scholarships, was nonetheless always relevant. God, they believe, used astute Christians in the political sphere, such as Henry Dunant, the founder of the international Red Cross, who, the ECI likes to point out, was a fervent Christian Zionist,[44] and God continues to do so in this century. They assert that since the re-establishment of the state of Israel their political participation is relevant more than ever before, given that the clearly outlined prophetic scenario in the Bible about the Second Coming of Christ is almost identical to current upheavals in the Middle East, according to their biblical hermeneutics.

The second section of the chapter discussed an aspect of the ECI's normative premise that advocates Europe's reassertion of its Judeo-Christian values and that at times gets politicised due to the ECI's deep dislike of Islam. Christian political involvement, the ECI believes, is crucial at this particular time in history, since it identifies a growing Islam as a spiritual and political challenge to Europe's values. The importance of taking a principled stance against any shade of an Islamist ideology is not only a spiritual matter, but extends also into the realm of an Earthly rule where contending for democratic principles is essential if Europe is to preserve its identity and its political culture. Consequently for the ECI the very demarcation of moderate and radical Islam is a problematic notion given that Islam is not only a religion, but is also a comprehensive system of intertwined religious, cultural, economic and social aspects that demands a superior position in a society.

The chapter went on to explain how the identification of Europe's social values, political culture and economic model with those of Israel is a political platform from which the ECI advocates for the EU's support of Israel and greater cooperation. The ECI specifically invokes human rights and good governance as the values with which to challenge the EU's approach to the Israeli–Palestinian conflict, since those values are at the core of the soft power EU and instruments of its foreign policy. In terms of its political affiliation the chapter explained that the ECI fits comfortably into the category of the European political centre right even though the ECI umbrella consists of diverse Evangelical persuasions from across Europe and activists from both left and right of the political spectrum.

The chapter ended with a section that explained the most significant normative dimension of the ECI's pro-Israel advocacy. Whereas American Christian Zionist advocacy certainly incorporates strategies that challenge antisemitism, this particular aspect is more profound in Europe as European Christian Zionism is in fact deeply defined by the painful history of European Jewry. One of the ECI's updates to its members points out: 'Although we may not have the critical numbers that exist in the US, we have a moral mandate that cannot be ignored by anyone.'[45] The eschatological element, therefore, although at the core of European Christian Zionism, is not that central to its pro-Israel advocacy, evidenced by the ECI's Founding Director who asserts that Christian Zionist eschatology 'should not be a pre-condition for supporting Israel'.[46] Such attitude explains, firstly, that contemporary Christian Zionism in Europe needs to be evaluated in its moral as much as in its religious context. Secondly, given that this moral context is forged in Europe's historical abuse of the Jewish people, European Christian Zionism therefore presents a certain comprehensive appeal to all groups and individuals, religious and secular, to join Christian Zionists in the struggle against the resurgent antisemitism, rather than a purely particularistic appeal that would attract Christians exclusively.

Therefore, having taken into consideration the importance of the ECI's normative premise for its advocacy, it is clear that the ECI has made a significant normative impact in EU agenda shaping and policy making. By taking up the problem of resurgent antisemitism in European societies and embedding it in the fabric of the EP, the ECI has made a lasting normative mark on the EU at the institutional level. The politicisation of the issue did not only place the battle against antisemitism as high-ranking in terms of prioritisation of identified problematic issues by the EU's agenda setters and policy makers, but it also affirmed the ECI as a respectable NGO that enhances the EU's value system. This effectively demonstrates how religious lobby groups and their diverse spiritual convictions and contested moral grounds make perhaps an even greater impact on the EU's decision making than has been previously imagined, which consequently calls for broadening of the academic scope within the normative studies of European integration.

CHAPTER 5

THE ECI STRATEGY

A large amount of literature has been written on the pro-Israel lobby in the US, most notably on the AIPAC, as well as on Christian Zionism, although Christian Zionist influence on US foreign policy has attracted far less media attention and academic interest than the secular pro-Israel groups. In the case of the EU, as the presence of interest representations grew exponentially, so did the interest in academia about the lobbying in the EU, although research into lobbying by religious groups remains largely under-explored. Consequently, by explaining the ECI strategy this chapter narrows the gap in the existing knowledge about the influence that the non-state religious actors try to exert in the EU's foreign policy.

As a lobby organisation the ECI engages in both defensive and offensive modes of lobbying depending on the nature and duration of the campaigns it conducts. The analysis of these campaigns, as well as the various instruments that the ECI uses in order to engage in its strategy, demonstrates on the one hand the level of efficiency with which the ECI co-ordinates and streamlines German and British Christian Zionist advocacy onto the EU level, and on the other hand it discusses whether there were any EU pro-Israel policies that were established directly or indirectly as a result of the ECI's successful lobbying. However, before the chapter draws conclusions regarding the level of lobby success that the ECI did, or did not, manage to achieve, it is necessary to provide a background of its advocacy. The initial section therefore provides an overview of the network in Brussels that the ECI maintains and is part of, namely the two Jewish organisations and several political figures from Brussels who most identify with the ECI values and goals, and who provide the organisation with the necessary resources to present their message and agitate for certain political positions. The second section presents the ECI's cooperation with the Jewish organisations from Europe (but outside of Brussels) and Israel, which is an important aspect to include given that an influential political lobby usually consists of numerous groups centrally organised, for which the AIPAC itself is a very good example.

The following section reviews the literature that is relevant specifically to the ECI lobby strategy and explains why it was conceptualised in a particular manner, and why some of the campaigns are conducted in an offensive or defensive style. By discussing the reasons behind the ECI's decision to isolate certain issues and turn them into campaigns, and whether these campaigns have produced any level of influence at the EU institutional level, the chapter evaluates how successful the ECI has been, and accordingly sections 5–8 engage in a contextualised analysis of the ECI lobbying, focusing on the EU funding of the PA, combating antisemitism, the two-state solution, and the ECI San Remo campaign respectively.

The Brussels network

One of the ECI's promotional leaflets contains the following statement: 'In the late 1990s Tomas Sandell, then an accredited journalist to the European Commission in Brussels, discovered that Israel had few friends in the European Union.'[1] Whether this statement reflects the number of politically influential individuals accurately is debatable, but if Sandell's observation refers to the number of organised pro-Israel voices in Brussels, then the statement was as true then as it is true to a degree now. David Cronin, in contrast, argues: 'In Europe, the pro-Israel lobby is in no way as well organised or resourced as that in the United States. But over the past few years, it has grown in both size and strength, a phenomenon that has gone unnoticed by most of the mainstream press' (Cronin, 2011: 137). Cronin starts his polemics with a highly charged emotional outburst that the lobby is responsible for the EU's reprehensible attitude and policies towards Palestinians and, sure enough, the conclusion likewise recommends the formation of a critical mass across Europe in order to enforce the boycott of Israel (2011:

159–63). Although Cronin's work is partial and his conclusions are of limited use to the author or a reader, he nevertheless does identify correctly three organisations that are based in Brussels and that contend, among other issues, for pro-Israel policies (Cronin, 2011: 136–56). Interestingly, however, he fails to identify the ECI, which works closely with the organisations that Cronin criticises.

The European Jewish Congress (EJC), a European branch of the World Jewish Congress (WJC), is the single largest Jewish pan-European organisation, which is headquartered in Paris and has its offices in several European cities, including Brussels since 2009 (EJC, n.d.). The EJC was established in 1986, soon after SEA, for the purpose of federating and coordinating national Jewish communities in Europe, and as such the organisation represents approximately 2.5 million Jews. No thorough research has been done so far to establish whether the degree and strategy of its advocacy resembles that of the AIPAC, but its own website lists a range of issues that the organisation raises with the Commission, most notably the concern over antisemitism and European policy towards Israel and the Middle East. Its latest conference on contemporary antisemitism was held in the EP and in cooperation with the European branch of B'nai B'rith International (EJC, 2012), whose website contains the following information:

> Extending the work of the B'nai B'rith Centre for Public Policy in Washington DC, and following the initiative taken by B'nai B'rith in the UK with the London Bureau of International Affairs, an office for Public Policy was opened at the headquarters in Brussels (BBE, Who We Are).

Given the recognition by both organisations of the importance of streamlining national advocacy onto the level of the EU, it is clear that the Israel lobby has asserted itself in Brussels; but whether the degree of its influence in the EU's institutions is as high as claimed by Cronin, is arguable.

Another group that contends for Israel's interests is the European Friends of Israel (EFI), which functions as a cross-party alliance of MEPs, and is, according to Cronin (2010), 'at least partly modelled on the American Israel Public Affairs Committee (AIPAC)'. This is conceivably true, as the organisation, which was launched in 2006, had 'an initial membership of some 1,000 members of Parliament from all of Europe's mainstream political parties, making it one of the largest pan European parliamentary groups of its kind' (EFI, 2006). Its Chairman, Marek Siwiec of the Progressive Alliance of Socialists and Democrats (S&D), a Polish MEP and a member of the Committee on Foreign Affairs, lent its support to the ECI by participating in its 'Israel and Arab Spring' conference in 2011 (more below). The EFI's Executive Committee comprises five MEPs, one of which is Hannu Takkula of the Alliance of Liberals and Democrats for Europe (ALDE) from Finland, and who sits in the Committee on Culture and Education and is a member of the Delegation for Relations with Israel. Takkula lends his support to the ECI often as being a host to the ECI's conferences, but also as a speaker who challenges some of the EU's policies towards Israel. For instance, *The Jerusalem Post* reported that in March 2012 Takkula received a report at the ECI conference (more below) about human rights abuses by the PA and Hamas, and promised that it would be distributed to EU officials (Lazarof, 2012).

It is somewhat surprising that the EFI was launched relatively late in view of the fact that the existence of intergroups in the EP goes as far back as the 1984–9 Parliament. Given that MEPs in the same parliamentary groups do not necessarily agree on all issues, the formation of intergroups of like-minded MEPs, where they could work towards achieving both broad-focused goals and specific interest goals, was a necessary and logical development in the EP. Over the years the number of such groups steadily grew, but not all have achieved official recognition, as such wide accreditation would mean that Parliament would have to provide the necessary logistics for them all, such as interpretation services and meeting rooms (Corbett et al., 1992: 160). In view of such restrictions, as well as the fact that the Friends of Israel group already existed in the EP (Corbet et al., 1992: 168), it was no small achievement for the EFI to be granted official recognition. This is possibly due to its strategy of bringing together parliamentary pro-Israel groups from all member states and pro-Israel groups within the EP, thereby exemplifying policy networking that contributes a much-needed legitimacy to the EU. As the intergroups are encouraged to cultivate contacts with the civil society/lobby groups in order to solidify their strategy, the EFI too fulfils its role in this democratic exchange where it clearly finds the ECI a competent partner in championing Israel's cause.

A notable MEP, who is a member of the EFI and supports the work of the ECI by performing a speaker's role at its annual policy conferences, is Bastiaan Belder of Europe of Freedom and Democracy (EFD). Belder has served as an MEP since 1999 and, like Siwiec, is a member of the Committee on Foreign Affairs, and perhaps even more importantly has since 2009 held the Chair of the Delegation for Relations with Israel. Belder's role in the Israel lobby is described by Cronin as such:

> Zionist zealots have pulled off something of a public relations coup within the Parliament. Since September 2009, the assembly's official delegation to the Knesset, Israel's parliament, has been headed by Bastiaan Belder, a Dutch Christian Fundamentalist (2010).

This description of an influential MEP is not incorrect, as Belder granted an interview to the author of this book in 2010 in which he explained that his political role is performed within a worldview that Europe needs to reassert its Judeo-Christian values, and that part of that struggle includes the support of Israel as the Jewish state because the restoration of the Jewish state is evidence of God's faithfulness to the Jewish people.[2] This worldview certainly places Belder in the camp of politically active Christian Zionists appreciated by the ECI. In one of its updates for members, for example, the ECI credits Belder with the EU's changed policy towards Iran:

> Despite personal attacks and political pressure from Iran, he [Belder] managed to write a highly critical report to the Parliament [EP, 2011]. His work was recognised last week [22nd January 2012] when the European Union finally decided to boycott Iranian oil in order to prevent Iran from developing nuclear capabilities.[3]

Belder, however, is not the only MEP who shares a common normative basis with the ECI. Hannu Takkula also argues that it is essential for Europe to honour its Judeo-Christian roots[4], as does Sari Essayah of European People's Party (EPP), who is also a Finnish MEP and occasionally hosts the ECI's annual policy conferences. Essayah is, most notably, a member of the Committee on Employment and Social Affairs and the Delegation for Relations with Israel, and uses her years-long experience to be a pro-Israel voice in the EP, but also to politicise the Christian faith.[5] She is an active member of the European Christian Political Movement (ECPM), whose website provides the following information: 'With the official status and the funding from Brussels the ECPM aims to become more visible in European politics and to become active in the European political debates' (ECPM, n.d.).

Timothy Kirkhope of European Conservatives and Reformists (ECR), a British MEP, who is a Vice-Chair of the Special Committee on Organised Crime, Corruption and Money Laundering and a member of the Delegation for Relations with the United States, supports the ECI in various ways. Most significantly, this support was manifested through his active endorsement of the ECI's San Remo campaign (more below) at the 2011 Jerusalem Day in the EP. He too refers to his Christian faith as one of the reasons for his strong support of the Jewish state and claims that the pro-Israel support in the EP is substantial: 'The pro-Israel lobby is strong – I am approached on a regular basis and the information is reliable and well delivered.'[6] Jana Hybaskova likewise, now a former MEP (EPP) from the Czech Republic, was a valuable asset to the ECI while she served until 2009 as Chair to the Delegation for Relations with Israel and sat on the Committee on Foreign Affairs. As a strong critic of Iran and the Palestinian political process, she too appeared in several of the ECI's policy conferences, most notably in 2006 where the ECI urged the suspension of financial aid to the PA, and Hybaskova reassured the audience that the ECI's action 'may in due time lead to a concrete proposal from the European Parliament',[7] which, of course, happened not long after the conference (more in section 5).

Clearly not all MEPs that support Israel are listed in the book; the above-noted MEPs are meant to illustrate how the EFI, an organisation that consists of MEPs whose pro-integrationist stance (exemplified in the EPP group) and anti-integrationist stance (taken by the EFD group), encompasses supporters from most of the EU's political spectrum, and as such reflects the centrist political flavour of the Israel lobby in Brussels. This is important to the ECI, since the organisation, as pointed out already, takes a pragmatist stance in terms of political/ideological affiliation and refuses to be branded as rightist or leftist.[8]

A 'Jewish view'

Chapter 3 discussed how the ECI works as an independent Christian Zionist lobby group in Brussels even though its structure incorporates an extended informal network across Europe and its strategy often demands the forming of ad hoc alliances with Jewish groups. It should be noted at this point that the ECI is very well aware that American Christian Zionists are frequently accused of religious fanaticism. Such perception explains precisely why many American Christian Zionist groups have over the years invited both criticism from, but at times also an enthusiastic endorsement by, the Jews. Reasons for both responses are numerous, and they all stem essentially from the dilemma of whether there can be any trust between the Jews and Christians given the last 2,000 years of history. If American Christian Zionism provokes such a polarising response from the Jewish communities and from Israel, then presumably European Christian Zionism too generates more or less the same reaction to its pro-Israel advocacy. When questioned regarding the issue of trust, the Director of EU Affairs of B'nai B'rith Europe, Nuno Wahnon Martins, gave a positive answer:

> The great advantage of Christian Zionism is the grassroots that support the movement and unconditionally support Israel. It's very hard to find this, especially in the Jewish organisations...
> I have been working with ECI in the past and it's my intention to continue this work.[9]

This attitude and the level of trust between the two organisations was evidenced in 2011 when the author had an opportunity to observe the ECI's lobby training sessions[10] in Brussels. A day of exchanging ideas and receiving instructions from experienced lobbyists included the presentation by Martins, who gave a crash course on lobbying to some 100 ECI members, elaborating on the most pressing issues for Israel, as well as explaining the practicalities in lobbying, and how to achieve lobby efficiency in national parliaments, as well as in Brussels.

   The ECI's reputation as an organisation that is not actively proselytising Jews is clearly a reason why certain Jewish groups find it easy to work with it. The issue itself, as explained in the previous chapter, causes division in the Christian Zionist movement, but it also causes deep suspicion about Christian motivations among Jewish communities, which could potentially undermine the effectiveness of Christian–Jewish cooperation. In the words of an Israeli official in Brussels:

> Of course, as Jews we always think how is it possible that Christians could be interested in Israel and the Jews for free. Because history has shown us that after the Inquisition, after the Second World War, after the Pogroms... that it was not in the past something free.[11]

Charlotte Gutman likewise, a PR professional based in Brussels who lobbies actively on behalf of Israel, explains that even though the ECI, as well as the Revelation TV station, may be good to work with, in general terms. nonetheless '[t]he question about the "hidden agenda" remains'.[12] Martins, in contrast, is more optimistic when musing over the issue of 'the so called conversion of Jews to Christianity' and adds that 'this is a tiny group that advocates it in the Christian Zionist Group'.[13]

Whatever current partnerships and campaigns the ECI pursues with Jewish groups, they are almost certainly the outworking of its initial partnership with the EJC, established at the beginning of ECI's advocacy in 2005 and explained in the previous chapter. The degree of trust that the ECI had earned among the Jewish communities is exemplified by the fact that EJC co-hosts the Holocaust Remembrance Day with the ECI in the EP, but also by the event that took place in Berlin in January 2012 where the Holocaust Survivors Association recognised publicly the work of the ECI Chairman Harald Eckert as a powerful example of genuine reconciliation between the Jews and Germans.[14] Outside of Brussels too, Jewish groups have found the ECI a valuable partner, most notably the Simon Wiesenthal Centre (SWC), based in Paris. In 2008 it welcomed the ECI, the only non-Jewish organisation, to participate at a strategic planning meeting in Geneva on the issues regarding the Durban II conference in 2009.[15] Following this meeting, the Director of International Relations at the SWC, Shimon Samuels, attended the 2008 ECI annual policy conference '70 Years After Kristallnacht'.[16] The ECI attached a great deal of importance to the SWC's endorsement of the ECI and described it as a significant indicator of 'a growing trust and cooperation between Christian and Jewish groups in Europe'.[17] The organisation, however, does not limit its cooperation to Jewish groups in Europe, but also tries to work effectively with organisations from Israel. One is the Jerusalem Institute for Justice (JIJ), which is not only a lobby organisation on behalf of Israel but also works to strengthen the democratic and social fabric of Israeli society (JIJ, About Us). In an interview with the author about the JIJ's cooperation with European Christian Zionists, the founder and chief counsel of JIJ, Calev Myers, explained that so far the JIJ has been 'moderately successful at mobilising members of the European Evangelical Christian community', but he expressed satisfaction with being involved with the ECI, singling out specifically 'a demonstration for Israel at the Durban II UNHRC conference in Geneva in 2009'.[18]

Another significant collaboration that strengthens ECI's lobbying in Brussels is between the ECI and the Palestinian Media Watch (PMW), whose credibility is affirmed by the fact that it has

> presented its findings before members of US Congress and to members of Parliament in numerous countries, including the European Union, Britain, France, Norway, Sweden, Holland, Switzerland, Canada and Australia, and has lectured at universities and conferences world wide (PMW, About Us).

As an Israeli organisation that was willing to participate at a policy conference of the only Christian Zionist lobby organisation in Brussels,[19] the PMW demonstrates how the ECI is identified as a respectable and potentially influential NGO in the EU. In addition, the participation of the PMW at an ECI conference demonstrates that the ECI is useful to Israel (even though the PMW is not a state-sponsored organisation but an independent NGO) since it is doubtful that many organisations at the EU level would be willing to expose the PA's antisemitic pronouncements and its periodic endorsement of terrorism (PMW Research Center), as the PA is understood to be, and claims to be, a genuine peace partner in conflict resolution.

An accurate picture of the extent to which Israel directly encourages lobby activities in Europe, specifically at Brussels, is a subject that is beyond the scope of this book and it merits, from the author's opinion, a separate enquiry. It suffices to mention Charlotte's Gutman's revealing view on the Israel lobby where she certainly approves of the EFI, but believes at the same time that 'the organisation didn't succeed with their initial objectives', and the way to improve the Israel lobby is to bring all pro-Israel groups in Brussels under a common and centralised strategy with a main office in Jerusalem.[20] Martins and Meyers are likewise candid in their evaluation of the Israel lobby in Brussels. 'I see it in a very negative way due to the extreme competition within all the pro-Israel groups. The majority are not effective and they try to undermine the good work of other groups. In one word, the future is challenging', exclaims Martins[21], while Myers bemoans: 'I see a trend of the European Jewish community taking a step back from Israel advocacy.'[22] Perhaps, for this reason, as well as the fact that the EU has, arguably, grown in significance and influence in international politics, Israel's appreciation of support from Christians in Europe is yet to take place. Meyers seems to believe this to be the case: 'I am optimistic that we can improve the relationship between Israel and the EU, and I think that the European Evangelical community is really the primary resource where we have to make progress.'[23] An Israeli official in Brussels, likewise, explains:

We have relations with some Christian organisations and churches in Europe, specifically in the Evangelical world... [T]hose churches are growing in Europe and I think they will become in the next years an interesting support and co-operative system for Israel.[24]

Finally, it is significant that Israel's specific recognition of the ECI's work took place in the Knesset on 22 November 2011 (Knesset, 2011; also available on Vimeo, 2011). The ECI members were informed that

the European Coalition for Israel was one of the organisations which were awarded with an official certificate of honor for its advocacy for the Jewish state. The certificates were presented by MK Lea Shemtov who is actively building bridges between Christians and the Israeli Knesset.[25]

A year previously the ECI also informed its members that the Israeli Foreign Minister, Avigdor Lieberman, took time to meet the ECI Founding Director during his official visit to Finland: 'A particular recognition was given to the groundbreaking work which the ECI has done in recent months in commemorating the 90th Anniversary of the

San Remo resolution which codified Israel's legal rights to the land under International Law' (ECI, 2010 August). This is particularly significant in light of the fact that one of the attendees and speakers at the launch of the ECI's San Remo Initiative in 2010 was Danny Danon, the Deputy Speaker of the Knesset.[26] It must be noted, however, that regardless of such affirmation of the ECI's work, recognition on the part of Israel is low key and limited, evidenced by an article in *The Jerusalem Post* that heavily criticised PM Netanyahu's government for not endorsing the ECI's campaign more aggressively: 'Disturbingly, instead of supporting efforts like the San Remo commemoration conference, and embracing staunch supporters of Israel from Rome to San Francisco to Jerusalem itself, the government is sitting on the fence' (Glick, 2010: 3).

Conceptualising the ECI strategy

The ECI's two-fold aim has remained consistent since its inception. Its website states that the organisation exists in order to address the issue of growing antisemitism and anti-Zionism and to

> inform members of the European Parliament and other political leaders in Brussels and other European capitals about the complex realities of the conflict in the Middle East by acknowledging the right for Israel, as the only democracy in the region, to exist within secure borders (ECI, About Us).

In order to evaluate the relative success that the ECI, as a numerically small and self-funding lobby organisation, managed to achieve, it is important to locate its advocacy in an appropriate political context. Coen provides a comprehensive overview of all interest representations in Brussels and points out that, even though the EC remains the primary focus of lobby activity, where the welcomed participation in policy making is conditioned by the lobby groups' ability to provide the Commission with reliable information and conciliatory consultation (2007: 334), the lobbying, nevertheless, is not restricted to the Commission. '[S]ophisticated EU interest groups', claims Coen, 'have recognised that the locus of activity is primarily a function of the policy cycle... [A]s we move along the policy cycle and assess different policy areas', he continues, 'we can expect feedback loops between the national and European institutions' (2007: 337). He rightly concludes that business interests are not the only lobby groups that have learnt how to become part of the policy cycle, but the public interests have also learnt how to 'create complex advocacy alliances and political presence via "gate keeping" and identity-creating functions' (2007: 341). The ECI is one among many such organisations that aim to influence EU politics by establishing distinct credentials at the supranational level, while incorporating and coordinating national advocacy into their strategy when required. Therefore conceptualising the ECI's strategy is important not only because it furthers general understanding of the interest politics in the EU, but it specifically contributes to the understanding of the workings of politico/religious groups, which brings certain implications for future policy making at the EU level.

Scott Thomas argues effectively about the future global impact of the religious NGOs, given the vast number of such organisations that exist in the form of sub-state and/or transnational actors, as well as inter-governmental organisations (2005: 97–105). His evaluation of religious groups being a part of wider transnational religious subcultures is pertinent to the ECI as he rightly claims that transnational NGO coalitions 'must be firmly connected to a local constituency, and are more likely to be effective when they are helped by the strength of domestic civil society in countries targeted for global action' (2005: 118). Thomas also points out that religious groups have to rely on soft power since their influence on foreign policy is minimal (2005: 110), which is accurate in the case of the ECI whose lobby strategy is always conducted within the normative framework of human rights and democratic principles. Thomas' conceptualisation is, however, limited since the ECI is not purely a religious group (as demonstrated in the previous chapter), but a politico-religious organisation whose campaigns in the EU institutions have primarily political objectives. Another useful approach is that of Jeffrey Haynes who affirms the soft power of religious actors and conceptualises religious non-state actors (both malign and benign) as Religious Transnational Actors (RTAs), which are not consistently or formally connected to states, and whose goals include spiritual, political and social concerns (2013: 94–100). Beyond this broad conceptualisation Haynes' categorisation of some RTAs as state-linked (2013: 110–12) is true to a degree in the case of the ECI, since national Christian Zionist movements in Europe aim to embed themselves in the political process of the state, but it is clearly inadequate in the post-Westphalian context of the EU.

On the other hand, Friederike Bollmann's insights into the political mobilisation of religious organisations in Brussels are helpful for conceptualising the ECI's adaptation to a political space beyond the nation state, specifically the two aspects that relate to the paths of mobilisation and types of interests the organisations are contending for (2010: 2–4). Firstly, her categorisation of religious representations into 'religions as traditional institutions' and 'faith-based organisations of civil society', is particularly useful, as the latter applies correctly to the ECI, and, secondly, her identification of the interest of non-members which some organisations are pursuing, in this case the ECI's advocacy on behalf of the Jews in Europe and the state of Israel. In the same way as Thomas and Haynes, she too refers to the soft power of religious organisations, i.e. their cultural capital, as the only available and suitable influence tool in contemporary pacifist European culture and the EU foreign policy (Bollmann, 2010: 6). This, however, in spite of the ECI's commitment to the EU's normative values and principles, is a problematic framework at times for the ECI, as the organisation is supportive of Israel's settlement policy and supports Israel's periodic military actions (more below).

Based on internal restructuring and the nature of the political campaigns, the ECI's strategy could be broadly categorised into internal expansion and external activism. Internal expansion refers to Christian groups and individuals in the ECI's network that contend against Replacement Theology and aim to broaden the pro-Israel base in churches. Typical examples would be C4I international ministry[27] and national CFI-sponsored the Kesher[28] course in Britain,[29] as well as periodically organised events in churches that have pro-Israel speakers.[30] Most importantly perhaps is the ECI's direct sponsoring and coordinating of the expansion into the youth ministry,[31] which has occurred as a result of the ECI's recognition that support for Israel among Christians under the age of 30 is very low:

> We want to invite young people (between 18 and 35) with passion and vision for seeing a new generation raised up in Europe in support of Israel. We believe there are many out there who can and will make a difference once they have been given a chance to connect with other like-minded people.[32]

To that end Calev Myers from JIJ conducted a seminar on human rights[33] at this particular event[34] (JIJ, 2012). A few months later, at the ECI's follow-up regional conference for young adults[35] in Oxford, Myers appeared again as one of the main speakers, where he explained the best strategy for campus pro-Israel advocacy and specifically taught the young people how to refute the arguments relating to Israel as an apartheid state.

The youth initiative marks a more aggressive stance by the ECI in terms of ensuring that the anti-Israel voice in European supersessionist churches, which inevitably influences young Christians, is mitigated by Christian Zionist active recruitment of young people for political activism. Secondly, the initiative reflects long-term thinking for solidifying the ECI through a numerical expansion, as well as achieving and sustaining its political stronghold in Brussels. Whether this strategic re-orientation towards broadening its appeal to younger generations will achieve the ECI's envisioned goals is clearly too early to judge, as the ECI is a pan-European Christian Zionist organisation, and for some countries, especially traditionally Euro-sceptic Britain, anything that is Brussels-based might not be worth pursuing. On the other hand, it is conceivable that European integration, which is facilitated in no small measure by religious actors (Bollmann, 2010: 2; Thomas, 2005: 166–72) could affect greater Christian Zionist mobilisation at the EU level, fostered particularly by the youth from pro-integrationist Germany.

Another campaign, which the ECI conducted in 2009,[36] could be, arguably, interpreted as the ECI's attempt at broadening its base and solidifying its network in Brussels, as its goal was the election of pro-Israel MEPs to the EP (ECI: Campaigns, 1). The main question that the ECI leadership and some 100 members were discussing was how to motivate people to vote in May 2009 elections that were neither popular nor exciting, and with limited resources. Thanks to the Romanian Alpha and Omega TV channel (discussed in Chapter 3) the ECI launched its campaign shortly before the elections by uploading three one-minute trailers on its website and YouTube channel (ECI: Campaigns, 4). This was announced in its press release: 'The campaign aims at mobilising constituencies in all 27 member states to take active part in the election campaign by educating themselves about the issues and by engaging in dialogue with the candidates.'[37] Given the short time in which the ECI tried to influence voters to elect pro-Israel MEPs it is difficult to establish whether all pro-Israel MEPs, such as Alf Swensson, Magdi Allam, Laslo Tokes and Lech Walesa[38] were elected as a result of the ECI's advocacy, and it remains to be seen whether the ECI will allocate greater resources, expertise and time to every subsequent European parliamentary election. What is far more significant in this particular instance is how the ECI, as a Brussels-based lobby group, played a role in legitimising the EU's political aspirations through mobilising political participation of European citizens and, as such, clearly confirms the Commission's correct assessment that the religious actor (as argued in the first chapter) is a significant section of Europe's civil society that plays its part in the reduction of the EU's democratic deficit.

Defensive and offensive lobbying

Regarding the ECI's external activism, its strategy is pursued mostly through the access mode, but it adopts both a defensive and offensive style. The ECI's overall long-term goals are the eradication of antisemitism in Europe and encouraging the EU's commitment to Israel's security as the Jewish state; and to that end it advocates greater political, economic and cultural cooperation between the EU and Israel (ECI, About Us). In terms of the ways in which the ECI pursues these goals, they are determined by several factors – the ECI's human and financial resources (explained in the previous chapter) and the fact that the organisation is a part of the network that includes national and pan-European, and at times also international, advocacy. Most pressure groups that have diffuse interests and that happen to have a wide and numerically high membership often resort to voice mode campaigning, i.e. public demonstrations and/or sustained media campaigns, when agitating for certain political directions and decisions. The ECI, due to its size, never resorts to organising mass rallies in Brussels, although some national organisations that are part of the ECI network, such as Mordecai Voice from the UK and Christensen fur Israel from Germany, do so occasionally. In answering the question whether he prefers lobbying through private meetings to mass rallies and demonstrations, an ECI board member David Adeola answered emphatically: 'Yes. It's more effective, because you're not exposing them [politicians]. You are not shouting about them, you are not putting their name on your placard... they will be more willing to actually talk to you.'[39] When the ECI does resort to the voice mode in pursuit of its goals, it is always done through media outlets, such as YouTube, Facebook, and occasionally national newspapers.

As an organisation that has limited resources and has to carve a political space for itself in a competitive political culture in Brussels, the ECI is first and foremost an organisation that conducts its strategy through the access mode, which confirms Beyers' findings about the policy network dynamics and voice/access strategy on a national and pan-European level (2002: 600–8; also Beyers, 2004: 213–20). Firstly, as an accredited lobby group the ECI organises delegations to meet with the existing, as well as with the upcoming, EU presidencies, where, on a general level, they demonstrate that Israel has an organised, vocal and committed constituency on a pan-European level. National governments and parliaments, as well as upcoming presidencies, as the ECI likes to remind its members occasionally, are equally important for pro-Israel lobbying, including the 'problematic ones', such as Sweden, Spain, Belgium and Ireland.[40] Specifically though, in light of the fact that the CFSP tends to function according to the lowest common denominator that is, from the ECI perspective, detrimental to Israel, the ECI seeks to exploit the CFSP disunity to Israel's advantage, usually by encouraging pro-Israel administrations, such as the Czech Presidency in the first half of 2009. Secondly, the ECI has access to both the EP and the Commission. For example its press release in 2006 states that at the ECI's meeting with Franco Frattini, the European Commissioner for Security and Freedom, and Vice-President of the EC, Frattini expressed his deep commitment to Israel as the Jewish homeland and his full support for the goals of the ECI.[41] Such high profile meetings are regularly reported to its members, but the contents of the discussions are, naturally, minimal. When the author raised the issue about transparency of the ECI in its dealings with the MEPs and Commissioners, Sandell maintained that the transparency level is high as all meetings are recorded, but the communication with the constituency is much more discreet: 'You know, it doesn't make sense to go on the record to say I saw this or that person, and he or she said that. So, you know sometimes it's public, it makes sense, [but] many times you have to keep it discreet and confidential.'[42]

Overall, while the ECI demonstrates an impressive level of competence by securing access to both the EP and the Commission, it is important to remember that its preferred point of access remains the EP rather than the Commission. Apart from the fact that, according to Sandell, the EP's power and influence in foreign policy is increasing, it also consists of politicians who are potentially future influential ministers in their own countries.[43] This confirms the research that Brussels-based interest representations carefully maintain policy networks that include national points of access, and that their focus on the EP is a logical strategy since they have access to the meetings of specialised committees through which they could influence the legislative process (Bouwen 2004: 482). In the case of the ECI, some MEPs, as demonstrated in the initial section of the chapter, do indeed sit (or have been sitting) in influential committees.

A final point to elaborate on in this section refers to the ECI's campaigning style. In view of the fact that in several years of its existence the ECI gradually improved its expertise in the use of media, and also successfully acquired a sufficient number of 'entry points' in order to disseminate information, it is possible to distinguish its lobby strategy as either defensive or offensive, depending on the nature, duration and aims of the campaigns. Firstly, however, it is important to clarify that the ECI typically conducts its lobbying in a non-adversarial manner, which is conditioned by the institutional framework in which it operates. Recent comparative work about lobbying in the US and the EU indicates that lobbying styles are different despite the similarities in tactics, hence the American 'winner takes all' approach, due to its fully established federal system, is unworkable in the EU consensus-building system that is preconditioned by a complex governance model (Woll, 2013: 193–5; also Mahoney, 2007). Rather than adopting a combative posture, which is counter-productive in Brussels, the EU-based interest groups 'have a strong incentive to formulate their policy demands in constructive terms, making reference to pan-European goals and principles rather than their immediate interests' (Woll, 2013: 209). In terms of the applicability of such tendencies to religious groups Bollman identifies and conceptualises this strategy as the 'common good' path of religious organisations' political mobilisation (2010: 2).

The ECI, at least partially, can appeal to the 'common good' of its pro-Israel advocacy, most notably when it is based on its appeal for the eradication of antisemitism in Europe, and when it emphasises the benefits of close political and economic EU–Israel relations. While the ECI conducts campaigns and pursues policies related to these issues, as well as issues relating to Israel's security, in both defensive and offensive styles, nonetheless it is always done, as already noted, in a framework of persuasive soft power, or dialoguing partnership.[44] As a concept, defensive lobbying was developed in the context of the lobbying culture in the USA, where interest groups aim to preserve long-established laws, and as such it proved to be a successful framework in Washington DC where 'the landscape is biased in many ways towards supporting the status quo policy' (McKay, 2012: 121; also Victor, 2007: 828–30). These laws are of course entrenched in a fully functioning federal system where any attempted legislative change provokes fierce opposition, particularly from well-established lobby groups. A good example would be the National Rifle Association (NRA),[45] a staunch defender of the Second Amendment, which consistently lobbies hard against any major legislative changes that would introduce greater state-sponsored gun control. Likewise the polarised debate about the health system in 2011 mobilised a number of groups to political action, most notably Planned Parenthood,[46] whose 'federal lobbying bill more than tripled in the first three months of the new Congress, as Republicans targeted the group for funding cuts' (Ackley, 2011).

In the EU, however, institutional fluidity and legislative evolution mean not only that interest groups need to operate in a more complex governance system, but also that the defensive strategy, which characterises so much of American lobby culture, rarely works for the Brussels-based lobby groups. The exceptional cases are the trade associations, according to Daniel Guegen, which use blocking strategy in order to prevent new regulations and protect their favourable conditions (2007: 55). This is understandable given that business interests spent decades lobbying the EU, while non-business associations, including religious lobby groups, only recently, as demonstrated in the first chapter, made inroads into the Brussels lobby culture. As the EU opened up to the possibility of becoming more than just an 'economic club' so too the value-driven NGOs became assertive and eager to exploit the new openness and influence EU politics (Guegen, 2007: 50–6). For that reason, the non-business organisations, especially the religious lobby groups, could hardly engage in a defensive lobby strategy as they are still in the process of asserting their influential and/or powerful positions in Brussels. Likewise the existing pro-Israel lobby in Brussels, including the ECI, cannot engage in a defensive strategy identical to that of the AIPAC, as that organisation had been operating as a powerful lobby for decades in American politics.

The ECI's lobby strategy (its positions and policy recommendations) is therefore most of the time offensive, though never aggressive in its demands, nor combative in its approach. This is so because the ECI, as the only Christian pro-Israel organisation in Brussels whose stance on the Israeli–Palestinian conflict (more below) is substantially different from the EU's official policy, had to 'break ground' in many ways and establish itself as a credible lobby organisation in a relatively short time. Compared to trade associations, claims Riss, Brussels-based NGOs are 'determined, combative and engaged' (quoted in Guegen, 2007: 56), and in that respect the ECI fulfils its part in the mobilisational process. Having said that, there are times when the ECI's lobbying is conducted in a defensive mode, usually at times when EU–Israel existing good trade relations are threatened in the EP, but it is also active in the media during times of periodic crisis when Israel faces severe criticism from different directions and the ECI seeks to prevent defamation and delegitimisation of the Jewish state. Some notable examples are the *Mavi Marmara*[47] incident in 2010 and the Third Intifada[48] Facebook launch in 2011.

Economic issues for political ends

The ECI's goal of committing the EU to Israel's well-being is its long-term vision where economic cooperation in particular is viewed as an area that exemplifies the benefits for both partners if pursued for pragmatic purposes. This important instrument, however, has not been necessarily used sufficiently enough in the ECI's advocacy, since the organisation never considered, until 2011 that EU–Israel trade relations could start deteriorating because of an uneasy political relationship. The EU's pragmatism has always been considered as the factor that overrides any political objections to the deepening of EU–Israel economic cooperation, which was demonstrated once again by the EU's 2012 upgrade, despite its critical position towards numerous Israeli official policies, and an opposition in the EP to the upgrade. Consequently, while the ECI raised its objections every time it considered that the decisions regarding the trade were politicised, at the same time the periodic campaigns against deepening EU–Israel trade relations were not considered a problematic issue that merited the ECI's special attention. This is evident throughout its press releases and monthly reports to its members and the fact that not a single policy conference was focused on these issues. This however changed in 2011, when the ECI announced to its members: 'As we support Israel it is important that we also consider aspects other than war and conflict. In the future ECI will focus more attention on presenting these little known facts about the miracle of the modern state of Israel.'[49]

This demonstrates, firstly, that the ECI seeks to preserve and defend Israel's image in the media and in the EU institutions as that of a vibrant democracy that 'contributes to economic prosperity in the region' (ECI, 2012: 4) by using economic instruments for peaceful purposes, which as a strategy resonates well with EU policy makers. Secondly, in view of the fact that the EU's official stance towards the two-state solution and status of Jerusalem (more in the last section) differs considerably from that of the ECI, it is perhaps logical that the ECI includes also a less confrontational instrument in its advocacy. Thirdly, the global BDS movement, which has advanced in Britain more than in other countries, is viewed by all Christian Zionists as damaging since its goal is to delegitimise Israel, even though it has achieved little success so far, according to Shay (2012) and Ehud Rosen, who notes that in Britain only the Department for the Environment, Food and Rural Affairs recommended voluntary labelling of Israeli and Palestinian goods produced in the West Bank (2010: 45). Nonetheless the CFI activists maintain that the tactics and aims of the BDS in Britain were alarming enough and needed to be discussed with MPs.[50] Even more disturbingly for the CFI, as well as for the ECI, was Yvette Cooper's (Labour Shadow Foreign Secretary) call to the British government in 2010 to pressure the EU and demand compulsory product labelling from the West Bank (Rosen, 2010: 45). A few years later, more calls from the EU for such a policy caused, according to Barack Ravid, deep concern in Israel because the initiative in May 2012 was 'unanimously approved by all 27 foreign ministers' (Ravid, 2012). For that reason CFI-ZF Lobby Day in 2012[51] made the BDS campaign its priority where over 300 activists met nearly 100 MPs and urged them to oppose boycotts in any form.

The ECI's decision to allocate more time to trade issues was exemplified by its cooperation with the AJC Transatlantic Institute in 2012 that started a 'Pass ACAA'[52] campaign, which called on the EU to finalise the pharmaceutical deal between the EU and Israel (ACAA, 2012). Evidently this was a short-term defensive campaign where the ECI was an active participant in an ad hoc coalition, although it did not conduct any direct lobbying in the EP. It was engaged mostly in a media campaign by encouraging over 8,000 of its Facebook members (at the time) to expand the EU citizen petition, which at the time of the Strasbourg plenary session on 23 October 2012 numbered over 2,500. After it passed, *The European Jewish Press* (EJP) branded it as a victory for pro-Israel supporters in the EP and singled out MEP Bastiaan Belder as an influential pro-Israel voice who criticised the politicisation of the issue by anti-Israel MEPs: 'For too long I've looked forward to the approval of this important trade agreement, I don't know why it's been delayed for so long' (Belder, quoted in Ryness, 2012).

While campaigns that lobby for favourable economic policies can be categorised as defensive regardless of whether they are fought in Brussels or in national parliaments, sometimes the ECI's approach is more aggressive, when it attempts to influence the EU policy. This was demonstrated very early in the ECI's existence as a pro-Israel lobby group in 2005 at its 4th annual policy conference[53] where the organisation challenged the Commissioner Allan Seatter, the then Head of Near East Division, about corruption in the PA and misuse of EU financial aid. 'During the conference', the ECI press release states, 'it was agreed that the Coalition will feed the European Commission with relevant material and documentation on the developments with regards to incitement to genocide or terrorism in the Palestinian territories'.[54] According to the ECI's Director: 'We presented this document to my recollection in September, and... I think it was December, the European Commission froze the funding to the Palestinian Authorities, quoting arguments in our leaflet.'[55] The influential document that Sandell refers to in his interview is titled 'European Leadership Funding' in which the ECI

call[s] upon the EU to address its own suggested steps with more determination. We strongly believe that European NGO funding directed to non-EU states should be firmly attached to clearly defined benchmarks with a view to increasing freedom, human rights and democracy as universally understood in the founding treaties of the Union (Buhler, 2005: 10).

Given that the initial suspension took place ten days before the Palestinian elections in January 2006, Sandell's claim that this was the outcome of the ECI's lobbying seems plausible. It could be argued that although the subsequent sanctions in April 2006 were put in place because of the electoral victory of Hamas, the earlier freeze of 35 million euros, nevertheless, was sanctioned because, in the words of the then Commissioner for External Affairs:

[W]e are not only pumping money into the Palestinians without asking for very clear benchmarks... Effective, functioning, democratic, Palestinian institutions are essential for the peace process. Without them we cannot lay the foundations for a viable Palestinian state living in peace with Israel (Benita Ferrero-Waldner, quoted in Lempkowicz, 2006).

The common reference to the EU benchmarks by the Commissioner and by the author in the ECI document, as well as the fact that suspension took place after the ECI presented documentation of financial abuse to the Commission and the MEPs, lends a certain level of credibility to Sandell's claim. Having said that, however, it must be noted that a lack of any other tangible evidence, such as an official acknowledgement by the Commission or the EP that the suspension of aid was credited directly to the ECI, makes clear corroboration very difficult to establish. Regardless of the effect that the ECI may or may not have had, it is possible also that the Commission's suspension was implemented in order to reiterate the EU's pressure on Hamas regarding the recognition of Israel and renunciation of terrorism, as well as to make its position clear to the Palestinian electorate.

In any case, since 2006 the ECI has not achieved any subsequent significant breakthroughs regarding EU policy on funding the PA, although it has continued to demand accountability from the policy makers, best demonstrated in 2008 at its 5th annual policy conference.[56] The overall framework for all the issues raised at the conference was the effectiveness of the EU Neighbourhood policy in the Mediterranean region where the representative from the UK Taxpayer's Alliance provided specific examples of the hate education in the Palestinian territories and demanded 'that the European Commission, being the single largest donor to the Palestinian Authorities, takes its full responsibility for better monitoring the Palestinian education system'.[57] The ECI also took the opportunity to present its new policy paper[58] at the conference, which was in essence a continuation of Buhler's 2005 document, but it failed to achieve its objective, namely to generate an investigation into whether EU funding is used for the promotion of human rights, democracy and peace education in the Middle East (ECI, 2008). While the document did not create the desired impact, it is nonetheless an interesting piece of evidence that reveals how fundamentally different the European Christian Zionist strategy is compared to that of American Christian Zionism:

> The EU prefers to use its 'soft power' to spread democracy and stability in its immediate Neighbourhood [sic] and in the world. The EU believes, rightly so, that regime change cannot be achieved through military means only, but by winning hearts and minds with one's message and values. At least in one respect the EU strategy of soft power has worked. Today a number of countries in its neighbourhood have aspirations to become candidate countries and later member states by already now preparing to meet up to the Copenhagen criteria, thus already now implementing measures which are in line with EU values and objectives (ECI, 2008).

Clearly, in terms of understanding the EU normative premise and foreign policy dynamics, the ECI commends the EU's 'biggest aid donor' status in the world. The problem exists, according to the organisation, in the EU's lack of consistent application of those values in the Middle East, hence the recommendation that the EU needs to 'identify and support opposition groups which subscribe to democratic values but are not engaged in military operations or terrorist organisations' (ibid.).

Battle against antisemitism

Groups that the ECI singles out as fundamentally opposed to EU values, particularly when they are engaged in obstructionist tactics in the peace process, are primarily Hamas and Hezbollah, but the PA is frequently referred to also as antisemitic and supportive of terrorism. Undoubtedly the ECI's challenge about the lack of monetary scrutiny by the EU at the 2005 annual conference was strengthened by the presence of Itamar Marcus, the Director of PMW, who effectively addressed the audience (perhaps most significantly the then Special Advisor on Religious Affairs to the Commission President Barroso), presenting evidence that the PA regularly 'permits the incitement to hatred or violence against members of a religion by its leaders, media or education system'.[59] Regarding the 'domestic' European context, the ECI's stated goal of eradicating European antisemitism is formed against the backdrop of not only Islamic but all types of Jew-hatred, and pursued with understanding that each member state has its own history of relations with the Jewish people.

The previous chapter explained why the issue of resurgent antisemitism is at the heart of the ECI, and why the organisation views the establishment of the annual Holocaust Memorial Day in the EP as its most important achievement. Fighting against old and new antisemitism is not only a foundational value of European Christian Zionism that sits alongside its eschatological hermeneutics, but it is also a decisive motivational factor that determines the ECI's advocacy for Israel's political issues. 'Together, we will look at how we can strengthen the Christian voice against antisemitism and Holocaust denial', the ECI members were informed, 'as we defend the legal rights of the Jewish people to live in security in their own ancestral homeland, Israel.'[60] Given that the ECI conflates the issues of anti-Israelism and antisemitism, its efforts to reach political circles, media, and churches with the message of a strong correlation between antisemitism and the delegitimisation campaign of the Jewish state is clearly in the category of its offensive strategy in pro-Israel advocacy (ECI, Learn From History). The institutionalising of the Holocaust memorial specifically is a demonstration that the ECI has achieved a significant milestone in its goal, but is also a demonstration that its campaign contributes to increased normative leverage of the EU, whose policy of criminalising xenophobia (The Council of the EU, 2008) further encourages the ECI, as well as Jewish groups, to participate in the political process at a supranational level. Additionally, such lobbying dynamics illustrate the normative impact of the above-noted Bollmann's concept of 'common good' that motivates religious representations' mobilisation in Brussels, where the ECI's proactive and assertive lobbying contributes to the EU's culture of tolerance, but also to the EU's image of a normative power.

At times however, the ECI's campaigns against resurgent antisemit-ism are not conducted exclusively within the framework of the EU's official stance against any form of discrimination, but very often they are politicised in order to highlight, in their view, the existential threats to the Jewish state. A very good example is the ECI's 2006 'Keep Ahmadinejad Out' campaign (ECI: Campaign, 3), organised (mainly) by German Christian Zionists and effectively reverberated across Europe, which was not surprising given the controversy that surrounded the then Iranian President. It was a short-term proactive political action conducted through the media (voice mode) that aimed to put pressure on the German government and FIFA.[61] After learning that the Iranian President was considering attending the FIFA World Cup in Germany, the ECI reported that 'concerned Christians across Europe have joined forces to ensure that [neither] Holocaust-denying Iranian President Mahmoud Ahmadinejad nor his deputy will be allowed to attend'.[62] As it happened, the Iranian leader did abandon his plans following a successfully coordinated action on a national/German and EU level: the combination of ECI's provocative advertisement in the German daily newspaper *Frankfurter Allgemeine Zeitung*,[63] demonstrations organised by Israel supporters on German streets, and the work of the ECI's network of MEPs, such as Charles Tannock and Jana Hybaskova (*Haaretz*, 2006). Ahmadinejad's reaction was published in another German paper in which he referred to the high profile campaign as something that was predictable 'because the network of Zionism is very active around the world, in Europe too' (*Der Spiegel*, 2006).

Given that the ECI's advocacy is firmly premised on eradication of antisemitism it is logical that this particular stream of lobbying is overwhelmingly shaped by German Christian advocacy, where under-standing of the special responsibility towards the Jewish people means 'to stand with Israel any time, always, to fight for the existence of Israel, to stand against the enemies of Israel'.[64] For that reason German Christian Zionist groups are a particularly welcome addition to the German pro-Israel network, most notably Israel Kongress[65] that convenes bi-annually in Frankfurt. According to one of its main organisers, Claudia Korenke, of all Christian groups in Germany it is

Christensen fur Israel that is most effective in recruiting new members for pro-Israel advocacy, particularly in the area relating to antisemitism.[66] Considering that Israel Kongress was initiated in 2010, its success a few years later, if it is to be measured by the extensive network of pro-Israel groups, seems remarkable, even though Korenke insists that 'it didn't go to the extent where we were able to move German politics'.[67] Even so, when compared with the absence of such high profile national gathering in other EU member states, the German pro-Israel umbrella is closest in resembling American AIPAC.

In Britain likewise the persistence of antisemitism is a pressing issue for Christian Zionists, demonstrated by the fact that it is a repeated item at every CFI/ZF annual lobby day, most notably in 2011.[68] In a somewhat similar manner to the German example, Britain also committed the Holocaust to perpetual memory by opening the Holocaust Memorial and Education Centre in north Nottinghamshire in 1995, which is described as 'a place of education, a place of memory, a place of testimony, a place of art, a place of academia' (The Holocaust Centre, Visit Us), but, surprisingly perhaps, it does not have any links with nor advocacy input into the ECI's work. Overall, British Christian advocacy is nowhere near as defined by the Holocaust as is the case with German Christian Zionism. It is rather affected considerably by the notion that Britain, after performing its initial instrumental role through the Balfour Declaration, betrayed the Jewish people at the onset, during, and after World War II, for which incidentally it lost its empire as a form of divine punishment, according to some prominent British Christian Zionists (*The Forsaken Promise* documentary, DVD). Hence the issues that tend to dominate British Christian Zionist advocacy relate to Israel's image, legitimacy and security, which, in view of the confrontational tactics that are embedded in British pluralist lobby culture (Eising, 2008: 7), have more chance of success in Westminster than in Brussels, where consensual lobbying is closer to the German corporatist model (Woll, 2006: 460–3).

The ECI and Israel's security

The welcoming of a confrontational tactic from the British lobbying stream, such as the noted Taxpayers' Alliance demand for greater scrutinising of the PA's expenditure, is not an anomaly in the ECI's strategy, but a necessity for the organisation as it seeks to influence EU policies that will enhance Israel's security. Since economic cooperation and combating antisemitism constitute issues that are lobbied within the normative context of the EU that the ECI wholeheartedly endorses, the tension level consequently is minimal (even when the ECI aims to create a hard political impact), and the consensual approach to problem-solving that characterises Brussels-based lobbying applies to the ECI as much as to the rest of the pan-European interest representations. The challenge for the ECI, however, is to remain within the same normative context when contending for policies that are contrary to the official EU positions. In this sense the ECI's strategy is by default offensive as it seeks to challenge the premise of the proposed two-state solution, and by extension the legality of Jewish settlements and the future status of Jerusalem.

The ECI subscribes to a particular narrative of the ongoing conflict and understands the threat to Israel as existential and imminent. Monthly reports and press releases regularly convey that the threat consists of periodic and/or sustained rocket attacks from Hamas-controlled Gaza, Hezbollah's menacing presence in Lebanon and, most problematically, Iran's nuclear aspirations. Therefore the ECI's endorsement of Israel's military operations is a natural attitude for an organisation that interprets Europe's twenty-first century pacifism as an appeasement policy: '[A]ppeasement and compromise can never give a foundation for true peace. When the world community again tries to find a solution to the Middle East conflict it will have to keep this in mind.'[69] Secondly, whether Israel's military operations are brief or prolonged, Christian Zionists understand them as defensive actions of the Jewish state, hence the ECI's support for IDF, such as during the *Mavi Marmara* confrontation, the war with Hezbollah in 2006, and the Operation Cast Lead Operation in 2008–9. This lenient outlook on Israeli militarism was exemplified at the ECI's policy 2011 conference where three specific issues generated the debate: the repercussions of the Arab Spring, the power of the Muslim Brotherhood, and the prospect of a nuclear Iran, and Sandell argued that the EU 'should step up the sanctions against Iran, but the [EU] parliament should support the pre-emptive strike if sanctions fail'.[70]

A further elaboration on Cast Lead in particular is pertinent at this point as it was a campaign, both reactive and defensive in its strategy, which brought the ECI to the forefront of the media battle. The operation, as well as the subsequent Goldstone Report and its endorsement in the EP, provoked a highly polarised reaction from around the world (Bolton, 2009; Falk, 2009; Kemp, 2009; NGO Monitor, 2009; Ghansay, 2010, Phillips, 2010), but it also exemplified the inadequacy of the CFSP given the differing policy agenda of member states. Indeed, contrary to the (previous) French Presidency that condemned Israeli actions, the Czech Presidency issued a statement describing the Israeli ground operation as self-defensive. Predictably this generated heavy criticism from many European countries and consequently forced the Czech President to issue a new statement, which included criticism aimed at Israel for the heavy loss of civilian life in Gaza. The ECI, of course, made sure in its press release to commend countries that took a more lenient stance towards Israel,[71] but far more significant was the ECI's immediate campaign to expose Mads Gilbert:[72]

[W]e sent out the breaking news to many media outlets, political leaders and activists about the fact that the Norwegian doctor who runs his news agency in Gaza with clear anti-Israel propaganda was a supporter of the terrorist attack on 9–11 in New York.[73]

Given the impact of Gilbert's reporting, *The Jerusalem Post* decided that the ECI's efforts were deserving of wider attention and promptly published Sandell's story about his 'discovery' of Dr Gilbert's real agenda:

The profile I discovered on Wikipedia was not one of a humanitarian icon but that of a political activist... What we do know by now is that Mads Gilbert and his friend Erik Fosse did not end up in Gaza by accident. They did not come only to help out in a hospital but with a clear political agenda to sell (Sandell, 2009).

In addition to its stance on military issues, the ECI's unequivocal support for Israel with regard to political issues conveys an image of an organisation that is uncritical of the Jewish state at all times. However, the issue of the status of Jerusalem in peace negotiations, i.e. the prospect of any Israeli government officially handing over any part of the city to the Palestinian jurisdiction, would probably provoke a strong negative reaction by the ECI. Such potential reaction is based on several convictions: firstly, that Jerusalem (more precisely the Old City, which is situated in East Jerusalem) has always held more spiritual significance for, and shaped the identity of, the Jewish people than any other religious or ethnic group; secondly, that '[o]nly Jewish sovereignty over Jerusalem can guarantee that the Old City and all of its Holy Places will be protected – Jewish, Christian and Muslim' (ECI, 2012: 11); and thirdly, the legitimacy of Jewish ownership of Jerusalem was established by international law in 1922 (more below). Other than that, and judging by the material and primary evidence that was available to the author, as well as witnessing the debates between the officials at a number of the ECI events and having many conversations with ECI activists, it became clear that the ECI sees itself as an organisation that champions Israel's cause, and as such it never criticises Israel openly since, it believes, Israel has never been short of critics. This is, arguably, a typically hawkish Christian Zionist attitude, which critics of Israel would find indistinguishable from the attitude of American Christian Zionists. While this may be accurate to a degree, it is nonetheless important to emphasise that the ECI is not unaware of the existing political and social problems in Israeli society, which is one of the reasons why it works in close partnership with the JIJ, an Israeli organisation that is patriotic, but very critical of Israel too. Its website states the following:

> JIJ has adopted various marginalised communities in Israel including Holocaust survivors, lone soldiers, Ethiopian new immigrants, human trafficking victims, refugees and migrant workers, abandoned children, and members of minority religious streams. We act as a voice for these populations by both gathering and distributing direct humanitarian aid while providing legal and public advocacy on their behalf (JIJ, About Us).

To what extent the ECI leadership endorses the causes that JIJ takes up, including controversial advocacy for the rights of the Messianic Jews (*Jewish Israel*, 2011), is not clear, but what is clear, however, is that the ECI steers clear of criticising Israel overtly. This is not least because its resources are limited and must be spent efficiently as the ECI contends against lobby groups that oppose Israel-friendly policies, but because it also promotes policies that are neither popular nor mainstream. As already pointed out, the ECI's attitude and its offensive strategy could potentially be characterised as a hawkish, right-wing, religiously induced Christian Zionism that is often used to portray American Christian supporters of Israel, which the organisation is keen to avoid since it seeks to contextualise its involvement in hard political issues along secular parameters and through international law. Accordingly its response[74] to the Palestinian statehood bid on 8 November 2012 at the UN was posted on its website and stated: 'Although the legal consequences of this resolution are perhaps debatable, its adoption would constitute a significant step towards the establishment of a new Islamic state of Palestine under international law' (ECI, 2012: 2). The document raises several points: mutual recognition, security, rights of the Jewish people, negotiations and Jerusalem, and argues that the Palestinian application is in conflict with the UN Charter. The ECI in particular rejects the 1967 armistice lines as future borders as they would conflict with the UN Security Council Resolution 242 and undermine the Oslo agreements (ibid.). As the Resolution states that lasting peace in the Middle East should include the application of two principles,[75] the document maintains that Israel has complied with the first principle and Palestinians are yet to fulfil the second one. In addition the ECI states that violation of the Oslo agreements would destroy a chance for peace, and (presumably) the Palestinian state, since Oslo II specifically calls for negotiations and warns against unilateralism (ECI, 2012: 10).

As the ECI is not explicitly against the creation of the Palestinian state, it is fair to assume that the organisation would genuinely accept such a state, provided it is an outcome of 'a negotiated solution to Middle East conflict',[76] but also a relinquished Palestinian claim to East Jerusalem and an end to the vilification of the Jewish settlements in the West Bank, referred to by the ECI as Judea and Samaria. These positions derive, as already noted, from a pro-Israel narrative of the conflict and it clearly presents a particular view of Resolution 242. For the ECI, as indeed for all diplomats, scholars and lawyers who undertook the task of interpreting the Resolution, the most contested sentence, regardless of what narrative to the conflict they subscribe to, is 'Withdrawal of Israeli armed forces from territories occupied in recent conflict', although the two other sections also proved to be an impediment, rather than the path, to peace: 'Termination of all... states of belligerency... and acknowledgement of the sovereignty... of every state in the area and their right to live in peace within secure and recognised boundaries', and

'A just settlement of the refugee problem' (IMFA). Essentially the
argument revolves around linguistics (Black, 1992), where Palestinians
contend that the Resolution (the French version) calls for Israeli
withdrawal from all territories that it captured from Syria, Jordan and
Egypt in the 1967 war, and refers specifically to 'inadmissibility of the
acquisition of territory by war'. Therefore, argues Abdulrahman
M. Ali, the existence of Jewish settlements in these territories is illegal
and violates international law (i.e. Resolution 242 and the fourth Geneva
Convention), which is a position that has been adopted by the European
Court of Justice (2012: 1–8). Finkelstein agrees with this positions and
contends that '[N]ot only has Israel used the 1967 war to bolster its
fledgling Zionist dream, due to high unemployment and brain drain
(2003a: 143–4), but its occupation generated 'systematic ruination of the
West Bank/Gaza economy' (2003a: 182). Likewise Kelman states:

> Israel's continued creation of the facts on the ground – the growth
> of Israeli settlements in the West Bank, the building of separate
> roads, the confiscation of land, the construction of the security
> barrier, the proliferation of checkpoints, the development of
> Jewish housing in East Jerusalem – have led an increasing number
> of Palestinians to the conclusion that a two-state solution is no
> longer possible (2011: 28).

The ECI emphatically rejects such application of Resolution 242 and
its consequent ramifications for the Jewish settlements on the basis of
the fact that the English version of the text omits the words 'all' and 'the'
(in the disputed section) when requiring withdrawal from the occupied
territories, thus clarifying that any withdrawals have to be negotiated.
The demands that Israel return to the 1949 armistice lines, argues the
ECI, are not substantiated either legally or historically as they were never
internationally recognised borders (ECI, 2012: 9–10). Secondly, such
borders, as already demonstrated in 1967, would be detrimental to
Israel's security (ibid.). Clearly the ECI's stance is at odds with the EU
official positions,[77] and therefore it is difficult to envisage precisely to
what degree the EU appreciates the ECI's contribution to the EU's
strategy of conflict resolution. In addition, the difficulty in envisioning
what the final outcome of a negotiated agreement between Israelis and
Palestinians would exactly look like involves the fact that application of

the Resolution might have to expand to areas that incorporate issues such as terrorism and environment, and might have to be pursued within the functional instead of territorial context (Lapidoth, 2007: 22).

San Remo Initiative

The ECI, as already noted, is capable of a certain amount of pragmatism since it is not inherently hostile to the idea of the Palestinian state, as long as that state does not appropriate East Jerusalem as its capital and incorporates all of the West Bank. From a strategic point of view its position paper (ECI, 2012) to the Palestinian statehood bid is clearly both defensive in its content and offensive in its aim. However, revealing though the interpretations of the Six Day War and Resolution 242 in the ECI document are, they are not the primary framework for the ECI's offensive lobbying since 2010.

While earlier in its existence the ECI took a more comprehensive approach and engaged in as many campaigns as possible, some of which were purely humanitarian in nature, such as pursuing the release of Gilad Shalit,[78] 2010 brought a significant shift in its priorities, in that the organisation became more focused on questions relating to hard politics and built its strategy around the 1920 League of Nations conference in San Remo, Italy. 'It is now clear', an ECI update to its members states, 'that there is an urgent need to inform Members of parliaments and governments as well as other opinion shapers about the history and the solid legal foundation of the Jewish state. This is urgently needed in these times as there are those in the international community who are pressing for a unilateral declaration of a Palestinian state.'[79] The San Remo Initiative was launched officially in 2010 in the EP and includes not only Christian Zionist activism in member states and Brussels, but in the international arena too. It engages in the area of international law and academic research in order to challenge, in the ECI's view, an anti-Israel narrative and distortion of the historical facts, with a central message about the legality of the Jewish state and Jewish jurisdiction over Jerusalem. A lengthy quote from the author's interview with Sandell effectively conveys the ECI's campaign framework and aims:

[T]he pledge that was made in San Remo on the 25th April 1920, then affirmed unanimously by the United Nations in 1922, was then carried over to the United Nations through Article 80, which means that any commitment that the League of Nations made is still valid. So, this means, legally speaking, that Judea, Samaria and Jerusalem, the right for Jewish people to settle, is legally unquestionable... [W]e have found after many years of working in the European Parliament and other parliaments that the historical knowledge of the Middle East, the Jewish State and other Arab States is very, very thin. If you ask the question for example, what is the legal foundation for the modern State of Israel, 9 out of 10 would say the Holocaust, or the partition plan in 1947, which is not true... And we also know from Christian sides, there is a misconception as well, to say that the Balfour declaration was the game changer, which is not true. It's partly true because what happened in San Remo, is that the Balfour declaration was incorporated into international law, accepted by the Supreme Council of the allied powers. This is what makes the legal case for the modern state of Israel.[80]

The intricacies of the legal arguments that would either endorse or reject such an interpretation of San Remo's determinative impact on subsequent UN resolutions regarding the Israeli–Palestinian conflict are beyond the author's competence and the scope of this book; the issue was raised merely for the purpose of conveying the significance of the campaign for the ECI as a lobby group. The San Remo Initiative was evidently in more than one way a turning point for the ECI's advocacy since the frequency and enthusiasm with which the ECI promoted the potentially successful campaign was very high between the end of 2009 and summer 2011.[81] Firstly, the ECI's commitment to long-term offensive campaigning on behalf of Israel took the organisation, as the only Christian Zionist group that operates outside the wider pro-Israel umbrella, to a playing field of hard politics. Secondly, focusing on one specific political goal further defined the ECI as a primarily political Christian Zionist organisation. Thirdly, this commitment meant that the organisation had to step up the acquisition of greater financial resources, initially for generating and organising educational material, and subsequently financing the ECI's advocacy expansion, which took on an international dimension, demanding that its leaders/delegations travel not only to the EU member states, but to Japan also, and frequently to the UN.

An obvious reason behind the selection of the national parliaments of Rome, Paris, London and Tokyo, where the ECI presented their material to policy makers, is in the fact that Italy, France, Britain and Japan constituted former members of the Supreme Council of the Principal Allied Powers of World War I that signed the San Remo Resolution[82] (Wallace, 2011: 37). The French and British[83] governments in particular needed a reminder about their legal obligations, according to the ECI, as their newly adopted positions seem to have moved 'towards accepting a unilateral declaration of a Palestinian State',[84] although the ECI is naturally keen for their educational material (ECI, Give Peace a Chance; ECI, San Remo Resources) to be disseminated as widely as possible among all policy makers in Europe. For that reason its members are encouraged to lobby their national parliaments, but the official ECI working visits were limited to those four capitals for the above-noted reasons, and in order to use the available resources as effectively as possible, namely to conduct their advocacy in the EU and at the UN. Given the constitutive roles that the two organisations hold in the Quartet, the ECI lobbying on the pan-European and international level makes sense, especially in view of the fact that no other pro-Israel lobby organisation uses the League of Nations document as the primary resource in challenging the existing legal and political framework of the Israeli–Palestinian conflict resolution.

The ECI also uses the media, mainly YouTube, the ECI Facebook page, and the ECI blog, as part of the San Remo campaign. This demonstrates that the organisation does not limit itself to approaching the agenda shapers and policy makers through the access mode only, but also uses a voice mode in its offensive strategy in order to create an impact. Although the use of the media inevitably affects the public to a degree, the lobby priority nonetheless remains focused on the policy-making institutions where the ECI aims to present information consisting mainly of work done by Jacques Gauthier (2012), Cynthia Wallace (2012 and 2011) and Howard Grief (2004), all experts in international law. While Grief made his research fully available to the ECI, Gauthier and Wallis took a more proactive role with the ECI, and provided the leadership not only with their research but also with their direct support by travelling with the ECI delegation and participating in meetings with members from other national delegations at the UN. Gauthier appears in the 'Give Peace a Chance' video, which was produced in 2011 and is an essential tool of the San Remo campaign (ECI, Give Peace a Chance) and available to the public on the YouTube channel. The video was initially presented in Brussels on 1 June 2011 as the highlight of the Jerusalem Day hosted in the EP by MEP Timothy Kirkhope, and subsequently presented also in several European capitals, as well as in the Japanese parliament[85] and in the UN (ECI: 2011, Video Reports from UN). Wallace also handed out hundreds of copies of her PhD thesis (Wallace, 2011) at the ECI's lobby training session in Brussels 2011,[86] and subsequently launched her book (2012) in New York at the official ECI event in the UN, where the former Governor and presidential candidate Mike Huckabee was a keynote speaker.[87] Clearly, the ECI's advocacy at the UN level is ambitious, as the organisation has already attended several annual General Assemblies, and met with many UN missions and key officials,[88] where the ECI lobbies not only to prevent the unilateral declaration of the Palestinian state but aims to make the growing antisemitism[89] a priority issue for the international community. In the EU likewise the ECI's ambitions are big and the task of lobbying regarding the issues surrounding the prospective Palestinian state is just as challenging as it is in the UN. It was in the EP in 2010 at its annual policy conference[90] that the ECI launched the San Remo Initiative, where it confirmed its consistently held positions since the organisation's inception as a lobby network, namely the indivisibility of Jerusalem, rejection of the 1967 lines as future borders, defence of Jewish settlements, and illegality of the unilaterally declared (and created) Palestinian state (Wallace, 2011: 18–34). It was rather telling that Catherine Ashton, who attended the Holocaust memorial, was conspicuously absent at this particular event, which was pointed out wryly in the ECI's press release, criticising her for failing 'to send a representative to the panel'; but it also mentioned that the conference 'included recorded messages from the Middle East Envoy of the Quartet Tony Blair and former Israeli Ambassador to the UN Dore Gold'.[91]

While the ECI cannot claim that it has exerted any substantial influence so far over EU policies, or over the policies of any non-European governments, towards Israeli–Palestinian conflict resolution, it has nonetheless ensured its visibility and forged a political space in relevant institutions where the impact of its offensive lobbying might yet take place. Christian Zionist concerns over security for the Jewish state clearly have an historical dimension, but they are essentially rooted in distrust towards the EU's political elite that pursues, in their view, the EU's Middle East policy with excessive pacifism. Hence the ECI's calls to the EU to support pre-emptive military action against Iran if sanctions fail to stop its nuclear programme, even though the ECI is aware that the EU is a power that rejects hard militarism and aims to spread its influence globally through the means of soft power. This soft power is exemplified, for example, by the EU's provision of peace-keeping assistance in order to facilitate conflict resolution, such as the Border Assistance Mission for the Rafah Crossing Point and the Police Mission for the Palestinian Territories (Sankowska, 2007: 2; also Pijpers, 2007: 5–6). As far as the ECI is concerned the EU's peace-keeping strategy is commendable (ECI, 2008), since the organisation believes that the peace that European countries have managed to maintain for the past seven decades is a truly remarkable achievement. Nevertheless, in a region such as the Middle East where the Arab Spring increased the existential threat to Israel, the ECI maintains, the EU should not expect Israel to entrust its security to goodwill and to accept a unilaterally declared solution to the conflict.

Conclusion

In view of the fact that the EU's institutional fluidity and its unique system of governance produces a conducive environment for the proliferation of interest representations, continued research in this area is essential where 'good qualitative studies can further our under-standing of interest politics' (Coen, 2007: 341). This is precisely why this chapter evaluated the ECI's advocacy at the policy-making level by presenting initially a brief overview of the ECI's network, which extends to the Commission, some Jewish groups, and the EP. Although the organisation has access to the Commissioners, who are sympathetic to its overall agenda, they are fewer in number compared to the MEPs, who wholeheartedly endorse the ECI's goals and provide the organisation with a platform to present its views and policy recommendations. The chapter utilised Haynes' (2013) and Thomas' (2005) conceptualisation of religious lobby groups, as both identify the increasing appeal of the soft power of religious actors in international relations. This is clearly relevant to the ECI given that it is an organisation that seeks to exert influence on an international level, but it is also embedded in national politics to a relatively[92] significant degree. Here the ECI effectively incorporates national expressions of German and British Christian Zionist advocacy, defined by different emphases on Christian–Jewish issues, which bring to the ECI a kind of variety that guarantees the ECI's strategic savvy and moral credibility. The combination of the ECI's values and its focus on political rather than religious issues characterises the ECI as a civil society faith-based organisation (Bollmann, 2010). This is no accident, as the ECI consciously maintains its initially self-defined status of an organisation that is at its core Evangelical, while functioning primarily as a political NGO.

Beyond the basic voice/access classification, the chapter conceptualised the ECI's strategy in terms of internal expansion, where the ECI recently made a strategic decision to prioritise an investment in the Christian youth and its active recruitment into the ECI network, and external activism, shaped and defined by both defensive and offensive styles. Defensive lobbying characterises political agitation in Washington DC where a long-established federal system and a high level of transparency precondition lobby groups for an aggressive and highly competitive performance, which for most of the time is reduced to retaining the status quo and preventing new, potentially unfavourable, legislation. That type of strategy, according to the selected literature, projects limited appeal and success in Brussels. Woll (2012) presents comparisons of, and distinctions in, the US and the EU lobby strategies, and concludes that lobby groups in Brussels are more consensual in their approach due to a lesser degree of transparency, but also a high degree of complexity, in the EU governance structures.

This evaluation is applicable to the ECI to a degree. As the ECI conducts its campaigns within the EU's normative parameters, its stated goal of eradicating antisemitism fits well within the EU's overall commitment to outlaw any form of discrimination. The consensual style of lobbying, however, gives way to a more contentious form when the ECI lobbies for pro-Israel policies that are contrary to the EU's official positions. The issues that the ECI takes up are inextricable from hard power politics, where, from a Christian Zionist perspective, the prolonged delegitimisation of the Jewish state affects not only the image of Israel but also aims for its destruction. Therefore the ECI's lobbying becomes offensive, which confirms Gueguen's (2007) assertion that the NGOs, unlike business representations, are far more proactive, seeking continuously to set the agendas, and offering solutions to the problems. Of course, the success of such strategy is not easy to establish given that the political influence of lobby groups is a highly contested subject, and it lacks uniform definition.

As demonstrated in this chapter the ECI's lobbying operates in two spheres. 'Domestically' the ECI's fight against resurgent antisemitism is a sphere where the ECI has so far achieved a great deal of influence. The success of a short-term, offensive 'Keep Ahmadinejad Out' campaign, although in essence fought by German Christian Zionists, is attributed to the ECI since it was initiated, coordinated and publicised by the ECI. Far more significant evidence of the ECI's political leverage on the agenda shaping is evidenced by the institutionalisation of the Holocaust Memorial Day in the EU. This was, and it continues to be, a long-term offensive campaign, which the ECI has taken to the UN[93] also. In terms of the ECI's influence on policy making in EU–Israel relations, the author has demonstrated the limited success of the ECI strategy and its aims. Even if the Commission's initial aid suspension to the PA in 2006 occurred as a result of the ECI's lobbying, as the organisation claimed, it was a temporary, isolated victory, as the EU's funding has since then been reinstated, and the ECI's subsequent pressures on the EU to stop the PA's profligacy produced no tangible results. Nonetheless, the ECI's presentation in the EP was an important breakthrough for the organisation, and it arguably carries greater significance than the suspension of aid itself in view of the fact that the organisation asserted its reputation in the EP as a trustworthy NGO capable of providing information to the EU policy makers in a coherent and professional manner.

This success can be attributed to the fact that even though the strategy was offensive and aimed at changing EU policy in the long run, it was pursued on the basis of the EU's benchmarks of good governance. However, challenging the EU's official position on conflict resolution and the two-state solution is a far more difficult context for the ECI for two reasons. Firstly, the EU's criticism of Israel for its 'disproportionate response' during periodic crises and Israel's internal dealings with its Arab minority are at odds with the ECI's analysis of Israel's conduct during the military confrontations and functioning of its democratic institutions. Secondly the EU's two-state formula policy is based on, and pursued according to, international law, and for that reason, the ECI's annual policy conference in 2010 failed to shift the EU's policy on the

1967 borders, Jewish settlements in the West Bank, and the status of Jerusalem. Therefore, when assessed comprehensively, the level of the ECI's influence on the EU's policy making in the Israeli–Palestinian conflict so far has been low. The ECI's successful performance in creating a positive normative impact through its fight against antisemitism has earned it a high level of respectability at the institutional level, but that achievement has so far failed to translate into a successful lobbying in power politics.

At the institutional level the ECI remains on the margins of political influence, and it is unlikely that this status will change in years to come, unless some specific changes take place in Israel itself, where an increasing number of intellectuals, politicians and lawyers call on the government to recognise the legal significance of the 1920 San Remo Resolution. This would indeed be the highest of all affirmations for the ECI, because the endorsement of the Israeli government would confirm that, though the ECI is a small lobby organisation, its goals are visionary and big. For the ECI, being on the margins of power politics is not something that affects its optimism and convictions. Its leader firmly believes that the legal weight of San Remo is too big to be ignored, which at some point will affect the EU, as it is an institution that adheres to international law. The most immediate need, the ECI maintains, is to create awareness at the highest political echelons that Israel's legitimacy and its territorial claims are legally unchallengeable. That is why it stresses in its advocacy that successful resolution to the Israeli–Palestinian conflict involves moving away from the Balfour Declaration and UN Security Council Resolution 242, and why it conducts its San Remo campaign for the time being not just as a political, but also an educational, campaign.

CONCLUSION

This book was conceived with the understanding that religious actors became significant factors in shaping international relations at the beginning of the twenty-first century. However, the religious factor that shapes the collective European identity has been under-explored thus far in studies that are concerned with EU Middle East policy, and consequently there exists a gap in understanding the direction in which the continually evolving European project is headed as a global power. By including the religious/cultural dimension in its discourse and policy making, Europe's normative values that the EU seeks to project in the Middle East will, arguably, have to be redefined to a substantial degree. In addition, the extensive research into the nature and ways in which the interest groups have sought over the decades to impact upon the EU's policy making have not included the various religious trends, hence a twofold weakness in the EU studies has ensued. Firstly, this exclusion of the new religious trends limits a comprehensive analysis of the new European identity and, secondly, lack of identification of the impact that religious lobby groups have on EU politics limits the analysis of their contribution to the reduction of the EU's democratic deficit, and their contribution in shaping Europe's contemporary multicultural framework.

The author reduces the gap in this particular academic field by presenting insights into the rise of European Christian Zionism through an in-depth study of the ECI, a politico-religious organisation launched officially in 2004 in Brussels. All Brussels-based lobby groups seek to establish their influence at the EU institutional level, and the ECI is not an exception. Its advocacy is framed by two aims – to raise awareness of, educate about, and fight against, antisemitism, and to promote good economic, political and cultural relations between the EU and Israel. In order to assess the degree of the ECI's success in attaining its goals and whether it has established itself as a professional and influential pro-Israel lobby organisation in Brussels, the writer sought to engage with the questions that relate to the ECI's organisational capacity, its ability to make a normative impact at the EU institutional level, its ability to incorporate national (German and British) Christian Zionist advocacy into the pan-European level, and its leverage in influencing the EU's policies in a pro-Israel direction. For that reason the book was structured in a way that initially provides and explains themes that are relevant to Christian Zionist advocacy, as well as the context of EU–Israel relations, followed by an analysis of the ECI in the last three chapters.

The first chapter focused on the themes that form essential parts of European Christian Zionist discourse. It initially evaluated the CFSP and its inconsistency due to the gradual transference of power away from member states, which caused the functional segmentation of the EU's institutions. The issues of identity, religion and religious lobby groups followed a review of the EU's normative values and principles. The review included questions regarding the assumptions about those values, i.e. their normative power and applicability in non-secular societies both within and outside of Europe. Within Europe these exclusively secular values have been challenged by a growing refutation that religious beliefs should remain private. This normative shift was exemplified during the controversy about the inclusion, or to put it more accurately the exclusion, of any reference to Christianity in the EU's constitution. Even though the reference would have a largely symbolic value, nevertheless, for a section of the European populace, including Christian Zionists, the institutionalising of Christianity would demonstrate a political will on the part of the EU's policy makers that Europe is seeking to restore some values that have been (possibly irretrievably) lost in a Europe that has been for some time characterised as post-Christian, neo-Pagan, and, increasingly, Islamic. The rise of Islam, as well as the reassertion of Europe's old religious identities, are demonstrated in the proliferation of religious lobby groups, which, the author maintains, is encouraged at the EU institutional level where they are seen as valuable assets in reducing the EU's democratic deficit.

Chapter 2 focused on several key areas of EU–Israel relations. By contextualising EU–Israel relations through the issues of the ENP and Islamism, EU's normative values and the rise of antisemitism, as well as the peace process and economic relations, the chapter further illuminated the Christian Zionist discourse. Through its neighbourhood policy the EU aims to build positive political, economic and cultural relations with Middle Eastern countries, and aims specifically to facilitate the democratic process through its various instruments, one of which is the conditionality principle. A dilemma that the EU needs to resolve (due largely to lack of unity in its foreign policy) stems from the question as to whether the EU should include Islamist parties in the political dialogue and the democratisation process. The ECI's view of the EU role in the Middle East, and specifically in the peace process, is based on its belief that good economic relations with Israel are beneficial and should continue to deepen, while criticism is aimed at the EU's lack of consistent application of the conditionality principle, most significantly its lenience regarding Palestinian financial corruption. The ECI also emphatically rejects inclusion of the Islamist parties and movements in a political dialogue and maintains that their obstructionism and inherent antisemitism damage the peace process. The chapter reviewed specifically Israel's current relations with Germany and Britain, as these two countries are embedded units of the case study. Aside from the fact that the two countries are among the most influential member states in terms of forming the EU's policy towards Israel, German and British Christian Zionism likewise constitute the most influential streams in the ECI, each bringing contributions to the ECI's advocacy, shaped by the political culture of their domestic environments and by the relations that their governments have with Israel. The last section provides an overview of the ECI, briefly discussing organisational capability, normative premise, and lobbying strategy, which are extensively analysed and discussed in Chapters 3, 4 and 5 respectively.

The third chapter specifically evaluated the ECI's structure. As stated in the overall introduction to the book, this was the first detailed study of a Brussels-based Christian Zionist organisation, and as such it had to evaluate its essential building block. While it is of a paramount importance for all lobby groups in Brussels to become thoroughly familiarised with the EU's institutional functioning if the lobbying process is to achieve any level of success, it is also equally important for lobby groups to structure themselves as a unit that enables their available resources to be used in a way that is cost-effective and with maximum impact. That is why the first criterion regarding the ECI's capacity to influence the EU's agenda-shaping and decision-making competence was applied to the ECI's organisational competence. Its leadership structure, membership and network, as well as its use of media and ability to sustain itself financially, demonstrated that, apart from the fact that the ECI achieved accreditation in the EP, its internal structure and the level of professionalism have been progressively modified since 2004 to the point where in 2012 the organisation solidified its image of an NGO that conducts its advocacy in a competent manner at the EU's institutional level.

Chapter 4 focused on values that inform and determine the ECI's lobbying and provide an elaborate clarification about European Christian Zionism, which shares certain common characteristics with the American variant. It is, however, significantly different in other areas, namely in its motivational factor for pro-Israel advocacy, based on special responsibility for centuries-long European antisemitism. The author demonstrated that the ECI has made a significant normative impact on EU agenda shaping and policy making. Although the ECI's belief that Europe should reassert its Judeo-Christian values may not be in the mainstream in European societies, and most definitely not in academia, it is the ECI's stated commitment to human rights, good governance and other democratic principles that reinforce the normative values that the EU seeks to uphold and promote. Of course, the most significant normative impact that the ECI has accomplished (and continue so to do) at the EU's institutional level is through its fight against antisemitism. The ECI's commitment to organising annually the commemoration of the Holocaust Day in the EP (in partnership with the EJC) led to its being declared in 2013 an official EP event by its President.

Chapter 5 demonstrated the level of the ECI's lobbying success, which essentially revolved around two specific factors – the efficiency with which the ECI co-ordinates and streamlines national (German and British) Christian Zionist advocacy on the EU level, and its ability to influence, directly or indirectly, EU pro-Israel policies. As this was the chapter that had to analyse and discuss the ECI's lobby strategy it initially discussed the ECI's network in the EP, then also its connections with the groups outside the EU institutions. Like all interest representations and NGOs that seek to increase and maintain their effectiveness, the ECI too seeks to form ad hoc alliances and maintain long-term partnerships. The Jewish organisations in particular, those from outside Israel as well as from Israel, have proved so far to be reliable partners in pursuing the same short-term and long-term goals. The concept of defensive strategy, it was argued, characterises lobbying in Washington DC for most of the time, but it is problematic to apply it to Brussels-based lobby groups due to several features in EU governance: high functional segmentation, less accountability in decision making, and less transparency in lobby regulation.

The ECI, particularly its network from Britain, occasionally engages in defensive tactics when it seeks to preserve good economic relations between the EU and Israel and contends for Israel's good image through the media in times of crises. Most of the time, however, the ECI's lobbying is offensive because it seeks actively to influence the EU's policy. Chapter 5 provided several examples of its lobbying in order to demonstrate that the campaigns, both short-term and long-term, have so far produced mixed results. Evidence showed that when the ECI engages in a constructive dialogue, or even challenges the status quo, at the institutional level, it succeeded because its lobbying was conducted within the framework of the EU values, i.e. good governance, antidiscrimination, economic prosperity etc. On the other hand, the ECI's position on issues that are constitutive to the peace process predisposes the organisation to a place where its consensual approach remains outside the ECI's strategy because it diverges significantly from the EU's position on a two-state solution and Jerusalem. Consequently, the ECI has failed to change the EU's policy on the Israeli–Palestinian conflict, which is essentially entrenched in the (contested) interpretation of Security Council Resolution 242, and which the EU maintains according to its role in the Quartet.

It is worth noting at the close of the book some issues regarding the ECI, which extend generally to European Christian Zionism. The last chapter made a point in singling out the ECI's pragmatism regarding the two-state solution and the fact that the organisation maintains its status as an advocacy group that is primarily concerned with political issues, while spiritual convictions remain largely outside the public space and are rarely used as an instrument with which the ECI champions Israel's cause at the institutional level. The ECI's official press releases clearly spell out the organisation's political position on all the contentious issues, but they are void of the spiritual dimension of the ECI's conviction. These are reserved as a periodic reminder for its members in monthly reports, such as the one that criticises the EU Swedish Presidency when it urged the declaring of Jerusalem as the shared capital of Israel and a future Palestinian state: '[I]t is a major blow in the battle for the city of the Great King [Jesus Christ] and is also a clear sign of the times of nations preparing to line up against Israel.'[1] Any Christian Zionist would immediately understand that this is a clear reference to a biblical prophecy in the book of Zechariah chapter 14, verse 2. This is, as demonstrated in the last chapter, part of the ECI's strategy of operating in a secular political environment, where its emphatic rejection of the partitioning of Jerusalem can be maintained publicly from a purely political position, and therefore it is not in conflict with its spiritual convictions. On the other hand, the ECI's pragmatism about the two-state solution, more precisely the support that it lends to Israel's official 'land for peace policy', demonstrates that the ECI's primary function in pro-Israel advocacy is in the political domain.

Having said that, it is important to remember that the political positions, as well as the spiritual convictions, are not uniform across the Christian Zionist landscape in Europe. Some groups, and indeed some individuals within the ECI network, do not approve of any pragmatism whatsoever, whether the issue in question is 'land for peace', or inter-denominational, ecumenical alliances, or proselytising the Jews, or Christian Zionist political involvement. In addition some Christian Zionists do not hold that dispensational pre-millennial eschatology is a necessary spiritual prerequisite for supporting the Jewish state. In fact, at times it is criticised as an over-emphasised biblical hermeneutic among American evangelicals, whose excessive fervour is used by the secular press to portray all Christian Zionists as warmongering, out of the mainstream, right-wing ideologues. All these issues, and many more, became apparent to the author during the field trips undertaken over the period of four years, where she met many Christian supporters of Israel from nearly every country in Europe, and where she learnt that European Christian Zionism, like all other movements that have a strong normative base, is not a monolithic and coherent expression of twenty-first century Christian philosemitism. On the contrary, there exists a multitude of divergent opinions regarding the spiritual, political, geo-strategic, and economic issues, formed in the specific historical setting of the Christian faith and relationship with the Jewish people. Significantly perhaps, the influence of American Christian Zionism is not negligible, due possibly to the rise of the Charismatic/Pentecostal movement in Europe in the last several decades, but also its propagation through the globalisation of media.

This is significant for two reasons. On a broader level, the rise of the Christian Zionist movement in European countries demonstrates the changing shape of European Christianity that, to some level, is impacting upon the process of the formation of the new European identity. Specifically though, in view of the fact that some Christian Zionist groups seek to influence national policies in Israel's favour, they are potentially significant influencers of foreign policy at the EU level. Given that the Christian Zionist movement is present across Europe, but has been investigated in only two countries so far, the scope for further research remains, as it does indeed into religious interest representations in general. While this book offers some insights into religious groups' adaptation onto the supranational level, there still remains a range of religious lobby groups and national lobby strategies, whose effects on the EU policy making remain unexplored. For that reason this book aims to encourage further research into Brussels-based lobby culture, where continuing academic enquiry would not only shed further light into the competing (or compatible) narratives and normative premise of the diverse religious groups, but would also demonstrate the degree to which different national lobby models impact upon or shape their lobby strategies in Brussels. For example, the diverse lobby strategies of national Christian Zionist groups may or may not emulate British pluralist or German corporatist modes when working for their goals in their national parliaments, but at the level of the EU, where the consensus-building antihierarchical model defines Brussels' political culture, their approach will always be modified according to the German style lobbying.

It is important to stress that this book selected only German and British Christian Zionist advocacy in order to analyse and draw certain conclusions about the ECI. The reasons for choosing these two particular member states were outlined in the second chapter, which were compelling enough scientifically to conduct an inquiry into, and construct a picture of, pan-European Christian Zionism. Although the findings, analysis and conclusions were based on the available evidence, which the author used to the best of her ability, it must be stressed that German and British Christian Zionist contributions to the ECI, though the most substantial, are nonetheless only two parts of the whole. For instance, the number of Dutch participants tends to be fairly high at the ECI's conferences, and their national influence, mainly through C4I, seems to have an effect that goes beyond the national parliament. Czech and Romanian participants, who are among the most fervent, bring an eastern European 'flavour', in terms of culture, but also lobbying experiences, to the ECI's gatherings. Further research into the ECI's network from other member states would not only provide a complete picture of Christian Zionist advocacy in Brussels, but detailed enquiry of national Christian Zionist networks would also reduce the gap in the literature about different levels of influence that NGOs are able, or allowed, to exert across Europe, and it would specifically discover the nature of alliances that Christian Zionist groups make in their national settings. For instance, are these alliances characterised by Christian–Jewish cooperation, as in the case of Germany and Britain, and if this is the case, does the size of the Jewish population, and (non)existence of Jewish advocacy groups determine, affect, or disqualify such networks?

A specific insight into Christian–Jewish cooperation is another area for further research where findings and analysis can offer a significant contribution to the studies of the normative lobby groups in the EU, but it can also provide a more accurate picture of the existence and level of influence of the Israel lobby in member states and the EU. This is important so that the existing assertions and sweeping statements about the Israel lobby can be either confirmed or disproved from a scientific point of view. With regard to the ECI, because it is a numerically small organisation in comparison to some large NGOs such as Friends of the Earth, and because the ECI likes to maintain its status of an independent NGO, it was relatively easy to compile the necessary evidence and identify the ECI's influence independently from other organisations that it works with. However, as demonstrated in the chapters that focused specifically on the ECI, it is apparent that whatever modest or significant success the ECI has achieved, the importance of its cooperation with the Jewish groups cannot be underestimated. This book clearly provides the evidence that the Israel lobby is well established in Brussels and, as such, it is an important source of information in constructing a comprehensive picture about the Israel lobby and its networking across Europe should such further academic inquiry take place.

Regardless of whether the Jewish–Christian–secular pro-Israel movement in Europe gathers pace or whether it does not move beyond its current level, Christian Zionism will continue in its quest for political influence, and become potentially in the near future one of the most significant and influential sources of support for the state of Israel. The case study of the ECI demonstrated how something so marginal on the landscape of power politics and numerically almost negligible among the well-funded and popular NGOs can become so relatively influential. In the space of eight years, and due to the combination of several factors: accreditation at the EU institutional level, professional information supply, endorsement by respectable Jewish organisations, and an official recognition at the Knesset, the ECI has managed to establish itself as a professional and trustworthy NGO. On the one hand, this confirms the correct assumption that, just as business interest groups that recognise the EU's power have to embed themselves in the unique policy network setting, so too the NGOs that are defined by norms have to go through the same process of adaptation to the Brussels political culture and develop their strategy in line with the EU's fluid institutional structures. Politically-minded Christian Zionists have observed that even though the EU's leverage in the Middle East, particularly in the Israeli–Palestinian conflict, might not be that high, due to traditional American power-brokering and Israel's preference for a bilateral approach to conflict-resolution, the EU has nevertheless asserted a unique role for itself in the region and its political power continues to grow with each successive treaty that aims to streamline its foreign policy. On the other hand, the ECI's successful embedding in the Brussels lobby scene also demonstrates the existence of the favourable environment for NGOs at the EU's institutional level, where a range of religious and/or politico-religious groups have an equal chance to contend for proposals and policies.

Obviously, the fact that the lack of statehood opens up the EU to influences from a wide range of actors does not guarantee a successful outcome for all lobby groups that seek to impact the EU's foreign policy, as the EU aims to act according to its assumed normative values and principles. Nevertheless the EU's particular openness to religious interest representations demonstrates recognition on the part of the policy makers that the clashing perceptions of secular and sacred worldviews need not impede the transformation of the EU from an economic club into a community of values. This was aptly expressed by Romano Prodi when he declared that '[t]here is no essence of Europe, no fixed list of European values' (European Commission, 2004), thereby affirming the notion that EU political culture has become conducive to an input from diverse religious and philosophical persuasions into the normative framework of the EU. This conduciveness is relative for the ECI as it is highly unlikely that European Christian Zionism will affirm the EU's universalism by blending in and negating its normative premise that advocates for Europe's return to its Christian roots. The movement is clearly aware that it has a limited appeal on an institutional level where multiculturalism and religious egalitarianism effectively prevent any faith expression from monopolising Europe's religious identity. Equally, it recognises that the only place in which it can exercise its credibility is in the political arena, where all actors that are involved in the political process can obtain some benefits. For the ECI specifically this means that beyond its contribution to the legitimisation process of the EU, it has a potential to exert its influence on the outcome of the peace process, providing that its network widens in years to come, not only numerically, but also in terms of securing a significant number of agenda setters and policy makers who are sympathetic to the ECI's goals.

NOTES

Prelims

* A conventional acronym for both Conservative Friends of Israel and Christian Friends of Israel is CFI. For the purpose of avoiding confusion the author has used CFI as an acronym for Christian Friends of Israel.

Introduction   Religion and Lobbying in the European Union

1. President of the European Commission Jacques Delors, text of speech given to Church leaders in Brussels, 4 February 1992, http://ec.europa.eu/dgs/policy_advisers/archives/activities/dialogue_religions_humanismssfe_en.htm accessed on 04/10/11.
2. The Article ensures that the EU institutions respect the national status of, as well as maintaining an open, transparent and regular dialogue with, the religious and non-confessional organisations.
3. Principles, methods and rules necessary for the interpretation of biblical texts.
4. Study of the End Times and the second coming of Jesus Christ. Three basic positions are known as post-millennialism, a-millennialism and pre-millennialism. A-millennialism denies the literal 1,000-year reign of Jesus, while post-millennialism asserts that the Kingdom was ushered at Christ's ascension, and the world is to be Christianised and handed to Jesus upon his return. Christian Zionists in contrast propagate pre-millennialism, i.e. Jesus' return before his literal 1,000-year reign on earth, since he alone has power and purity to establish a perfect kingdom.
5. Known also as Replacement Theology which teaches that the Church has replaced Israel/Jews in God's divine plan for humanity.

Chapter 1   Europe's Values and Religion

1. The worldwide community of Muslim believers that transcends race, ethnicity, nationality and class.
2. An Islamic law that incorporates both civil and criminal justice, as well as regulating the personal and moral conduct of an individual.

Chapter 2   EU–Israel Relations in Context

1. Romano Prodi interview with *Time Magazine*, 23 April 2006, http://www.time. com/time/magazine/article/0,9171,1186540,00.html.
2. The most accurate and respectable source that monitors and documents Palestinian-sponsored antisemitism is Palestinian Media Watch (PMW).
3. Binyamin Netanyahu's inclusion of Avigdor Lieberman' right-wing Yisrael Beiteinu party in a coalition caused concern for the human rights of Israeli Arab citizens.
4. See BICOM (2012) and JURIST (2011) notes and analysis.
5. The Boycott, Divestment and Sanctions movement started in 2005 by Palestinian NGOs. Call for an academic boycott of Israel is particularly strong in the British Association of University Teachers (AUT).

Chapter 3   The ECI Structure

1. ECI original booklet, p.1.
2. Ibid.
3. Sandell T. 2011 interview.
4. The four principal Allied Powers of World War I met in 1920 in San Remo, Italy where it was decided to incorporate the 1917 Balfour Declaration into the British mandate for Palestine.
5. Salmi K. 2011 interview.
6. Sandell T. 2011 interview.
7. Eckert H. 2010 interview.
8. Ibid.
9. Tucker A. 2010 interview.
10. Ibid. follow-up interview.
11. Adeola D. 2012 interview.
12. Ibid. where he referred to Moses and Aaron from the book of Exodus in the Bible. As long Aaron and Hur held Moses' arms the Israelites were winning in the battle against the Amalekites.
13. One of the largest Pentecostal churches in Britain.
14. Adeola D. 2012 interview.
15. ECI monthly report, August 2008.
16. Fjell L. 2010 interview.
17. Ibid.

18. Salmi K. 2011 interview.
19. ECI press release, 1 May 2008.
20. ECI monthly report, September 2008.
21. Sandell T. 2011 interview.
22. Ibid.
23. I.e. a conviction that God has led him to establish a Christian pro-Israel voice in Brussels.
24. Study of the Holy Spirit, the third Person of Christian deity. Charismatics and Pentecostals are frequently criticised by other denominational Protestants for attributing some excessive spiritual experiences, which are not mentioned in the Bible, to the workings of the Holy Spirit.
25. Christian Zionists base this particular contention on many scriptures (mostly, but not exclusively, from the Old Testament), of which 'valley of the dry bones' from the prophet Ezekiel 37: 1–14 seems to be most popular.
26. Sandell T. 2011 interview.
27. Tucker A. 2010 interview.
28. Ibid. follow-up interview.
29. Salmi K. 2011 interview.
30. ECI press release, 12 May 2008.
31. ECI monthly report, March 2008.
32. Ibid., January 2009.
33. Tucker A. 2012 follow-up interview; Eckert H. 2011 interview.
34. Facebook membership doubles, on average, every year.
35. Sandell T. 2012 follow-up interview.
36. ECI press release, 12 May 2008.
37. ECI monthly report, September 2008.
38. Eckert H. 2010 interview.
39. ECI monthly report, May 2008.
40. Ibid., June 2009.
41. Salmi K. 2011 interview.
42. At a workshop in Brussels, November 2011, British Christian Zionists shared with some 100 ECI members from across Europe how to lobby national parliaments, and how to organise protests and demonstrations.
43. Eckert H. 2011 interview.
44. Ibid.
45. Klein L. 2012 interview.
46. Ibid.
47. Ibid.
48. The biggest pro-Israel network in Germany of over 140 organisations, including Christian groups, that gathered in Frankfurt, October 2011. The estimated attendance was 3,000 people.
49. Based on the Kairos Palestine document the British Methodist conference produced a resolution that was very critical of Israel.
50. Sandell T. 2011 interview.

51. The majority of young people who attended the symposium in the EP were from the UK. Several months later, in August 2012, an ECI-sponsored 'Trowel and Sword' youth conference was held in Oxford, with the aim of encouraging Christian Zionist youth to be active in influential institutions and in churches.
52. At the 2012 lobby day the lobbyists urged about 300 MPs to oppose the BDS campaign, to take the Iranian nuclear threat seriously, and to take action against the plight of Christian minorities in Arab countries.
53. Vince J. 2011 interview.
54. Mordecai was a spiritual adviser to Esther, a Jewish queen, during the reign of the Persian king Ahasuherus. He urged her to take action against Haman, a high-ranking political adviser, who plotted to enact genocide of the Jewish people. The current crisis between Iran and Israel is interpreted by Christian Zionists as an historical repeat of the same existential threat against the Jewish people.
55. Although many religious Jews from a variety of expressions of Jewish faith could be described as Messianic Jews, the term has become an acceptable expression that identifies those Jews who accept that Jesus Christ is the long-awaited Jewish Messiah.
56. Gutmann T. 2011 interview.
57. Richard Bartholomew's article on Mordecai Voice http://barthsnotes.com/2011/12/31/christian-zionist-counter-protest-at-israeli-embassy-in-london/ also Ben White's warning about the organisation http://pulsemedia.org/2011/09/15/israels-advocates-in-the-uk-cosy-up-to-christian-right/.
58. Gutmann T. 2011 interview.
59. Sandell T. 2012 follow-up interview.
60. Ibid.
61. ECI monthly report, June 2009.
62. www.roku.com.
63. Barrett S. 2012 interview.
64. 22–23 March 2012 'In the Eye of the Storm' Conference. The ECI made a strategic decision to expand its network by active recruitment of young people.
65. Barrett S. 2012 interview.
66. Ibid.
67. ECI monthly report, January 2010.
68. Ibid., March 2012.
69. January, June, July, August, November and December 2010 monthly reports.
70. ECI monthly report, March 2011.
71. Sandell T. 2011 interview.
72. Ibid.
73. ECI monthly report, January 2012.
74. Ibid., March 2010.
75. Tamagnini M. 2011 interview.
76. Eckert H. 2011 interview.
77. Tucker A. 2012 follow-up interview.

Chapter 4   The ECI Values

1. Dispensationalism divides human history into (usually) seven dispensations: Innocence, Conscience, Human Government, Promise, Law, Grace and Millennial Kingdom. The more extreme form of dispensationalism teaches two distinct plans of salvation for Gentiles and the Jews.
2. Tucker A. 2010 interview.
3. Eckert H. 2010 interview.
4. ECI monthly report February 2008.
5. Ibid. 2011.
6. After the annual conference in the EP, January 2010, some 200 members attended the church service in the Pentecostal/Charismatic church within the vicinity Brussels.
7. After the first ECI 'Youth Ministry' in Brussels, March 2012, about 300 members spent a weekend in La Foresta Christian retreat centre outside of Brussels.
8. A Christian practice and a form of authentication of spiritual authority, recorded in the book of Acts (the Bible).
9. The 2010 annual conference was titled: 'Israel, EU and the intercultural dialogue: How will the demographic and cultural changes in Europe change relations with Israel?'.
10. ECI press release, 25 September 2006.
11. ECI monthly report, May 2008.
12. Sandell T. 2011 interview.
13. Ibid.
14. ECI press release, October 20 2006.
15. On July 22 2003, however, senior European officials gathered in Brussels and announced that Hezbollah's military wing would be added to the EU's list of banned terrorist groups.
16. ECI monthly report, February 2009.
17. At its 8th annual Policy Conference in the EP on Arab Spring, November 2011, the ECI expressed its concern about the rise of Islamic radicalism across the region and urged the EU policy makers to prioritise the Iranian nuclear threat.
18. ECI press release, January 30 2006.
19. ECI monthly report, October 2011.
20. Ibid., February 2011.
21. Sandell T. 2011 interview.
22. ECI monthly report, April 2010.
23. A Turkish ship, organised by 'Gaza Freedom Flotilla' and 'Foundation for Human Rights and Freedom and Humanitarian Relief 'that aimed to break the Israeli blockade of Gaza. The IDF raid of the ship left nine people dead.
24. ECI press release, June 4 2010.
25. ECI monthly report, August 2009.
26. Barrett S. 2012 interview.
27. Sandell T. 2011 interview.
28. ECI monthly report, June 2008.

29. ECI monthly report, November/December 2008.
30. 'Israel is more than Holocaust and conflict – Start up nation Israel – a light to the nations'.
31. ECI monthly report, December 2011.
32. ECI press release, 13 December 2011.
33. ECI monthly report, April 2010.
34. Ibid., March 2008.
35. ECI monthly report, July 2009.
36. Sandell T. 2011 interview.
37. ECI monthly report, February 2009.
38. Gnosticism essentially regarded the physical body as evil, the God of the Old Testament as a false God and Jesus as a pure spirit that represents a religion designed to provide an escape from the material world. This escape is preconditioned by a possession of a hidden wisdom or knowledge – a privilege that only a select group of highly spiritual people can obtain.
39. Scholasticism was a method that emphasised dialectical reasoning and disputations, which Christian Western scholars felt was necessary in order to reconcile the ancient classical philosophy with biblical texts.
40. Eckert H. 2010 interview.
41. ECI press release, 23 January 2013.
42. ECI monthly report, January 2012.
43. Ibid., December 2011.
44. ECI press release, 1 November 2010.
45. ECI monthly report, March 2012.
46. Sandell T. 2011 interview.

Chapter 5   The ECI Strategy

1. The ECI booklet.
2. Belder B. 2010 interview.
3. ECI monthly report, February 2012.
4. Takkula H. 2010 interview.
5. Essayah S. 2010 interview.
6. Kirkhope T. 2011 interview.
7. ECI press release, May 4 2006.
8. Sandell T. 2011 interview.
9. Martins N. 2012 interview.
10. 8 November 2011 workshop, 'How to win the battle of narratives – one heart and one mind at a time' that took place in Brussels prior to the ECI's annual conference in the EP.
11. Drai S. 2011 interview.
12. Gutman C. 2012 interview.
13. Martins N. 2012 interview.
14. ECI monthly report, February 2010; also ECI press release, 27 January 2012.

15. ECI monthly report, May 2008.
16. Shimon Samuels presented a message that defamation and condemnation of Israel at the Durban I and (the forthcoming) Durban II is in its essence the globalisation of antisemitism.
17. ECI monthly report, June 2009.
18. Myers C. 2012 interview.
19. At the ECI annual policy conference, September 2005, the PMW Director Itamar Markus argued that the PA funding is not being sufficiently scrutinised.
20. Gutman C. 2012 interview.
21. Martins N. 2012 interview.
22. Myers C. 2012 interview.
23. Ibid.
24. Drai S. 2011 interview.
25. ECI monthly report, November 2011.
26. ECI press release, 26 April 2010.
27. Tucker A. 2010 interview.
28. In Hebrew 'making the connection', in this case between Judaism and Christianity, and in such a way as to undermine the supercessionist stream, as well as predispose undecided Christians in a pro-Israel direction.
29. Vince V. 2011 interview.
30. In November 2012, among three other speakers, a Palestinian Christian from the West Bank spoke about her journey from being virulently anti-Israel to becoming an advocate for the Jewish state. She urged the audience to become involved in political advocacy on behalf of Israel.
31. 22 March 2012, 'In the Eye of the Storm' Youth Symposium in the EP drew around 50 young enthusiastic adults from Britain, the Netherlands, Hungary, France, Finland and Switzerland, who attended a series of workshops on topics related to Israel in media and academia, as well as 'lawfare' tactics in the political domain.
32. ECI monthly report, February 2012.
33. 'Palestinian Responsibility for Human Rights – Facing the Facts on the Ground' Myers presented a report about the human rights abuses by Hamas and the PA, as well as Europe's double standards towards the human rights abuses.
34. ECI press release, 22 March 2012.
35. 17–19 August 2012, 'Sword and Trowel' youth conference where two prominent Christian theologians taught the history of the persecution of the Jewish people by the Church, and pre-millennial eschatology. Other speakers encouraged youth to be active politically on behalf of Israel, and to contend for the Christian faith.
36. 'Pray and Vote 2009' campaign for the European parliamentary elections.
37. ECI press release, 20 May 2009.
38. ECI monthly report, August 2009.
39. Adeola D. 2012 interview.
40. ECI monthly report, July 2009.

41. ECI press release, 2 February 2006.
42. Sandell T. 2011 interview.
43. Ibid.
44. This specific concept of religious representations advocacy is particularly emphasised by COMECE and CEC.
45. A US non-profit organisation founded in 1871 that promotes the right of citizens, as a civil right, to bear arms.
46. The largest US provider of reproductive health services, including cancer and HIV screening, contraception and abortion.
47. Within hours after the IDF boarded the vessel, the ECI was sending out information bulletins to friends and supporters through e-mails, Twitter and Facebook (ECI, 2010 MR June), as well as posting videos on the internet conveying the message that the Gaza flotilla was not a humanitarian but a military operation. It agitated in the EP through Bastiaan Belder (Chairman of the EU–Israel parliamentary delegation) and Gabriele Albertini (Chairman of the foreign affairs committee).
48. A pro-Palestinian group announced the start of the Third Intifada page on 15 May. The ECI initiated a massive response from pro-Israel users causing Facebook to shut down the page (CiF Watch, 2011).
49. ECI monthly report, December 2011.
50. Concerns over the BDS are raised at every CFI-ZF Annual Lobby Day, which takes place in Westminster.
51. The lobby day was reported in Israeli media as one of the largest and most influential so far.
52. Agreements on Conformity Assessment and Acceptance of Industrial Products.
53. The conference was titled 'Promoting the reform process in the Middle East – what role can the European Union play?' and hosted by MEP Hannu Takkula.
54. ECI press release, 23 September 2005.
55. Sandell T. 2011 interview.
56. The conference was titled 'Faith and Values in Europe – 70 Years after Kristallnacht' and hosted by MEP Hannu Takkula.
57. ECI press release, 12 November 2008.
58. The 2008 document is titled 'European Coalition for Israel contribution for a new EU mechanism for supporting peace building and conflict prevention in EU external relations'.
59. ECI press release, 23 September 2005.
60. ECI monthly report, December 2011.
61. ECI press release, 31 May 2006.
62. Ibid., 9 June 2006.
63. Hitler's and Ahmadinejad's pictures were placed next to each other and the caption read 'Just a Game? In the summer of 1936 this man [Hitler] hijacked the Berlin Olympics. This summer 2006 don't let this man [Ahmadinejad] do the same'.
64. Klein L. 2012 interview.

65. In 2011 it was attended by over 140 Jewish and Christian, as well as secular, organisations, and prominent political figures from Germany and Israel. The ECI, Christensen fur Israel and Saxony Friends of Israel conducted jointly a very-well attended seminar where speakers presented the history and aims of the organisations.

66. Korenke C. 2012 interview.

67. Ibid.

68. This particular lobby demanded an investigation into, and challenging of, Islamic radicalism and antisemitism at British campuses. It also demanded the creation of a safe environment for Jewish students.

69. ECI press release, 1 July 2008.

70. The ECI's Founder and Director T. Sandell's argued at the ECI 2011 'Arab Spring' annual policy conference that the EU needs to take Israel's security concerns more seriously.

71. ECI press release, 6 January 2009.

72. A Norwegian doctor whose reports about Israeli atrocities were broadcast worldwide on prominent media networks, such as ABC, BBC, CBS and CNN.

73. ECI monthly report (Special Report), 13 January 2009.

74. 'Unilateral Palestinian Statehood: Why the Palestinian application for advanced status in the United Nations should be rejected'.

75. 1.'Withdrawal of Israeli armed forces from territories occupied in the recent conflict' and 2.'Termination of all claims or states of belligerency and respect for and acknowledgement of the sovereignty, territorial integrity and political independence of every State in the area and their right to live in peace within secure and recognised boundaries free from threat or acts of force.' http://www. mfa.gov.il/MFA/Peace%20Process/Guide%20to%20the%20Peace%20Process/ UN%20Security%20Council%20Resolution%20242.

76. ECI press release, 12 October 2012.

77. Most difficult for the ECI to challenge is the EU's position on the 1967 borders, division of Jerusalem, as well as the expansion of Jewish homes in East Jerusalem. http://www.eeas.europa.eu/mepp/eu-positions/eu_positions_en. htm.

78. An IDF soldier, abducted by Hamas in June 2006 and released in October 2011 as part of a prisoner exchange deal.

79. ECI monthly report, December 2010.

80. Sandell T. 2011 interview.

81. Nearly all ECI monthly reports to its members in this initial period of the campaign contain reminders of the legal significance of the San Remo conference in 1920, as well as requests for prayer for the ECI delegations, and an occasional appeal for increased financial support in order to conduct lobbying efficiently.

82. Text available in the appendix section of the author Wallace C.D. (2011).

83. The meeting in Britain was hosted by MP Jeffrey Donaldson who warned that dividing up cities is not a formula for peace, and it can lead to years of negative experiences, his own home town of Belfast providing an apt example.
84. ECI press release 8 July 2011.
85. Ibid., 25 April 2012.
86. 8 November 2011, 'How to win the battle of narratives – one heart and one mind at a time'.
87. ECI press release, 23 May 2012.
88. At the 2012 UN General Assembly gathering the ECI delegation met with Jan Eliasson, the UN Deputy Secretary General (ECI, PR 1 December).
89. The ECI 'Ban Holocaust Denial at the UN' campaign was concluded at the 2012 UN General Assembly.
90. The conference was titled 'The legitimacy of Israel – from San Remo to Brussels', and was hosted by MEP Bastiaan Belder.
91. ECI press release, 17 November 2010.
92. An in-depth research in all 27 member states would provide an accurate and comprehensive answer to the extent of Christian Zionist political participation in Europe.
93. The ECI initiated a global citizen petition in 2012 aimed at the UN to outlaw Holocaust denial at the UN.
94. ECI monthly report, December 2009.

BIBLIOGRAPHY

PRIMARY SOURCES

Interviews

(Posts that were held by interviewees at the time of interview indicated. Interviews listed in chronological order)

2010

Lennart Fjell:	30 January (Pastor of the Word of Life church, Sweden; member of the ECI board)
Harald Eckert:	31 January (Chairman of the board of Christensen fur Israel, Initiative 27 January, and the ECI)
Andrew Tucker:	1 March (Executive Director of Christians for Israel; member of the the ECI board)
Roy Thurley:	2 March (former Director of CFI UK; North Wales CFI representative)
Phil Margolis:	5 March (Chairman of the Leeds branch ZF)
Lee Scott:	9 March (MP; Member of CFofI)
Bastian Belder:	26 March (Dutch MEP, member of EPP; Chairman of European Parliamentary Delegation to Israel)
British official:	28 April (Permanent Representations member, Brussels)
German official:	28 April (Permanent Representations member, Brussels)
Hannu Takkula:	29 April (Finnish MEP; member of ALDE; Chairman of the Knesset–Christian Allies Caucus in the EU)
Jacob Vince:	16 March (Director of the CFI UK; member of the General Synod of the Church of England)

2011

Tomas Sandell:	30 May (Founding Director of the ECI)
Monica Tamagnini:	8 November (former ECI representative, Brussels)
Katariina Salmi:	9 November (Personal Assistant to Tomas Sandell)
Harald Eckert:	9 November (follow-up interview)
Claudia Korenke:	17 November (Vice-President German–Israeli Friendship Society)
Ben Garrett:	21 November (Head of Policy and Research Labor Friends of Israel)
Mathew Harris:	29 November (Vice Chairman of Liberal Democrat Friends of Israel)
Tim Gutmann:	9 December (Pastor of Junction 28 Church, UK; Founder of Mordecai Voice)
Timothy Kirkhope:	13 December (British MEP; member of ECR)
Sari Essayah:	21 December (Finish MEP; member of EPP)

2012

German Christian Zionist:	16 February (prominent position in Initiative 27 January)
Lothar Klein:	26 February (Chairman of Saxon Friends of Israel; former MEP; former CDU deputy)
David Adeola:	24 March (Leader in Kensington Temple; member of the ECI board)
Samuel Drai:	25 March (serving in Israeli Embassy, Brussels)
Nathalie Tamam:	11 April (Political Director of Conservative Friends of Israel)
Simon Barrett:	12 April (Broadcaster and Journalist, Revelation TV)
Tomas Sandell:	8 May (follow-up interview)
Andrew Tucker:	16 May (follow-up interview)
Israeli official:	12 June (serving in Britain)
Charlotte Gutmann:	13 August (Founder of CGP Europe, Brussels)
Calev Myers:	7 September (Founder of Jerusalem Institute for Justice)
Israeli official:	15 September (serving in Germany)
Nuno Wahnon:	16 October (Director of EU Affairs, B'nai B'rith)

Participant observation

Brussels:	
11 November 2008:	'Seventy years after Kristallnacht' ECI annual policy conference, European Parliament

13 November 2008:	Sunday service in a Charismatic/Pentecostal church, organised by the ECI, city of Brussels
28 January 2009:	Holocaust Memorial Day, ECI-EJC, European Parliament
28 January 2010:	'Israel, the EU and the intercultural dialogue: How will the demographic and cultural changes in Europe change relations with Israel?' ECI annual policy conference, European Parliament
31 January 2010:	Sunday service in a Charismatic/Pentecostal church, organised by the ECI, outskirts of Brussels
8 November 2011:	'How to win the battle of narratives – one heart and one mind at a time' ECI-sponsored advocacy training day
9 November 2011:	'Israel and the Arab Spring: How can the EU promote peace and democracy in the Middle East'? ECI annual policy conference, European Parliament
22 March 2012:	'In the Eye of the Storm' ECI Youth Symposium, European Parliament
23 March 2012:	'Israel and Lawfare' ECI seminar, European Parliament
24 March 2012:	ECI Prayer summit, Christian retreat centre in La Foresta

Britain:

20 January 2010:	Annual Lobby Day CFI-ZF, Westminster
26 January 2011:	Annual Lobby Day CFI-ZF, Westminster
29 January 2012:	Christian Youth advocacy training day, London
18–19 August 2012:	'Sword and Trowel' ECI Youth Conference, Oxford
18 November 2012:	'Israel's Future and Ours' CFI-sponsored conference, York

Germany:

| 23 October 2011: | Israel Kongress, Frankfurt |

ECI monthly reports

(available on request from the researcher)

2008:   January, February, March, April, May, June, September, November/ December
2009:   January, 13 January (Special Report), February, June, July, August
2010:   January, March, April, June, July, August, November/December
2011:   February, April, August/September, October, November, December
2012:   January, February

ECI press releases

available at www.ec4i.org/index.php?option=com_content&view=category&id
= 74&Itemid = 53

2005: 27 September, 2 December

2006: 18 January, 2 February, 28 February, 4 May, 25 September, 20 October

2008: 12 May, 15 May, 1 July

2009: 6 January, 20 May, 9 June, 15 July

2010: 26 April, 4 June, 1 November, 17 November, 21 December

2011: 10 March, 18 March, 11 November, 13 December 2012 – 22 January,
27 January, 22 March, 25 April, 12 October, 1 December

2012: 23 January

ECI official documentation

Buhler, J. (2005) 'European Leadership Funding – Investing for Peace in the Middle
East' (The European Coalition for Israel) http://int.icej.org/sites/default/files/en/
pdf/EU%20Leadership%20Funding.pdf, accessed on 5 October 2009.

ECI (2008) 'The ECI's contribution for a New EU mechanism for supporting peace
building and conflict prevention in EU external relations' available on request
from the researcher.

——— (2012) 'Unilateral Palestinian Statehood: Why the Palestinian application
for advanced status in the United Nations should be rejected' available on request
from the researcher.

JIJ (Jerusalem Institute for Justice) (2012) 'The Status of Human Rights in the West
Bank and the Gaza Strip' (The European Coalition for Israel) www.jij.org.il/
download_file.php?id=13, accessed on 15 June 2012.

ECI campaigns and resources

ECI   (About   Us)   http://www.ec4i.org/index.php?option=com_content&
view = article&id = 13&Itemid = 40, accessed on 3 September 2009.

——— (About Us) 'What is European Coalition for Israel' www.ec4i.org/index.php?
option=com_content&view = article&id = 13&Itemid = 40, accessed on 15
March 2009.

——— (Campaigns, 1) 'Pray and Vote 2009' http://www.ec4i.org/index.php?
option=com_content&view = category&id = 83&Itemid=59.

——— (Campaigns, 2) 'International Holocaust Remembrance Day' http://www.ec4i.
org/index.php?option=com_content&view=category&id=83&Itemid=59.

——— (Campaigns, 3) 'Football World Cup '06 – Keep Ahmadinejad Out' http://
www.ec4i.org/index.php?option=com_content&view=category&id=83&
Itemid=59.

——— (Campaigns, 4) 'Learn From History' http://www.ec4i.org/learnfromhistory/.

——— brochure http://www.ec4i.org/images/stories/eci-brochure.pdf, accessed on
5 July 2012.

——— (Give Peace a Chance) The video and the book http://www.givepeaceachance.
info/, accessed on 12 October 2012.

———— (San Remo Resources) http://www.ec4i.org/index.php?option=com_content& view=category&layout=blog&id=85&Itemid=63, accessed on 12 October 2012.
———— (2012) (Coalition Events) 'Seventy Years After Wannsee' http://www. coalitionevents.com/wannsee, accessed on 14 September 2012.
———— (2011) Video Reports from UN http://www.ec4i.org/index.php?option=com_ content&view = article&id = 132:please-watch-our-video-reports-from-new-york&catid = 74:press-releases&Itemid = 53, accessed on 17 December 2011.
———— original booklet (available on request from the researcher).
———— booklet (available on request from the researcher).

SECONDARY SOURCES

Books

Abbas, T. (ed.) (2007) *Islamic Political Radicalism, A European Perspective*, Edinburgh University Press, Edinburgh.
Adler, G. (2005) 'Israel in the Land – A Legal View' in Wright, F. (ed.) *Israel – His People, His Land, His Story*, Thankful Books, East Sussex.
Alecu de Flers, N. and Regelsberger, E. (2005) 'The EU and Inter-regional Cooperation' in Hill, C. and Smith, M. (eds) *International Relations of the European Union*, Oxford University Press, Oxford.
Appleby, S.R. and Marty, M.E. (eds) (1993) 'Conclusion: Remaking the State: The Limits of the Fundamentalist Imagination' in *Fundamentalisms and the State*, The University of Chicago Press, Chicago and London.
Awad, M. (2008) 'Their Theology, Our Nightmare' in Brown, W.H. and Penner, P. (eds) *Christian Perspectives on Israeli-Palestinian Conflict*, Neufeld Verlag, Schwarzenfeld.
Al-Azmeh, A. and Fokas, E. (eds) (2007) *Islam in Europe: Diversity, Identity and Influence*, Cambridge University Press, Cambridge.
Balabkins, N. (1971) *West German Reparations to Israel*, Rutgers University Press, New Jersey.
Balfour, R. (2006) 'Principles of Democracy and Human Rights' in Lucarelli, S. and Manners, I. (eds) *Values and Principles in EU Foreign Policy*, London and New York.
Bard, M. (2002) *Myths and Facts – A Guide to Arab-Israeli Conflict*, American-Israeli Cooperative Enterprise, USA.
Barder, C. (2001) *Oslo's Gift of 'Peace': The Destruction of Israel's Security*, ACPR Publishers, Israel.
Barnes, C. (2013) The Denouement of Triumphalist Supersessionism: The European Churches and the Holocaust in Calvin L. Smith (ed) The Jews, Modern Israel and the New Supersessionism, Kings Divinity Press, Kent, UK.
———— (2014) They Conspire Against Your People, The European Churches and The Holocaust, Kings Divinity Press, Kent, UK.
Bellier, I. (1997) 'The Commission as an Actor: An Anthropologist's View' in Wallace, H. and Young, A.R. *Participation and Policy–Making in the European Union,* Clarendon Press, Oxford.
Bialer, U. (2005) *Cross on the Star of David*, Indiana University Press, USA.

The Bible (1995) New American Standard Bible, Zondervan, Michigan.

———— (1998) New International Version (Prophecy Study), Zondervan, Michigan.

Bicchi, F. and Gillespie, R. (2011) *The Union for the Mediterranean*, Routledge, London.

Black, E. (1992) *Parallel Realities: A Jewish/Arab History of Arab/Palestine*, Paradigm Press, USA.

Bouwen, P. (2009) 'The European Commission' in Coen, D. and Richardson, J. (eds) *Lobbying the European Union*, Oxford University Press, Oxford.

Bostom A.G. and Warraq I. (eds) (2008) *The Legacy of Islamic Antisemitism,* Prometheus Books, New York.

Bretherton, C. and Vogler, J. (2006) *The European Union as a Global Actor,* Routledge, New York.

Bruce, F.F. and Payne, D.F. (1997) *Israel and the Nations*, Paternoster Press, UK.

Bruce, S. (1999) *Choice and Religion*, Oxford University Press, Oxford.

Burge, G.M. (2003) *Whose Land? Whose Promise?*, The Pilgrim Press, USA and Paternoster Press, UK.

Bynum, R. (2011) *Allah is Dead: Why Islam is not a Religion*, Kindle edition, Amazon.

Cahill, T. (1998) *The Gifts of the Jews*, Bantam Doubleday Dell Publishing Group, New York.

Caldwell, C. (2010) *Reflections on the Revolution in Europe: Can Europe be the Same with Different People in It?,* Penguin Books, London.

Casanova, J. (2006) 'Religion, European Secular Identities, and European Integration', in Byrnes, T.A. and Katzenstein, P. (eds) *Religion in an Expanding Europe*, Cambridge University Press, Cambridge.

Cameron, D. (2010) *Minor Prophets and the End Times*, John Ritchie Ltd, Kilmarnock.

Carmi, A. and Carmi, J. (2003) *The War of Western Europe Against Israel*, Devora Publishing, Jerusalem and New York.

Chapman, C. (2002) *Whose Promised Land?,* Lion Publishing, London.

Clark, V. (2007) *Allies for Armageddon – the Rise of Christian Zionism*, Yale University Press, US.

Coen, D. (2009) 'Business Lobbying in the European Union' in Coen, D. and Richardson, J. (eds) *Lobbying the European Union*, Oxford University Press, Oxford.

———— and Richardson, J. (2009) 'Learning to Lobby in the European Union: Twenty Years of Change' in Coen, D. and Richardson, J. (eds) *Lobbying the European Union*, Oxford University Press, Oxford.

Cohen, A.S. (1982) *English Zionists and British Jews*, Princeton University Press, Princeton, New Jersey.

Cohen, E. (1997) 'The Interplay of Corporate, National and European Interests' in Wallace, H. and Young, A.R. *Participation and Policy–Making in the European Union,* Clarendon Press, Oxford.

Cohn-Sherbok, D. (2006) *The Politics of Apocalypse*, One World, Oxford.

Corbett, R. et al. (1992) *The European Parliament*, The Longman Group, UK.

Cox et al. (2003) 'Toward a broader leadership development agenda: extending the traditional transactional-transformational duality by developing directive, empowering, and shared leadership skills' in Murphy, S. and Riggio, R. (eds) *The Future of Leadership Development*, Lawrence Erlbaum Associates, New York.

Crombie, K. (2008) *For the Love of Zion – Christian witness and the Restoration of Israel*, Terra Nova Publications, Bradford.

———— (2008a) *Restoring Israel – 200 Years of the CMJ Story,* Nicolayson's, Jerusalem.

Cronin, D. (2011) *Europe's Alliance with Israel – Aiding the Occupation*, Pluto Press, London and New York.

De Haan, M.D. (1944) *The Second Coming of Jesus*, Zondervan, Michigan.

Devine, F. (1995) 'Qualitative Analysis' in Marsh, D. and Stoker, G. (eds) *Theory and Methods in Political Science*, Macmillan Press, Basingstoke and London.

Diez, T. and Manners, I. (2007) 'Reflecting on Normative Power Europe' in Berenskoetter, F. and Williams, J. (eds) *Power in World Politics*, Routledge, London and New York.

Diprose, R.E. (2004) *Israel and the Church*, Authentic Media, Milton Keynes.

———— (2008) 'A Biblical Theology of Israel and the Recent History of the Near East' in Brown, W.H. and Penner, P. (eds) *Christian Perspectives on Israeli-Palestinian Conflict*, Neufeld Verlag, Schwarzenfeld.

Dixon, M. (2006) *Israel, Land of God's Promise*, Sovereign World, Lancaster.

Dolan, D. (2003) *Holy War for the Promised Land*, Broadman and Holman Publishers, Nashville, Tennessee.

Dumper, M. (2002) *The Politics of Sacred Space – the Old City of Jerusalem in the Middle East Conflict*, Lynne Rienner Publishers, Colorado and London.

Eldridge, M. (2009) 'Churchill and the Jews: An Assessment of Two Recent Studies and Their Contemporary Relevance', Olive Press.

Finkelstein, N. (2003) *The Holocaust Industry*, Verso, London and New York.

———— (2003a) *Image and Reality of the Israel-Palestine Conflict*, London and New York.

Fisher, J. (2008) *Israel's New Disciples*, Monarch Books, Michigan.

Fox, J. and Sandler, S. (2004) *Bringing Religion into International Relations*, Palgrave, New York and Basingstoke.

Gabriel, M.A. (2003) *Islam and the Jews – The Unfinished Battle*, Charisma House, Lake Mary, Florida.

———— (2004) *Jesus and Muhammad. Profound Differences and Surprising Similarities*, Charisma House, Florida.

Garvey J.H. (1993) 'Fundamentalism and American Law' in Appleby, S.R. and Marty, M.E. (eds) *Fundamentalisms and the State*, The University of Chicago Press, Chicago and London.

Gelvin, J.L. (2005) *The Israel-Palestine Conflict*, Cambridge University Press, Cambridge.

Giddens, A. (1989) *Sociology*, Polity Press, Cambridge.

Gilbert, M. (2005) *The Routledge Atlas of the Arab-Israeli Conflict*, Routledge, Oxford.

———— (2007) *Churchill and the Jews*, Simon & Schuster, London.

Glaser, D. (1995) 'Normative Theory' in Marsh, D. and Stoker, G. (eds) *Theory and Methods in Political Science*, Macmillan Press, Basingstoke and London.

Gold, D. (2007) *The Fight for Jerusalem*, Regnery Publishing, Washington DC.

Gold, S. (2002) *The Israeli Diaspora*, Routledge, London.

Gray, N. (2005) 'Generations of Poverty: The Question of Palestinian Refugees', in Wright, F. (ed) *Israel – His People, His Land, His Story*, Thankful Books, East Sussex.

Greenwood, J. (2003) *Interest Representation in the European Union*, Palgrave Macmillan, Basingstoke, UK.

———— (2010) 'Regulating NGO Participation in the EU; A De-Facto Accreditation System Built on Representativness' in Steffek, J. and Hahn, K. (eds) *Evaluating Transnational NGOs*, Palgrave Macmillan, Basingstoke.

Gueguen, D. (2007) *European lobbying*, Europolitics, Brussels.

Harrison, L. (2001) *A Guide to Writing a Politics Dissertation*, Routledge, London.

Haseler, S. (2004) *Super-State, The New Europe and Its Challenge to America*, I.B.Tauris, London, New York.

Hayness, J. (2013) *An Introduction to International Relations and Religion*, Pearson, Harlow.

Henry, D.V. and Agee, B.R. (eds) (2003) *Faithful Learning and Christian Scholarly Vocation*, Wm. B. Eerdmans Publishing, Michigan and Cambridge.

Heschel, S. (2008) *The Aryan Jesus, Christian Theologians and The Bible in Nazi Germany*, Princeton University Presss, Princeton and Oxford.

Hill, C. (2003) *The Changing Politics of Foreign Policy*, Palgrave Macmillan, Basingstoke and New York.

Hinnebusch, R. (2005) 'The Politics of Identity in Middle East International Relations' in Fawcet, L. (ed.) *International Relations of the Middle East*, Oxford University Press, Oxford.

Hocking, D. (2000) *The Coming World Leader*, HFT Publications, USA.

Honderich, T. (1995) (ed.) *The Oxford Companion to Philosophy*, Oxford University Press, Oxford.

Horner, B. (2013) Parting of the Ways: Jewish-Christian relations in the Post-Apostolic Period, in Calvin L. Smith (ed) The Jews, Modern Israel and the New Supersessionism, Kings Divinity Press, Kent, UK.

Hornstra, W. (2008) 'Western Restorationism and Christian Zionism: Germany as a Case Study' in Brown, W.H. and Penner, P. (eds) *Christian Perspectives on the Israeli-Palestinian Conflict*, Neufeld Verlag, Schwarzenfeld.

Howorth, J. (2005) 'From Security to Defence: the Evolution of CFSP', in Hill, C. and Smith, M. (eds) *International Relations of the European Union*, Oxford University Press, Oxford.

Hunter, S. (ed.) (2002) *Islam, Europe's Second Religion: The New Social, Political and Cultural Landscape*, Praeger, Connecticut and London.

Huntington, S. (2002) *The Clash of Civilizations*, The Free Press, UK.

Hyde-Price, A. (2008 a) 'Christian Ethics and the Dilemmas of Foreign Policy' in Blewett, T., Hyde-Price, A. and Rees, W. (eds) *British Foreign Policy and the Anglican Church*, Ashgate Publishing, Aldershot.

Jenkins, P. (2002) *The Next Christendom, The Coming of Global Christianity*, Oxford University Press, Oxford.

Jorgensen, K.E. (2006) 'Theoretical Perspectives on the Role of Values, Images and Principles in Foreign Policy' in Lucarelli, S. and Manners, I. (eds) *Values and Principles in EU Foreign Policy*, Routledge, London and New York.

Karr, K. (2006) *Democracy and Lobbying in the European Union*, The University of Chicago Press, Chicago.

Kendall, R.T. and Rosen, D. (2006) *The Christian and the Pharisee*, Hodder & Stoughton, London.

Khasson, V. et al. (2008) 'Everybody Needs Good Neighbours': The EU and Its Neighbourhood in *Europe's Global Role, External Policies of the European Union*, Orbie, J. (ed.), Ashgate Publishing, Aldershot.

Kieval, G.R. and Reich, B. (1991) *Israeli Politics in the 1990s*, Greenwood Press, Westport.

Kilpatrick, W. (2000) *Christianity, Islam, and Atheism: The Struggle for the Soul of the West*, Penguin Books, London.

Koenig, W. (2006) *Eye to Eye, Facing the Consequences of Dividing Israel*, About Him Publishing, Alexandria.

Kohler-Koch, B. (1997a) 'Organised Interests in European Integration: The Evolution of a New Type of Governance' in Wallace, H. and Young, A.R. (eds) *Participation and Policy – Making in the European Union*, Clarendon Press, Oxford.

Kohlman, E.F. (2004) *Al-Qaida's Jihad In Europe: The Afghan-Bosnian Network*, Berg, Oxford.

Lambert, L. (2002) *The Uniqueness of Israel*, Kingsway Communications, Eastbourne.

Laqueur, W. (2004) *No End to War – Terrorism in Twenty-First Century*, Continuum, New York and London.

Larres, K. (2000) (ed.) *Uneasy Allies: British-German Relations and European Integration Since 1945*, Oxford University Press, Oxford.

Lavi, G. (1996) *Germany and Israel, Moral Debt and National Interest*, Frank Cass, London.

Lehman, W. (2009) 'The European Parliament' in Coen, D. and Richardson, J. (eds) *Lobbying the European Union*, Oxford University Press, Oxford.

Leister, D. (2006) *Writing Research Papers in the Social Sciences*, Pearson Longman, New York and London.

Leonard, M. (2005) *Why Europe Will Run the 21st Century*, Fourth Estate, London and New York.

Lewis, D.M. (2010) *The Origins of Christian Zionism: Lord Shaftesbury and Evangelical Support for a Jewish Homeland*, Cambridge: Cambridge University Press.

Lewis, B. (2003) *The Middle East*, Phoenix, London.

———— (2004) *The Crisis of Islam*, Phoenix, London.

Liebman, C.S. (1993) 'Jewish Fundamentalism and the Israeli Polity' Appleby, S.R. and Marty, M.E. (eds) in *Fundamentalisms and the State*, The University of Chicago Press, Chicago and London.

Littman, D.G. (2005) 'Universal Human Rights and Human Rights in Islam' in Spencer, R. (ed.) *The Myth of Islamic Tolerance*, Prometheus Books, New York.

———— and Wadlow R. (2005) 'Dangerous Censorship of a UN Special Rapporteur' in Spencer, R. (ed.) *The Myth of Islamic Tolerance*, Prometheus Books, New York.

Lloyd, S. (2002) 'The Crusading Movement' in Riley-Smith, J. (ed.) *The Oxford History of the Crusades*, Oxford University Press, Oxford.

Loconte, J. (2004) *The End of Illusions*, Rowman and Littlefield Publishers, Lanham, New York.

Lucarelli, S. and Menotti, R. (2006) 'The Use of Force as a Coercive Intervention' in Lucarelli, S. and Manners, I. (eds) *Values and Principles in EU Foreign Policy*, Routledge, London and New York.

Mackenstein, H. and Marsh, S. (2005) *The International Relations of the European Union*, Pearson Longman, London and New York.

Madeley, J. et al. (eds) (2009) *Religion, Politics and Law in the European Union*, Routledge, UK.

Maltz, S. (2013) The Real Roots of Supersessionism, in Calvin L. Smith (ed) The Jews, Modern Israel and the New Supersessionism, Kings Divinity Press, Kent, UK.

Manners, I. (2006) European Union, Normative Power and Ethical Foreign Policy in Chandler, D. and Heins, V. (eds) *Rethinking Ethical Foreign Policy*, Routledge, London.

——— (2006a) The Constitutive Nature of Values, Images and Principles in the European Union in Lucarelli, S. and Manners, I. (eds) *Values and Principles in EU Foreign Policy*, Routledge, London and New York.

——— (2008a) 'The European Union's Normative Strategy for Sustainable Peace' in Fischer, M. and Rittberger, V. (eds) *Strategies for Peace: Contributions of International Organisations, States and Non-State Actors*, Barbara Budrich, Verlag.

Marr, P. (1998) 'The United States, Europe and the Middle East, Cooperation, Co-optation or Confrontation?' in Roberson, B.A. (ed.) *The Middle East and Europe, The Power Deficit*, Routledge, London and New York.

Marsden, L. (2008) *For God's Sake*, Zed Books, London and New York.

Massignon, B. (2007) 'Islam in the European Commission's system of regulation of religion' in Al-Azmeh, A. and Focas, E. (eds) *Islam in Europe, Diversity, Identity and Influence*, Cambridge University Press, Cambridge.

McCormick, J. (2007) *The European Superpower*, Palgrave Macmillan, Basingstoke and New York.

McGrath, A. (2006) *The Twilight of Atheism*, Galilee Doubleday, New York and London.

Mearsheimer, J.J. (2001) *The Tragedy of Great Power Politics*, Norton, New York.

——— and Walt, S.M. (2007) *The Israel Lobby and U.S. Foreign Policy*, Farrar, Straus and Giroux, New York.

Meijer, R. and Bakker, E. (eds) (2012) *The Muslim Brotherhood in Europe*, Columbia University Press, US.

Merkley, P.C. (2001) Christian Attitudes Towards the State of Israel, McGill-Queen's University Press, London.

Milton-Edwards, B. (1999) *Islamic Politics in Palestine*, I.B.Tauris, London.

Mirbagheri, F. (2012) *War and Peace in Islam: A Critique of Islamic/ist Political Discourses*, Palgrave MacMillan, UK.

Murray, I.H. (1971) *The Puritan Hope*, The Banner of Truth Trust, Edinburgh.

Nazir-Ali, M. (2006) *Conviction and Conflict*, Continuum, London and New York.

Nerel, G. (2005) Spiritual Intifada of Palestinian Christians and Messianic Jews in Wright, F. (ed.) (2005) *Israel – His People, His Land, His Story*, Thankful Books, East Sussex.

Noakes, D. (2005) The Restoration of All Things in Wright, F. (ed.) (2005) *Israel – His People, His Land, His Story*, Thankful Books, East Sussex.

Nonneman, G. (1993) (ed.) *The Middle East and Europe*, Federal Trust for Education and Research, London.

Orbie, J. (2008) 'A Civilian Power in the World? Instruments and Objectives in European Union External Policies' in Orbie, J. (ed.) *Europe's Global Role, External Policies of the European Union*, Ashgate Publishing, Aldershot.

Ottolenhgi, E. (2009a) *Under A Mushroom Cloud: Europe, Iran and the Bomb*, Profile Books, London.

Pawson, D. (2008) *Defending Christian Zionism*, Terra Nova Publications, Bradford.

Peck, J.M. (2007) *Being Jewish in the New Germany*, Rutgers University Press, US.

Peters, J. (2002) *From Time Immemorial*, JKAP Publications, Chicago.

Peterson, J. and Bomberg, E. (1999) *Decision-making in the European Union*, Macmillan Press, Basingstoke and London.

—— and O'Toole, L.J. (2001) 'Federal Governance in the United States and the European Union: A Policy Network Perspective', in Kalypso, N. and Howse, R. (eds) *The Federal Vision – Legitimacy and Levels of Governance in the United States and the European Union*, Oxford University Press, Oxford and New York.

Phillips, M. (2006) *Londonistan*, Encounter Books, New York.

Pipes, D. (2005) 'Jihad and the Professors' in Spencer, R. (ed.) *The Myth of Islamic Tolerance*, Prometheus Books, New York.

Pollack, M.A. (2005) 'Theorising EU Policy-Making' in Wallace H. et al. *Policy-Making in the European Union*, Oxford University Press, Oxford.

Prasch, J. (2007) *Israel, the Church and the Jews*, St Matthew Publishing, UK.

Price, T. (2005) 'Reading and Understanding Scripture' in Wright, F. (ed.) *Israel – His People, His Land, His Story* by Thankful Books, East Sussex.

—— (2005a) 'The Restoration of Israel and the Kingdom of God' in Wright, F. (ed.) *Israel – His People, His Land, His Story* by Thankful Books, East Sussex.

Prince, D. (2003) *Promised Land*, Zondervan, Michigan.

Rapaport, L. (1997) *Jews in Germany After the Holocaust*, Cambridge University Press, Cambridge, New York and Melbourne.

Rauf, F.A. (2004) *What's Right With Islam: A New Vision for Muslims and the West*, Harper-Collins, San Francisco.

Richardson, J. (1996) 'Actor-based Models of National and EU Policy Making' in Kassim, H. and Menon, A. (eds) *The European Union and National Industrial Policy*, Routledge, London.

Riley-Smith, J. (2002) (ed.) *The Oxford History of the Crusades*, Oxford University Press, Oxford.

Risse, T. (2011) 'Nationalism and Collective Identities: Europe Versus the Nation-State?' in Heywood, P.M. et al. (eds) *Developments in European Politics*, Palgrave Macmillan, Basingstoke.

Roberson, B.A. (1998) 'Islam and Europe, An Enigma or a Myth'?, in Roberson, B.A. (ed.) *The Middle East and Europe, The Power Deficit*, Routledge, London and New York.

Roof, W.C. (1986) 'The New Fundamentalism: Rebirth of Political Religion in America' in Hadden, J.K. and Shupe, A. (eds) *Prophetic Religions and Politics* by Paragon House, New York.

Rosen, M. (2006) *Christ in the Passover*, Moody Publishers, Chicago.

Rosenberg, J.C. (2006) *Epicenter*, Tyndale House Publishers, Illinois.

Santala, R. (2002) *The Midrash of the Messiah*, Kaivokatu, Heinola.

Saurugger, S. (2009) 'COREPER and National Governments' in Coen, D. and Richardson, J. (eds) *Lobbying the European Union*, Oxford University Press, Oxford.

Schmidt, B.C. (2007) 'Realist Conceptions of Power' in Berenskoetter, F. and Williams, M.J. (eds), *Power in World Politics*, Routledge, New York.

Scott, T.M. (2005) *The Global Resurgence of Religion and the Transformation of International Relations*, Palgrave Macmillan, New York.

Shepherd, R. (2009) *A State Beyond the Pale, Europe's Problem with Israel*, Weidenfeld and Nicolson, London.

Shindler, C. (2008) *A History of Modern Israel*, Cambridge University Press, Cambridge.

Shorrosh, A.A. (1988) *Islam Revealed*, Thomas Nelson Publishers, Nashville.

Silvestri, S. (2007) 'Asserting Islam in the EU: Actors, Strategies and Priorities' in Foret, F. (ed.) *L'espace public européen à l'épreuve du religieux*, Brussels: Editions de l'Université de Bruxelles.

———— (2007a) 'Europe and Political Islam: Encounters of the twentieth and twenty-first centuries' in Abbas, T. (ed.) *Islamic Political Radicalism, A European Perspective*, Edinburgh University Press, Edinburgh.

———— (2010) 'Moderate Islamist Groups in Europe: The Muslim Brothers' in Hroub, K. (ed.) *Political Islam, Context versus Ideology*, Saqi Books, London.

Sizer, S. (2004) *Christian Zionism, Road Map to Armageddon*, Inter-Varsity Press, Leicester.

Sjursen, H. (2006a) 'The European Union between values and rights' in Sjursen, H. (ed.) *Questioning EU Enlargement: Europe in Search of Identity*, Routledge, USA and Canada.

Smith, C.L. (ed.) (2009) *The Jews, Modern Israel and the New Supercessionism*, King's Divinity Press, UK.

Smith, E.K. (2008) *European Union Foreign Policy in a Changing World*, Polity Press, Cambridge.

Spencer, R. (2005) *The Politically Incorrect Guide to Islam (and the Crusades)*, Regnery Publishing, Washington.

———— (2005a) 'Islamic tolerance: Myth and Reality' in Spencer, R. (ed.) *The Myth of Islamic Tolerance*, Prometheus Books, New York.

Stoker, G. (1995) 'Introduction' in *Theory and Methods in Political Science*, Marsh D. and Stoker, G. (eds), Macmillan Press, Basingstoke and London.

Trifkovic, S. (2002) *The Sword of the Prophet*, Regina Orthodox Press, Boston.

Tsukahira, P. (2003) *God's Tsunami*, Carmel Communications, Israel.

Tuchman, B.W. (1984) *Bible and Sword, England and Palestine from the Bronze Age to Balfour*, New York University Press, New York.

Vidino, L. (2010) *The New Muslim Brotherhood in the West*, Columbia University Press, New York and Chichester, West Susex.

Wallace, C.D. (2012) *Foundations of the International Legal Rights of the Jewish People and the State of Israel*, Creation House, Florida.

Wallace, H. (2005) 'An Institutional Anatomy and Five Policy Modes' in Wallace, H. et al. *Policy-Making in the European Union*, Oxford University Press, Oxford.

Wallace, W. (2005) 'Post-sovereign Governance: The EU as a Partial Polity' in Wallace, H. et al. *Policy-Making in the European Union*, Oxford University Press, Oxford.

Wallis, J. (2006) *God's Politics*, Lion Hudson, Oxford.

Waltz, K. (1979) *Theory of International Politics*, Random House, New York.

Walvoord, J.F. (1994) *Major Bible Prophecies*, Harper Paperbacks, New York.

Warraq, I. (2003) (ed.) *Leaving Islam*, Prometheus Books, New York.

———— (2005) 'The Genesis of a Myth' in Spencer, R. (ed.) *The Myth of Islamic Tolerance*, Prometheus Books, New York.

———— (2005a) 'Honest Intellectuals Must Shed Their Spiritual Turbans' in Spencer, R. (ed.) *The Myth of Islamic Tolerance*, Prometheus Books, New York.

Weber, T.P. (2004) *On the Road to Armageddon, How Evangelicals Became Israel's Best Friend*, Baker Academic, USA.

Wessels, W. (1997) 'The Growth and Differentiation of Multi-Level Networks: A Corporatist Mega-Bureaucracy or an Open City'? in Wallace, H. and Young, A.R. (eds) *Participation and Policy-Making in the European Union*, Clarendon Press, Oxford.

White, D. (2005) 'The Road to Holocaust' in Wright, F. (ed.) *Israel – His People, His Land, His Story* Thankful Books, East Sussex.

Wilkinson, P.R. (2007) *For Zion's Sake – Christian Zionism and the Role of John Nelson Darby*, Paternoster, Milton Keynes.

Wilson, M.R. (1989) *Our Father Abraham, Jewish Roots of the Christian Faith*, William B. Eerdemans Publishing Michigen and Center for Judaic-Christian Studies, Dayton, Ohio.

Wong, R. (2005) 'The Europeanisation of Foreign Policy' in Hill, C. and Smith, M. *International Relations and the European Union*, Oxford University Press, Oxford.

Wright, F. (2002) *Father Forgive Us*, Monarch Books, London.

————— (2005) 'The Jewish People in the End Times' in Wright, F. (ed.) *Israel – His People, His Land, His Story*, Thankful Books, East Sussex.

Ye'or, B. (2005) 'Aspects of the Arab-Israeli Conflict' in Spencer, R. (ed.) *The Myth of Islamic Tolerance*, Prometheus Books, New York.

————— (2006) *Eurabia*, Fairleigh Dickinson University Press, USA.

Yin, K.R. (2003) *Case Study Research: Design and Methods*, Sage Publications, Beverly Hills, London, New Delhi.

Zacharias, R. (1994) *Can Man Live Without God?*, W Publishing Group, Nashville.

————— (2004) *The Real Face of Atheism*, Baker Books, Michigan.

Journal articles

Aggestam, L. and Hill, C. (2008) 'The Challenge of Multiculturalism in European Foreign Policy', *International Affairs*, Vol. 84 No. 1, 97–114.

Antonsich, M. (2008) 'The Narration of Europe in 'National' and 'Post-national' Terms: Gauging the Gap between Narrative Discourses and People's Views', *European Journal of Social Theory*, Vol. 11 No. 4, 505–22.

Assenburg, M. (2003) 'The EU and the Middle East Conflict: Tackling the Main Obstacle to Euro-Mediterranean Partnership', *Mediterranean Politics*, Vol. 8 No. 2, 174–93.

Bailes, A.J. (2008) 'The EU and a "Better World": What Role for the European Security and Defence Policy?', *International Affairs*, Vol. 84 No. 1, 115–30.

Beloff, M. (1994) 'The Diaspora and the Peace Process', *Israel Affairs*, Vol. 1 No. 1, 26–40.

Bennett, A. and Elman, C. (2007) 'Case Study Methods in the International Relations Subfield', *Comparative Political Studies*, Vol. 40 No. 2, 170–95.

Beyers, J. (2002) 'Gaining and seeking access: The European adaptation of Domestic Interest Associations', *European Journal of Political Research*, No. 41, 584–612.

————— (2004) 'Voice and Access: Political Practices of European Interest Associations', *European Union Politics*, Vol. 5 No. 2, 211–40.

Bicchi, F. and Martin, M. (2006) 'Talking Tough or Talking Together? European Security Discourses Towards the Mediterranean', *Mediterranean Politics*, Vol. 11 No. 2, 189–207.

————— (2006) '"Our Size Fits All": Normative Power Europe and the Mediterranean', *Journal of European Public Policy*, Vol. 2 No. 13, 206–303.

Blom-Hansen, J. and Brandsma, G.J. (2009) 'The EU Comitology System: Intergovernmental Bargaining and Deliberative Supranationalism?', *Journal of Common Market Studies*, Vol. 47 No. 4, 719–40.

Bohmelt, T. (2012) 'The temporal dimension of the credibility of EU conditionality and candidate states' compliance with the *acquis communautaire*, 1998–2009', *European Union Politics*, Vol. 14 No. 2, 250–72.

Bollmann, F. (2010) 'How Many Roads Lead to Brussels? Decisive Factors for Political Mobilisation of Religious Organisations in the European Public Sphere', 2010 Conference: Does God Matter? Representing Religion in the European Union and the United States, Aston Centre for Europe, Aston University.

Borragan, N.P. (2004) 'EU Accession and Interest Politics in Central and Eastern Europe', *Perspectives on European Politics and Society*, Vol. 5 No. 2, 243–72.

Borzel, T. (2010) 'European Governance: Negotiation and Competition in the Shadow of Hierarchy', *Journal of Common Market Studies*, Vol. 48 No. 2, 191–219.

Bouwen, P. (2004) 'The Logic of Access to the European Parliament: Business Lobbying in the Committee on Economic and Monetary Affairs', *Journal of Common Market Studies*, Vol. 42 No. 3, 473–95.

Bull, M.J. (2009) 'Religion and Politics – American and European Experiences and Contrasts', *European Political Science*, Vol. 8 No. 3, 270–2.

Burgat, F. (2009) 'Europe and the Arab World: The dilemma of recognising counterparts', *International Politics*, Vol. 46 No. 5, 616–35.

Caporaso, J.A. and Min-hyung, K. (2009) 'The Dual Nature of European Identity: Subjective Awareness and Coherence', *Journal of European Public Policy*, Vol. 16 No. 1, 19–42.

Carey, S. (2002) 'Undivided Loyalties: Is National Identity an Obstacle to European Integration?', *European Union Politics*, Vol. 3 No. 4, 387–413.

Cattaruzza, M. (2005) 'Political Religions as a Characteristic of the 20th Century', *Totalitarian Movements and Political Religions*, Vol. 6 No. 1, 1–18.

Cavatorta, F. and Tonra, B. (2007) 'Normative Foundations in EU Foreign, Security and Defence Policy: the Case of the Middle East Peace Process – a View from the Field', *Contemporary Politics*, Vol. 13 No. 4, 349–63.

Challand, B. (2009) 'From Hammer and Sickle to Star and Crescent: the Question of Religion for European Identity and a Political Europe', *Religion, State and Society*, Vol. 37 Nos 1 & 2, 65–80.

Chelini-Pont, B. (2009) 'Papal Thought on Europe and the European Union in the Twentieth Century', *Religion, State and Society*, Vol. 37 No. 1&2, 131–46.

Coen, D. (1999) 'The Impact of U.S. Lobbying Practice on the European Business-Government Relationship', *California Management Review*, Vol. 41 No. 4, 27–44.

————— (2007) 'Empirical and Theoretical Studies in EU lobbying', *Journal of European Public Policy*, Vol. 14 No. 31, 333–45.

Constantelos, J. (2007) 'Interest Group Strategies in Multi-level Europe', *Journal of Public Affairs*, Vol. 7, 39–53.

Cross, J.P. (2012) 'Everyone's a winner (almost): Bargaining success in the Council of Ministers of the European Union', *European Union Politics*, Vol. 40 No. 1, 70–94.

Davidson, L. (2010) 'Christian Zionism and the Formulation of Foreign Policy' (Book Review), *Diplomatic History*, Vol. 34 No. 3, 605–9.

De Vreese et al. (2009) 'Introduction: Religion in the European Union', *West European Politics*, Vol. 32 No. 6, 1183–9.

Dieckhoff, A. (2005) 'The European Union and the Israeli-Palestinian Conflict', *Inroads Journal*, No. 16, 52–62.

Doe, N. (2009) 'Towards a 'Common Law' on Religion in the European Union', *Religion, State and Society*, Vol. 37 No. 1 & 2, 147–66.

Dolezal, M. et al. (2010) 'Debating Islam in Austria, Germany and Switzerland: Ethnic Citizenship, Church-State Relations and Right-Wing Populism', *West European Politics*, Vol. 33 No. 2, 171–90.

Don Harpaz, M. (2008) 'Israel's Trade Relations with the European Union: The Case for Diversification', *Mediterranean Politics*, Vol. 13 No. 3, 391–417.

Eising, R. (2004) 'Multilevel Governance and Business Interests in the European Union', *Governance: An International Journal of Policy, Administration and Institutions*, Vol. 17 No. 2, 211–40.

——— (2008) 'Interest Groups in EU Policy-making', *Living Reviews in European Governance*, Vol. 3 No. 4, 1–32.

Ensher, E.A. and Murphy, S.E. (2008) 'A qualitative analysis of charismatic leadership in creative teams: The case of television directors', *The Leadership Quarterly*, No. 19, 335–52.

Esposito, J.L. and Voll, J.O. (2000) 'Islam and the West: Muslim Voices of Dialogue', *Millenium: Journal of International Studies*, Vol. 29 No. 3, 613–39.

Fath, S. (2005) 'Evangelical Protestantism in France: An Example of Denominational Decomposition', *Sociology of Religion*, Vol. 66 No. 4, 399–418.

Focas, E. (2011) 'Islam in Europe: The Unexceptional Case', *Nordic Journal of Religion and Society*, Vol. 24 No. 1, 1–17.

Foret, F. and Schlesinger, P. (2006) 'Political Roof and Sacred Canopy? Religion and the EU Constitution', *European Journal of Social Theory*, Vol. 9 No. 1, 59–81.

——— (2009) 'Religion: a Solution or a Problem for the Legitimisation of the European Union?', *Religion, State and Society*, Vol. 37 No. 1, 37–50.

FRA (European Agency for Fundamental Rights) (2011) Antisemitism – Working Paper, April 2011.

Fraser, C.R. et al. (2001) 'Does Religion Matter?: Christianity and Public Support for the European Union', *European Union Politics*, Vol. 2 No. 2, 191–217.

Fukuyama, F. (1995) 'Reflections on the End of History, Five Years Later', *History and Theory*, Vol. 34 No. 2, 27–43.

Greenwood, J. (1998) 'Regulating Lobbying in the European Union in The Regulation of Lobbying: Experiences in Parliamentary Democracies in the Western World', *Parliamentary Affairs*, Vol. 51 No. 4, 587–99.

——— (2011) 'The Lobby Regulation Element of the European Transparency Initiative: Between Liberal and Deliberative Models of Democracy', *Comparative European Politics*, Vol. 9 No. 3, 317–43.

Gregory, F. (2011) 'Why the Middle East Studies Missed the Arab Spring', *Foreign Affairs*, Vol. 90 No. 4, 1–6.

Grieco, J.M. (1988) 'Anarchy and the Limits of Cooperation', *International Organisation*, Vol. 42 No. 3, 485–507.

Grossman, E. (2004) 'Bringing Politics Back In: Rethinking the Role of Economic Interest Groups in European Integration', *Journal of European Public Policy*, Vol. 11 No. 4, 637–54.

Harpaz, G. (2007) 'Normative Power Europe and the Problem of a Legitimacy Deficit: An Israeli Perspective, *European Foreign Affairs Review*, No. 12, 89–109.

———— (2008) 'Mind the Gap: Narrowing the Legitimacy Gap in EU-Israel Relations', *European Foreign Affairs Review*, No. 13, 117–37.

———— and Shamis, A. (2010) 'Normative Power Europe and the State of Israel: An Illegitimate EUtopia?', *Journal of Common Market Studies*, Vol. 48 No. 3, 579–616.

Hasenclever, A. and Rittberger, V. (2000) 'Does Religion make a Difference? Theoretical Approaches to the Impact of Faith on Political Conflict', *Millenium: Journal of International Studies*, Vol. 29 No. 3, 641–74.

Herman, L. (2006) 'An Action plan or plan for action? Israel and the European Neighbourhood Policy', *Mediterranean Politics*, Vol. 11 No. 3, 371–94.

Hill, M. (2009) 'Voices in the Wilderness: the Established Church of England and the European Union', *Religion, State and Society*, Vol. 37 Nos 1 & 2, 167–80.

Hix, S. (1994) 'The Study of the European Community: The Challenge to Comparative Politics', *West European Politics*, Vol. 17 No. 1, 1–30.

———— et al. (2003) 'The Party System in the European Parliament: Collusive or Competitive?', *Journal of Common Market Studies*, Vol. 41 No. 2, 309–31.

———— (2003a) 'Fifty Years On: Research on the European Parliament', *Journal of Common Market Studies*, Vol. 41 No. 2, 191–202.

Hofhansel, C. (2010) 'Accommodating Islam and the Utility of National Models: The German Case', *West European Politics*, Vol. 33 No. 2, 191–207.

Holden, P. (2009) 'The European Union's Mediterranean Policy in Theory and Practice', *Mediterranean Politics*, Vol. 14 No. 1, 125–34.

Hollis, R. (1994) 'The Politics of Israeli-European Economic Relations', *Israel Affairs*, Vol. 1 No. 1, 118–34.

Houston, K. (2009) 'The Logic of Structured Dialogue between Religious Associations and the Institutions of the European Union', *Religion, State and Society*, Vol. 37 No. 1 & 2, 207–22.

Huber, D. (2008) 'Democracy Assistance in the Middle East and North Africa: A Comparison of US and EU Policies', *Mediterranean Politics*, Vol. 13 No. 1, 43–62.

Hyde-Price, A. (2006) 'Normative Power Europe: A Realist Critique', *Journal of European Public Policy*, Vol. 13 No. 2, 217–34.

———— (2008) 'A "Tragic Actor"? A Realist Perspective on "Ethical Power" Europe', *International Affairs*, Vol. 84 No. 1, 29–44.

Inbar, E. (1998) 'Improving Israel-EU Relations: The European Economic Area as a Possible Model', *Israel Affairs*, Vol. 5 No. 1, 109–26.

Juneman, A. (2003) 'Repercussions of the Emerging European Security and Defence Policy on the Civil Character of the Euro-Mediterranean Partnership', *Mediterranean Politics*, Vol. 8 No. 2, 38–53.

Kentmen, C. (2008) 'Determinants of Support for EU Membership in Turkey: Islamic Attachments, Utilitarian Considerations and National Identity', *European Union Politics*, Vol. 9 No. 4, 487–510.

Kirchner, E.J. (2006) 'The Challenge of European Union Security Governance', *Journal of Common Market Studies*, Vol. 44 No. 5, 947–68.

Klausen, J. (2009) 'Why Religion has Become More Salient in Europe: Four Working Hypotheses about Secularisation and Religiosity in Contemporary Politics' (Symposium), *European Political Science*, Vol. 8 No. 3, 289–300.

Kohler-Koch, B. (2010) 'How to Put Matters Right? Assessing the Role of the Civil Society in EU Accountability', *West European Politics*, Vol. 33 No. 5, 1117–41.

Kubalkova, V. (2000) 'Towards an International Political Theology', *Millennium: Journal of International Studies*, Vol. 29 No. 3, 675–704.

Kumar, K. (2008) 'The Question of European Identity: Europe in the American Mirror', *European Journal of Social Theory*, Vol. 11 No. 1, 87–105.

Laudrup, C. (2009) 'A European Battlefield: Does the EU Have a Soul? Is Religion In or Out of Place in the European Union?', *Religion, State and Society*, Vol. 37 No 1&2, 51–63.

Laurence, J. (2009) 'The Corporatist Antecedent of Contemporary State-Islam Relations', *European Political Science*, Vol. 8 No. 3, 301–15.

Lausten, C.B. and Waever, O. (2000) 'In Defence of Religion: Sacred Referent Objects for Securitization', *Millennium: Journal of International Studies*, Vol. 29 No. 3, 705–39.

Leustean, L.N. (2009) 'Towards an Integrative Theory of Religion and Politics', *Method and Theory in the Study of Religion*, Vol. 17, 364–81.

——— (2009a) 'What is the European Union? Religion between Neofunctionalism and Intergovernmentalism', *International Journal for the Study of the Christian Church*, Vol. 9 No. 3, 165–76.

——— and Madeley, T.S. (2009) 'Religion, Politics and Law in the European Union: an Introduction', *Religion, State and Society*, Vol. 37 Nos 1 & 2, 1–18.

Litvak, M. (2006) 'The Islamic Republic of Iran and the Holocaust: Antisemitism and Anti-Zionism', *The Journal of Israeli History*, Vol. 25 No. 1, 267–84.

Mackenzie, D. (2005) 'End of the Enlightenment: Why is so much of the world bent on rejecting reason, tolerance and freedom of thought?', *New Scientist*, Vol. 188 No. 2520, 39.

Madeley, J. (2009) 'Unequally Yoked: The Antinomies of Church-State Separation in Europe and the USA' (Symposium), *European Political Science*, No. 8, 273–88.

Mahoney, C. (2007) 'Lobbying Success in the United States and the European Union', *Journal of Public Policy*, Vol. 27 No. 1, 35–56.

Manners, I. (2002) 'Normative Power Europe: A Contradiction in Terms?', *Journal of Common Market Studies*, Vol. 40 No. 2, 235–58.

——— (2008) 'The Normative Ethics of the European Union', *International Affairs*, Vol. 84 No. 1, 45–60.

Markovits, A.S. (2006) 'An Inseparable Tandem of European Identity? Anti-Americanism and Antisemitism in the Short and Long Run', *The Journal of Israeli History*, Vol. 25 No. 1, 85–105.

Matesan, I.E. (2012) 'The Impact of the Arab Spring on Islamist Strategies', *Journal of Strategic Security*, Vol. 5 No. 2, 27–46.

Mayer, J.D. (2004) 'Christian fundamentalists and Public Opinion Toward the Middle East: Israel's New Best Friends', *Social Science Quarterly*, Vol. 85 No. 3, 695–712.

McKay, A. (2012) 'Negative Lobbying and Policy Outcomes', *American Politics Research*, Vol. 40 No. 1, 116–46.

Mead, W.R. (2008) 'The New Israel and the Old – Why Gentile Americans Back the Jewish State', *Foreign Affairs*, Vol. 87 No. 4, 28–46.

Mihut, L. (2011) 'Lobbying – A Political Communication Tool for Churches and Religious Organisations', *Journal for the Study of Religions and Ideologies*, Vol. 10 No. 29, 64–86.

Milbank, J. (2009) 'Multiculturalism in Britain and the Political Identity of Europe', *International Journal for the Study of the Christian Church*, Vol. 9 No. 4, 268–81.

Miller, R. (2006) 'Troubled Neighbours: The EU and Israel', *Israel Affairs*, Vol. 12, No. 4, 642–64.

——— (2011) 'Europe's Palestine Problem', *Foreign Affairs*, Vol. 20 No. 5, 8–12.

——— and Mishrif, A. (2005) 'The Barcelona Process and Euro-Arab Economic Relations, 1995–2005', *Middle East Review of International Affairs*, Vol. 9 No. 2, 94–108.

Minerby, S. (2009) 'Benedict XVI, the Lefebvrians, the Jews, and the State of Israel', *Jerusalem Center for Public Affairs*, Vol. 21 Nos 3 & 4, 7–29.

Minkenberg, M. (2009) 'Religion and Euroscepticism: Churches in the EU Member States', *West European Politics*, Vol. 32 No. 6, 1190–211.

Mitzen, J. (2006) 'Anchoring Europe's Civilising Identity: Habits, Capabilities and Ontological Security', *Journal of European Public Policy*, Vol. 13 No. 2, 270–85.

Moravcsik, A. (1993) 'Preferences and Power in the European Community: A Liberal Intergovernmentalist Approach', *Journal of Common Market Studies*, Vol. 31 No 4, 473–524.

Muller, P. (2011) 'The Europeanisation of Germany's Foreign Policy toward the Israeli-Palestinian Conflict: Between the Adaptation to the EU and National Projection', *Mediterranean Politics*, Vol. 16 No. 3, 385–403.

Neuberger, B. (1999) 'Religion and State in Europe and Israel', *Israel Affairs*, Vol. 6 No. 2, 65–84.

Nye, J.S. (2004) 'The Decline of America's Soft Power', *Foreign Affairs*, Vol. 83 No. 3, 1–4.

Pace, M. (2007) 'The Construction of EU Normative Power', *Journal of Common Market Studies,* Vol. 45 No. 5, 1041–64.

Pahre, R. (2005) 'Formal Theory and Case Study Methods in EU Studies', *European Union Politics*, Vol. 6 No. 1, 113–46.

Pastorelli, S. (2009) 'The European Union and the New Religious Movements', *Religion, State and Society*, Vol. 37 No. 1, 193–206.

Pertes, V. (2000) 'The Advantages of Complementarity: US and European Policies Towards the Middle East Peace Process', *The International Spectator*, Vol. 35 No. 2, 41–56.

Pijpers, A. (2007) 'The EU and the Palestinian–Israeli Conflict: The Limits of the CFSP', *Netherlands Institute for International Relations*, 1–6.

Rammy, M.H. (2006) 'The Armageddon Lobby: Dispensationalist Christian Zionism and the Shaping of US Policy Towards Israel-Palestine', *Holy Land Studies: A Multidisciplinary Journal*, Vol. 5 No. 1, 75–95.

Richardson, J. (2000) 'Government, Interest Groups and Policy Change', *Political Studies*, Vol. 48 No. 5, 1006–25.

Risso, L. (2009) 'Cracks in a Façade of Unity: the French and Italian Christian Democrats and the Launch of the European Integration Process, 1945–1957', *Religion, State and Society*, Vol. 37 No. 1, 99–114.

Sadeh, T. (1998) 'The European Union and Israel: The Customs Union Alternative', *Israel Affairs*, Vol. 5 No. 1, 87–108.

Sandholtz, W. and Zysman, J. (1989) '1992: Recasting the European Bargain', World Politics, Vol. 42 No 1, 95–128.

Scott, T.M. (2001) 'Faith, History and Martin Wight: The Role of Religion in the Historical Sociology of the English School of International Relations', *International Affairs*, Vol. 77 No. 4, 905–29.

Shamir, B. (1995) 'Social Distance and Charisma: Theoretical Notes and an Exploratory Study', *The Leadership Quarterly*, Vol. 6 No. 1, 19–47.

Shindler, C. (2000) 'Likud Camp, the Christian Dispensationalists: A Symbiotic Relationship', *Israel Studies*, Vol. 5 No. 1, 153–82.

Silvestri, S. (2005) 'EU Relations with Islam in the Context of the EMP's Cultural Dialogue', *Mediterranean Politics*, Vol. 10 No. 3, 385–405.

——— (2009) 'Islam and Religion in the EU Political System', *West European Politics*, Vol. 32 No. 6, 1212–39.

Sjursen, H. (2006) 'The EU as a 'Normative' Power: How Can This Be?', *Journal of European Public Policy*, Vol. 13 No. 2, 235–51.

Smith, A.D. (1995) 'Zionism and Diaspora Nationalism', *Israel Affairs*, Vol. 2 No. 2, 1–19.

Smith, E.K. (2000) 'The End of Civilian Power EU: A Welcome Demise or Cause for Concern?', *The International Spectator*, Vol. 35 No. 2, 11–23.

Stavridis, S. (2008) 'The Euro-Mediterranean Partnership: Perspectives From the Mediterranean EU Countries' (Conference Report), *Mediterranean Politics*, Vol. 13 No. 1, 103–7.

Steven, M. (2009) 'Religious Lobbies in the European Union: from Dominant Church to Faith-Based Organisation?', *Religion, State and Society*, Vol. 37 No. 1, 181–91.

Streeck, W. and Schmitter, C. (1991) 'From National Corporatism to Transnational Pluralism: Organised Interests in the Single Market', *Politics and Society*, Vol. 19 No. 3, 133–63.

Tachau, F. (1995) 'The Knesset and the Peace Process', *Israel Affairs*, Vol. 2 No. 2, 142–55.

Thatcher, M. (1998) 'The Development of Policy Network Analysis: From Modest Origins to Overarching Frameworks', *Journal of Theoretical Politics*, Vol. 10 No. 4, 389–416.

Thompson, G.F. (2007) 'Religious fundamentalisms, territories and globalisation', *Economy and Society*, Vol. 36 No. 1, 19–50.

Totten, M. (2012) 'Arab Spring or Islamist Winter?' *World Affairs Journal*, January/February.

Urban, S.Y. (2009) 'The Jewish Community in Germany: Living with Recognition, Antisemitism and Symbolic Roles', *Jerusalem Center for Public Affairs*, Vol. 21 Nos 3 & 4, 31–55.

Van Der Brug, W. et al. (2009) 'Religion and Party Choice in Europe', *West European Politics*, Vol. 32 No. 6, 1266–83.

Varella, P. et al. (2012) 'A Model of Instrumental Networks: The Roles of Socialised Charismatic Leadership and Group Behaviour', *Organisation Science*, Vol. 23 No. 2, 582–95.

Venneri, G. and Ferrara, P.O. (2009) 'Alcide De Gasperi and Antonio Messineo: a Spiritual Idea of Politics and a Pragmatic Idea of Religion?', *Religion, State and Society*, Vol. 37 No. 1&2, 115–29.

Victor, J.N. (2007) 'Strategic Lobbying: Demonstrating how Legislative Context Affects Interest Groups Tactics', *American Politics Research*, Vol. 35 No. 6, 826–45.

Vidino, L. (2005) 'The Muslim Brotherhood's Conquest of Europe', *Middle East Quarterly*, Winter, 25–34.

Ward, S. and Williams, R. (1997) 'From Hierarchy to Networks? Sub-central Government and EU Urban Environment Policy', *Journal of Common Market Studies*, Vol. 35 No. 3, 440–64.

Weber, T. (2003) 'Antisemitism and Philosemitism among British and German Elites: Oxford and Heidelberg before the First World War', *English Historical Review*, 118 (475), 86–119.

Wagner, W. (2006) 'The Democratic Control of Military Power Europe', *Journal of European Public Policy*, Vol. 13 No. 2, 200–16.

Wilcox, C. (1994) 'Premillennialists at the Millennium: Some Reflections on the Christian Right in the Twenty-first Century', *Sociology of Religion*, Vol. 55 No. 3, 243–61.

Willaime, J. (2009) 'European Integration, Laicite and Religion', *Religion, State and Society*, Vol. 37 Nos 1 & 2, 23–35.

Woll, C. (2006) 'Lobbying in the European Union: From Sui Generis to a Comparative Perspective', *Journal of European Public Policy*, Vol. 13 No. 3, 456–69.

——— (2012) 'The brash and soft-spoken: Lobbying styles in a transatlantic comparison', *Interest Groups and Advocacy*, Vol. 1 No. 2, 193–214.

Zunes, S. (2005) 'The Influence of Christian Right in US Middle East Policy', *Middle East Policy*, Vol. 12 No. 2, 73–8.

Internet sources

Abramson, S. et al (2011) 'Key Trends in the British Jewish Community: A Review of Data on Poverty, the Elderly and Children', *Institute for Jewish Policy Research*. http://www.jpr.org.uk/downloads/Wohl%20report.pdf, accessed on 7 November 2012.

ACAA (2012) 'ACAA Fact Sheet' http://passacaa.files.wordpress.com/2012/10/facts heet.pdf, accessed on 10 October 2012.

Ackley, K. (2011) 'Planned Parenthood dramatically ups lobby tab', *Roll Call* http://www.rollcall.com/news/planned_parenthood_dramatically_ups_lobby_tab-205075–1.html, accessed on 12 February 2013.

AFI (Anglican Friends of Israel) (2006) 'Christians support Holocaust Day initiative' http://www.anglicanfriendsofisrael.com/2006/11/christians-support-holocaust-day-initiative/, accessed on 1 July 2012.

Ali, A.M. (2012) 'Jewish Settlements in the Rulings of the European Court of Justice', *Middle East Monitor* http://wwwmidleeastmonitor.com/articles/guest-writers/3334-jewish-settlements-in, accessed on 5 February 2013.

Alpha Omega TV 'History and Values' http://alfaomega.tv/partners/623-alfa-omega-tv-history-and-values#axzz20VNvEqBP, accessed on 12 July 2012.

All-Party Parliamentary Inquiry Into Antisemitism (2006) Report http://www.antis emitism.org.uk/wp-content/uploads/All-Party-Parliamentary-Inquiry-into-Antisemitism-REPORT.pdf, accessed on 2 February 2010.

Asamoah-Gyadu, K. (2008) 'African-led Christianity in Europe: Migration and Diaspora Evangelism', *Lausanne World Pulse (Themed articles)*, www.lausanneworldpulse.com/themedarticles.php/973?pg=all, accessed on 12 December 2009.

Assenburg, M. (2010) 'Ending the Gaza Blockade – But How?', Stiftung Wissenschaft und Politic/German Institute for International and Security Affairs http://www.swp-berlin.org/fileadmin/contents/products/comments/2010C18_ass_ks.pdf, accessed on 5 May 2011.

Aslan, R. (2012) 'Political Islam in the Middle East', *Council of Foreign Relations*, http://www.cfr.org/middle-east/political-islam-middle-east/p29622, accessed on 5 January 2013.

Aston University (2010) 'Does God Matter? Representing Religion in the European Union and the United States' Conference, Aston Centre for Europe http://www1.aston.ac.uk/lss/research/centres-institutes/aston-centre-europe/projects-grants/religion-eu/conference/, accessed on 12 December 2010.

Ataman, M. (2003) 'The Impact of Non-State Actors on World Politics: A Challenge to Nation-States', *Alternatives – Turkish Journal of International Relations*, Vol. 2 No. 1 www.alternativesjournal.net/volume2/number1/ataman2.htm, accessed on 14 December 2008.

Ayadi, R. and Sessa, C. (2011) 'What scenarios for the Euro-Mediterranean in 2030 in the wake of the post-Arab spring?' MEDPRO Policy Paper No. 2, *The Centre for European Policy Studies,* www.ceps.eu/book/what-scenarios-euro-mediterranean-2030-wake-post-arab-spring, accessed on 31 October 2011.

Bard, M. (n.d.) 'British Restrictions on Jewish Immigration', *Jewish Virtual Library* http://www.jewishvirtuallibrary.org/jsource/History/mandate.html, accessed on 1 April 2012.

Bastiaan Belder European Parliament/MEPs http://www.europarl.europa.eu/meps/en/4507/Bastiaan_BELDER.html, accessed on 5 July 2012.

Bauchard, D. (2009) 'Europe's role in averting a Middle East tragedy', *Europe's World* www.europesworld.ogr/NewEnglish/Home/Article/tabid/191/ArticleType/Article, accessed on 3 December 2009.

Bartholomew, R. (2011) 'Christian Zionist counter-protest at Israeli embassy in London', *Richard Bartholomew blog* http://pulsemedia.org/2011/09/15/israels-advocates-in-the-uk-cosy-up-to-christian-right/, accessed on 5 July 2012.

BBC online (2006) 'Europe fills Palestinian aid gap', 27 February, news.bbc.co.uk/1/hi/world/middle_east/4754580.stm, accessed on 30 March 2006.

BBE (B'nai B'rith Europe) 'Who We Are' http://www.bnaibritheurope.org/bbeurope/en/who-we-are, accessed on 7 July 2012.

Beck, E. (2010) 'Israel's friend in Europe: Stanislaw Tillich, minister-president of the Free State of Saxony, is one of Jewish state's greatest supporters in Germany, all of Europe', *Ynetnews* http://www.ynetnews.com/articles/0,7340,L-3922006,00.html, accessed on 6 January 2011.

Behr, T. (2011) 'Europe's flawed Arab Spring. Is the EU really willing to support Arab democracy?', *The Finnish Institute of International Affairs*, March, http://policypointers.org/Page/View/12563, accessed on 20 October 2011.

Belkin, P. (2007) 'Germany's Relations with Israel: Background and Implications for German Middle East Policy', *CRS Report for Congress*, 19 January, www.ftp.fas.org/sgp/crs/row/RL33808.pdf, accessed on 5 January 2009.

Berman, Y. (2006) 'Top Palestinian Muslim cleric okays suicide bombing', *The Middle East News Source*, 17 October, www.themedialine.org/news/news_detail.asp?NewsID=15404, accessed on 16 November 2006.

Besser, J. (2007) 'New coalition to fight any Jerusalem division', *The Jewish Week* www.thejewishweek.com/viewArticle/c40_a603/News/Israel.html, accessed on 3 December 2009.

Berzi, T. (2009) 'European Reactions to Israel's Gaza Operations', *Jerusalem Center for Public Affairs*, www.jcpa.org/JCPA/Templates/ShowPage.asp?DBID=1& LNGID=1&TMID=1, accessed on 23 March 2009.

────── (2011) 'The European Union: Challenges for Israeli Diplomacy', *Jerusalem Center for Public Affairs*, www.jcpa.org/JCPA/Templates/ShowPage.asp?DBID =1&LNGID=1&TMID=111&FID=442&PID=0&IID=6797, accessed on 7 October 2011.

────── and Gerstenfeld, M. (2009) 'The Gaza War and the New Outburst of Antisemitism', *Jerusalem Center for Public Affairs*, www.jcpa.org/JCPA/Templates/ ShowPage.asp?DRIT=3&DBID=1&LNGID=1, accessed on 23 March 2009.

Besussi, E. (2006) 'Policy Networks: Conceptual Developments and their European Applications', Working Paper Series, University College London http://eprints. ucl.ac.uk/3280/1/3280.pdf, accessed on 1 April 2011.

Bethune, B. (2002) 'In the beginning was the word', *Maclean's*, Vol. 115 No. 49, 42–49 web13epnet.com/citation.asp?tb=1&_ug=sid+36224AF7%2D41B3%, accessed on 7 February 2006.

BICOM (Britain Israel Communications and Research Centre) (2012) 'Foreign Office Minister: UK leading international campaign to halt Iran's nuclear programme' http://bicom.org.uk/news-analysis-article/4633/, accessed on 20 January 2012.

Blake, D. (2006) 'International leaders call for urgent action to heal Muslim-West conflict', *Christian Today*, 13 November, www.christiantoday.com/articledir/ print.htm?id=8312, accessed on 16 November 2006.

Bolton, J. (2009) 'Israel, the U.S. and the Goldstone Report', *The Wall Street Journal* http://online.wsj.com.article/SB10014240527487045006045744809329245 40724.html, accessed on 19 November 2009.

Borzel, T. (1997) 'What's So Special About Policy Networks? – An Exploration of the Concept and Its Usefulness in Studying European Governance', *European Integration Online Papers*, Vol. 1 No. 16. http://eiop.or.at/eiop/texte/1997–016a. htm, accessed on 26 October 2011.

Boyd, J. and Graham, D. (2010) 'Committed, concerned and conciliatory: The attitudes of Jews in Britain toward Israel', *Institute for Jewish Policy Research* http://www.jpr.org.uk/downloads/JPR%20Israel%20survey%20report%2015. pdf, accessed on 10 April 2011.

Brandon, H. (2008) 'Israel anti-terrorism Jerusalem Summit meets German Christian Zionists on Islamic Apartheid', *Israel News Agency* www.israelnews agency.comislamicapartheidterrorismisraeljerusalemsummit, accessed on 30 January 2009.

Bridges for Peace (About) 'Our Mission' www.bridgesforpeace.com/about, accessed on 17 April 2012.

Brimmer, R.J. (Rev.) (2002) 'Standing with Israel is standing with God', *Bridges For Peace*, www.bridgesforpeace.com/modules.php?name=news&file=article& sid=2361, accessed on 9 October 2006.

Carrera, S. and Parkin, J. (2010) 'The Place of religion in European Union Law and Policy – Competing Approaches and Actors inside the European Commission', Working Paper No. 1, *Religare* http://papers.ssrn.com/sol3/papers.cfm?abstract_ id=1688252, accessed on 1 January 2011.

Carson, J.D. (2005) 'The not-so-golden age of Islamic philosophy', *The American Thinker* http://www.americanthinker.com/2005/08/the_notsogolden_age_of_islamic.html, accessed on 10 December 2009.

CBN youtube (2011) 'Aznar on his "Friends of Israel" initiative' http://www.youtube.com/watch?v=H23kvw85tWs, accessed on 7 July 2012.

CERM (n.d.) (Christian Education Resource Material), 'Liberal Christianity' www.cerm.info/bible_studies?Topical_liberal_christianity.htm, accessed on 8 March 2009.

CGP European Public Relations, Section Lobbying www.cgpeurope.com/index_lobby.html, accessed on 4 May 2012.

Chandler, D. (2006) 'Moral grandstanding in the Middle East', *Spiked*, www.spiked-online.com/index.php?/site/article/1598, accessed 07 November 2006.

Charrad, K. (2004) 'Lobbying the European Union', Westfälische Wilhelms-Universität Münster http://nez.uni-muenster.de/download/Charrad_Literaturbericht_Lobbying_mit_Deckblatt.pdf, accessed on 10 March 2011.

Charrad, K. and Eisele, G. (2004) 'Project 24 – Accountability/Participation of Civil Society in New Modes of Governance', *NEWGOV New Modes of Governance* http://tarantula.ruk.cuni.cz/CESES-136-version1–6D_NMG_Interest_groups_in_EU_governance_Pleines.pdf#page=22, accessed on 10 March 2011.

CFI (Christian Friends of Israel) Links, https://www.cfi.org.uk/links.php, accessed on 1 January 2011.

CiF Watch (2011) 'Facebook shuts down "Third Intifada" page' http://cifwatch.com/2011/03/29/facebook-shuts-down-third-intifada-page/, accessed on 20 October 2012.

Clark, P. (2008) 'Global Pentecostalism: A European Perspective' http://pmgermany.com/wp-content/uploads/2010/08/global_pentecostalism_a_european_perspective.pdf, accessed on 13 December 2012.

Coen, D. (2007) 'Lobbying in the European Union', *Constitutional Affairs*, (European Parliament) http://www.eurosfaire.prd.fr/7pc/doc/1211469722_lobbying_eu.pdf, accessed on 10 March 2011.

———— and Richardson, J. (2009a) 'A commitment to consultation', *European Voice* http://www.europeanvoice.com/article/imported/a-commitment-to-consultation/65898.aspx, accessed on 2 March 2011.

Cohen, B. (2005) 'Evaluating Muslim-Jewish Relations in Britain', *Jerusalem Center for Public Affairs* http://jcpa.org/jl/vp527.htm, accessed on 16 February 2010.

CONECCS, (2009) 'Measuring the Size and Scope of the EU Interest Group Population' http://www.unc.edu/~fbaum/papers/ECPR-2009-IG-Population.pdf, accessed on 10 February 2011.

Council of the EU (2001) 'Conclusions and Plan of Action of the Extraordinary European Council Meeting on 21 September 2001', *Official Journal of the European Union* www.eur-lex.europa.eu/LexUriServ/LexUriServ.do?=OJ:L:2005:253:0022:0024:EN:PDF, accessed on 17 November 2006.

———— (2006) 'Council Conclusions of the Middle East, 13 and 14 November 2006' www.delwbg.cec.eu.int/en/whatsnew/comclusions_mepp.doc, accessed on 20 October 2006.

———— (2006a) 'Council Joint Action 2006/119/CFSP', *Official Journal of the European Union*, 20 February www.eur-lex.europa.eu/LexUriServ/LexUriServ.do?uri=OJ:L:2006:049:0008:0010:EN:PDF, accessed on 17 November 2006.

———— (2008) 'Council Framework Decision 2008/913/JHA of 28 November 2008 on combating certain forms and expressions of racism and xenophobia by means of criminal law' http://eur-lex.europa.eu/LexUriServ/LexUriServ.do?uri= CELEX:32008F0913:EN:HTML, accessed on 10 May 2012.

———— (2011) 'Go-ahead given to the European citizen's initiative' http://www. consilium.europa.eu/uedocs/cms_data/docs/pressdata/EN/genaff/119272.pdf, accessed on 22 March 2011.

Cowles, M.G. (1997) 'The Changing Architecture of Big Bussines', 1997 5th Biennial ECSA Conference, Seattle WA, May 29, http://aei.pitt.edu/2560/1/002508_1. pdf, accessed on 7 October 2012.

Cronin, D. (2010) 'How the Israel lobby dictates EU policy', *David Cronin Blog* http:// dvcronin.blogspot.co.uk/2010/11/how-israel-lobby-dictates-eu-policy.html, accessed on 5 July 2011.

C4I (Christians for Israel International) (n.d.) Section Prayer 'Coming of the Messiah' http://www.c4israel.org/c4i/prayer/coming_of_the_messiah, accessed on 17 April 2012.

———— About Us 'Rev Glashouwer' www.c4israel.org/c4i/about_us/rev_glashouwer, accessed on 3 May 2012.

Darring, J. (n.d.) 'A Catholic Time Line of Events Relating to Jews, Anti-Judaism, and the Holocaust From the 3rd. Century to the Beginning of the Third Millennium', *Sullivan*, http://web2.shc.edu/theolibrary/resources/timeline.htm, accessed on 13 March 2007.

Dembinski, M. and Joachim, J. (2006) 'From an Intergovernmental to Governance System? Non-Governmental Organisations and the EU's Common Foreign and Security Policy', Paper presented to Pan-European Conference on European Politics - Istanbul, Turkey. www.jhubc.it/ecpr-istanbul/virtualpaperroom/033. pdf, accessed on 10 December 2008.

De Vlieger, P. (2012) 'Religious lobbying at the European level: strengthened and professional', *Observatore des Religions et de la Laicite* http://www.o-re-la.org/ index.php?option=com_k2&view=item&id=413:religious-lobbying-at-the-european-level-strengthened-and-professional&Itemid=85&lang=fr, accessed on 18 October 2013.

De Waay, B. (n.d.) 'Pre-Millennialism and the Early Church Fathers', *Critical Issues Commentary/Scholarly* www.cicministry.org/scholarly.php, accessed on 22 May 2008.

D'Hippolito, J. (2006) 'Pontificating against Israel', *Front Page Magazine*, July, www. frontpagemag.com/Articles/ReadArticle.asp?ID=23484, accessed on 9 October 2006.

Diedrichs, U. (2004) 'The European Parliament in CFSP: More Than a Marginal Player?', *The International Spectator*, 31–36. www.assembly-weu.org/en/presse/ articles/2004/Udo_DiedrichsIntSpectator2_04.PDF, accessed on 8 January 2009.

———— (2007) 'The Impact of Intergovernmentalism on the Evolution of CFSP' – Policy Memorandum, *NewGov* http://www.eu-newgov.org/database/DELIV/ D01D59_Policy_Memo_Impact_Intergovernmentalism_CFSP.pdf, accessed on 9 October 2008.

Ebenezer (About Us) 'Operation Exodus – International Vision' http://operation-exodus.org/international-vision.html, accessed on 17 April 2012.

ECPM (European Christian Political Movement) 'What is ECPM?' http://www.ecpm. info/en/page/9340, accessed on 5 July 2012.

Edd, D. (1998) 'Desecularisation', *Humanist*, Vol. 58 No. 4, 37–38, web22.epnet. com/DeliveryPrintSave.asp?tb+1&_ug=sid + 3D5CABE2–99BO-46, accessed on 7 March 2006.

EEA (European Evangelical Alliance) (About) http://www.europeanea.org/, accessed on 5 January 2013.

EEAS (European External Action Service) (2000) 'Euro-Mediterranean Agreement', *Official Journal of the European Communities* www.eeas.europa.eu/delegations/ israel/documents/eu_israel/asso_agree_en.pdf, accessed on 20 December 2011.

———— (2011) 'Catherine Ashton statement following her meeting with the President Mahmoud Abbas – 15/12/11' www.consilium.europa.eu/uedocs/cms_ Data/docs/pressdata/EN/foraff/126936.pdf, accessed on 20 December 2011.

———— Delegation of the European Union to Israel – Agreements http://eeas.europ a.eu/delegations/israel/eu_israel/political_relations/agreements/index_en.htm, accessed on 10 October 2011.

———— 'EU positions on the Middle East peace process' http://eeas.europa.eu/mepp/ eu-positions/eu_positions_en.htm, accessed on 28 February 2013.

EFI (European Friends of Israel) (2006) About EFI http://www.efi-eu.org/index.php? option=com_k2&view=item&layout=item&id=269&Itemid=145 http:// www.youtube.com/watch?v=EqONN0cdmjk&feature=relmfu, accessed on 7 July 2012.

EJC (European Jewish Congress) About Us http://www.eurojewcong.org/ejc/news. php?id_article=134.

———— 'Germany – History and Demography' http://www.eurojewcong.org/ communities/germany.html, accessed on 4 July 2012.

Ekklesia (2004) 'Christian scholars gather to study the dangers of Zionism', www. ekklesia.co.uk/content/news_syndication/article_040426zionism.shtml, accessed on 9 October 2006.

EP (European Parliament) (2011) 'Report on the EU's approach toward Iran', Committee on Foreign Affairs Rapporteur Bastiaan Belder http://www.europarl. europa.eu/sides/getDoc.do?type=REPORT&reference=A7–2011–0037& language=EN, accessed on 8 September 2012.

Eran, O. (2007) 'Israel and the European Union' in Gerstenfeld, M., European-Israeli Relations: Between Confusion and Change?', *Jerusalem Centre for Public Affairs*, www.jcpa.org/JCPA/Templates?ShowPage.asp?DRIT=6&DBID=1&LNGID=1, accessed on 7 January 2009.

———— (2009) 'Why Europe and Israel need to bury the hatchet', *Europe's World*, www.europesworld.org/NewEnglish/Home_old/Article/tabid/191/ArticleType/a, accessed on 20 January 2010.

Erlanger, S. (2009) 'The Anti-Germans – The Pro-Israel German Left', *Jewish Political Studies Review*, Vol. 21 Nos 1 & 2, *Jerusalem Center for Public Affairs* http://jcpa.org/ article/the-anti-germans-the-pro-israel-german-left/, accessed on 4 March 2010.

Esposito, M. (n.d.) 'Dispensationalism', *End Times.org*, www.endtimes.org/dispens. html, accessed on 3 March 2006.

EU Funding.org (2006) 'EU Suspends Funding to the Palestinians' http://www. eufunding.org/accountability/SuspendsFunding.html, accessed on 9 May 2012.

EU@UN (2011) 'EU Parliament supports Palestine's "legitimate" bid for statehood' www.eu-un.europa.eu/articles/en/article_11441_en.htm, accessed on 10 January 2012.

EurActiv (2005) 'EU and US approaches to lobbying' www.euractiv.com/en/pa/eu-us-approaches-lobbying/article-135509, accessed on 1 November 2010.

EuroMed ' The EuroMed Partnership' http://www.enpi-info.eu/medportal/content/340/About%20the%20EuroMed%20Partnership, accessed on 20 January 2013.

———, 'The Amsterdam Treaty: A Comprehensive Guide' www.europa.eu/scadplus/leg/en/lub/a19000.htm, accessed on 26 November 2006.

———, 'Treaty of European Union (TEU), Title V – Provisions on the Common Foreign and Security Policy' www.europa.eu.int/en/record.mt/heads/html, accessed on 26 November 2006.

——— (2011) 'EU response to the Arab Spring: the SPRING Programme' http://europa.eu/rapid/pressReleasesAction.do?reference=MEMO/11/636&format=HTML&aged=0&language=EN&guiLanguage=en, accessed on 21 October 2011.

——— (2011a) 'Palestinian people and local business at the heart of the Commission's new assistance package' http://europa.eu/rapid/pressReleasesAction.do?reference=IP/11/976&format=HTML&aged=0&language=EN&guiLanguage=en, accessed on 21 October 2011.

——— (2009) 'Treaty of Lisbon – Taking Europe into the 21st century' http://europa.eu/lisbon_traty/faq/index_en.htm, accessed on 20 December 2009.

——— (2001) 'Council Common Position of 27 December 2001 on the application of specific measures to combat terrorism' (2001/931/CFSP), *Official Journal of the European Communities* http://eur-lex.europa.eu/LexUriServ/LexUriServ.do?uri=OJ:L:2001:344:0093:0096:EN:PDF, accessed on 9 August 2011.

European Commission (2001) 'European Governance – White paper 2001' www.aei.pitt.edu/1188/01/european_governance_wp_COM_2001_428.pdf-, accessed on 10 May 2009.

——— (2004) 'The Spiritual and Cultural Dimension to Europe' http://cordis.europa.eu/documents/documentlibrary/104214451EN6.pdf, accessed on 10 March 2011.

——— (2005) 'Social Values, Science and Technology', *Eurobarometer*, 1–336. www.ec.europa.eu/public_opinion/archives/ebs/ebs_225_report_en.pdf, accessed on 29 January 2009.

——— (2006) 'European Neighbourhood and Partnership Instrument – Israel, Strategy Paper 2007–2013 and Indicative Programme 2007–2010' www.ec.europa.eu/world/enp/pdf/country/enpi_csp_nip_israel_en.pdf, accessed on 30 December 2008.

——— (2006a) 'Position Paper to the Green Paper European Transparency Initiative' http://ec.europa.eu/transparency/eti/docs/contributions/97_c7_ch1_comece.pdf, accessed on 9 October 2012.

——— (2008) 'Lobbying – a US-EU comparison', *EU Insight,* No. 8 www.eurunion.org/News/eunewsletters/EUInsight/2008/EUInsight-Lobbying-Sept08.pdf, accessed on 1 February 2011.

European Commission Delegation to Israel, 'European Instrument for Democracy and Human Rights' http://www.delisr.ec.europa.eu/english/content/cooperation_and_funding/4.asp, accessed on 6 February 2009.

European Commission, BEPA (Bureau of European Policy Advisors) 'Dialogue with religions, Churches and Humanisms' http://ec.europa.eu/dgs/policy_advisers/archives/activities/dialogue_religions_humanisms/sfe_en.htm, accessed on 4 October 2011.

——— 'Dialogue with churches, religious associations and communities and philosophical and non-confessional organisations' http://ec.europa.eu/bepa/activities/outreach-team/dialogue/index_en.htm, accessed on 4 October 2011.

European Council (2003) 'A secure Europe in a better world', European Security Strategy www.consilium.europa.eu/uedocs.ansUpload/78367.pdf, accessed on 5 November 2009.

——— (2006) 'Laying down general provisions establishing a European Neighbourhood and Partnership Instrument (Regulation No. 1638/2006)', *Official Journal of the European Union* www.ec.europa.eu/world/enp/pdf/oj_I310_en.pdf accessed 05 November 2009.

Europe in Israel (2011) 'Coming soon: EU citizens empowered to propose legislation', No. 8 http://d157696.si27.siteam.co.il/eu-news/index.cfm?aId=88&eId=17, accessed on 22 March 2011.

Falk, R. (2009) 'The Goldstone report and battle for legitimacy', *Electronic Intifada* http://electronicintifada.net/v2/article10788.shtml, accessed on 8 December 2009.

Fathollah-Nejad, A. (2010) 'Silencing Critics of Israel: Germany's Finkelstein Phobia', *Global Research* http://www.globalresearch.ca/silencing-critics-of-israel-germany-s-finkelstein-phobia/17925, accessed on 23 November 2011.

FCO (2009) 'Middle East Peace Process' http://ukinisrael.fco.gov.uk/en/about-us/working-with-israel/mepp/, accessed on 9 December 2009.

Fendel, H. (2010) 'Mass European Rally for Israel', *Arutz Sheva* http://www.israelnationalnews.com/News/News.aspx/139880, accessed on 10 October 2012.

Fernandez-Morera, D. (2006) 'The Myth of the Andalusian Paradise', *The Intercollegiate Review* http://www.mmisi.org/ir/41_02/fernandez-morera.pdf, accessed on 20 April 2010.

Finke, B. (2007) 'Civil Society Participation in EU Governance', *Living Reviews in European Governance*, Vol. 2 No. 2, 1–31. www.livingreviews.org/lreg-2007–2, accessed on 7 March 2011.

Fitzgerald, H. (2003) 'Annals of Christian Zionism: De Witt Talmage', *Christian Zionism*, http://christianactionforisrael.org/annals_cz.html, accessed on 13 March 2007.

Fossum, J.E. (2001) 'Identity Politics in the European Union', *ARENA Working Papers* WP 01/17, 1–30. www.arena.uio.no/publications/wp01_17.htm-220k, accessed on 23 January 2009.

Franko, M. (2011) 'Can the pope recapture Europe?', *The Guardian*, www.guardian.co.uk/commentisfree/belief/2011/sep/27/pope-recapture-europe-catholic, accessed on 30 October 2011.

Fraser, R. (2005) 'The Academic Boycott of Israel: Why Britain?' (Post-Holocaust and Antisemitism), *Jerusalem Center for Public Affairs*, No. 36. www.jcpa.org.phas/phas-36.htm, accessed on 29 September 2009.

Friedman, G. (2000) 'Popular Trust in Palestinian Islamic Factions' (Analysis of Palestinian Public Opinion on Politics), *Jerusalem Media & Research Communication Centre – Research*, www.jmcc.org/research/reports/study2.htm, accessed on 20 January 2006.

Gauthier, J. (2012) 'Jerusalem Sovereignty Over Jerusalem and Its Old City', YouTube, *Shalom TV* http://www.youtube.com/watch?v=zf8cF1HYqN8, accessed on 10 October 2012.

Gerstenfeld, M. (2005) 'European Politics: Double Standards Toward Israel', *Jewish Political Studies Review*, Vol. 17 No. 3–4, 1–42. www.jcpa.org/phas/phas-gers tenfeld-1-f05.htm, accessed on 10 October 2008.

Glazier, R. (2007) 'Bringing Religion into International Relations: Exploring the Effects of Providential Beliefs', Paper presented at the *American Political Science Association*, Chicago. http://www.allacademic.com//meta/p_mla_apa_research_ citation/2/1/0/6/7/pages210677/p210677–1.php, accessed on 10 October 2009.

Gledhill, R. and Owen, R. (2006) 'Carey backs Pope and issues warning on violent Islam', *Times Online*, www.timesonline.co.uk/article/0,2–2366419,00.html, accessed on 9 October 2006.

Gold, D. (2012) 'The Levy Report and the "Occupation" Narrative', *New English Review*, http://www.bing.com/search?q=http%2F%2Fwww.newenglishreview. org%2Fblog_print_link.cfm%2Fblog_id%2F43092&src=IE-SearchBox& FORM=IE8SRC, accessed on 5 February 2013.

Goldberg, M. (2005) 'Jews and Christian Right: Is the honeymoon over?', *Salon.com*, http://dir.salon.com/story/news/feature/2005/11/29/foxman/index.html, accessed on 25 February 2007.

Goldman, S. (2005) 'The Fatah-Hamas Rivalry – Palestinian domestic competition and Israeli withdrawal from Gaza' (Working Paper), *EastWest Institute* www. mafhoum.com/press8/248P55.pdf, accessed on 30 November 2009.

Grant, C. (2011) 'A new neighbourhood policy for the EU', *Centre for European Reform*, www.cer.org.uk/publications/archive/policy-brief/2011/new-neighbou rhood-policy-eu, accessed on 30 October 2011.

Grief, H. (2004) 'Legal Rights and Title of Sovereignty of the Jewish People to the Land of Israel and Palestine Under International Law', *Native Online – A Journal of Politics and the Arts* http://www.acpr.org.il/ENGLISH-NATIV/02-issue/grief-2.htm, accessed on 7 July 2011.

Guitta, O. (2010) 'Muslim Brotherhood Parties in the Middle East and North Africa (MENA) Region', *Centre for European Studies* (Ethics, Values and Religion), www.thinkingeurope.eu/showdocumentsbytopics.asp?topicId=5A, accessed on 30 October 2011.

Hailes, S. (2012) 'Embassy hosts Christian Young Adults event', (CFI) *In Touch*, p. 9 http://cfi.org.uk/resources/newsletter40.pdf, accessed on 20 January 2013.

Halevy, E. (2007) 'How the European Union's attitude toward Israel evolved' in Gerstenfeld, M. 'European-Israeli Relations: Between Confusion and Change?', *Jerusalem Centre for Public Affairs*, www.jcpa.org/JCPA/Templates/ShowPage. asp?DBID=1&LNGID=1&TMID=1, accessed on 6 January 2009.

Hamas (1988) 'The Covenant of the Islamic Resistance Movement' www.jewishvirtu allibrary.org/jsource/Terrorism/Hamas_covenant_complete.html, accessed on 1 February 2007.

Hannu Takkula 'European Parliament/MEPs' http://www.europarl.europa.eu/meps/ en/28316/HANNU_TAKKULA.html, accessed on 5 July 2012.

Harrison, R. and Shiloh, I. (2007) 'Amen for Israel, say Christian Zionists', *Mail and Guardian Online* www.mg.co.za/article/2007–10–02-amen-for-israel-say-chris tian-zionists, accessed on 3 January 2009.

Holocaust Centre (Visit Us) http://holocaustcentre.net/?page_id=3, accessed on 1 March 2012.

Hornstra, W. (2006) 'Christian Zionism Among Evangelicals in the Federal Republic of Germany' http://www.christianzionism.de/media/thesis1.pdf accesses on 07 July 2011.

House of Commons (2009) Library – European Parliament Elections 2009, Research Paper 09/53, 17 June http://www.parliament.uk/documents/commons/lib/research/rp2009/rp09–053.pdf, accessed on 10 October 2011.

HR (Honest Reporting) (2009) 'The Goldstone Report: Rewarding Palestinian Terror' www.honestreporting.com/articles/45884734/critiques/new/The_Goldstone_Report, accessed on 19 November 2009.

———— (2009a) 'Stop the spread of the Swedish blood libel' www.honestreporting.com/articles/45884734/critiques/new/Stop_the_Spread_of, accessed on 3 December 2009.

Hucklesby, S. (2010) 'Justice for Palestine and Israel', British Methodist Report http://www.methodist.org.uk/downloads/conf10a-14-pal-israel-160211.pdf, accessed on 1 November 2010.

IBCC (The Israel-Britain Chamber of Commerce) http://www.ibcc.org.il/, accessed on 5 December 2012.

Ice, T. (n.d.) 'Dispensational Hermeneutics' (Miscellaneous), Pre-Trib Research Center www.pre-trib.org/article-view.php?id=21, accessed on 8 March 2009.

ICEJ (About) 'Inside the Embassy' http://fi.icej.org/category/main-menu/about?page=1, accessed on 17 April 2012.

Initiative 27 Januar (Home) 'Non-governmental organisation in the federal capital' http://translate.google.co.uk/translate?hl=en&sl=de&u=http://www.initiative27januar.org/&prev=/search%3Fq%3Dinitiative%2B27%2Bjanuar%26hl%3Den%26tbo%3Dd%26rls%3Dcom.microsoft:en-gb:IE-SearchBox&sa=X&ei=6GIWUY3HAqXJ0AWtloCQDQ&ved=0CDcQ7gEwAA, accessed on 7 July 2011.

Intercultural Dialogue (1999) 'Intercultural Dialogue – Basis for Euro-Mediterranean Partnership', 1995 Conference in Barcelona www.coe.int/...transmediterranean_dialogue/...InterculturalDialogue_Euro-Mediterranean_Partnership.pdf, accessed on 10 April 2009.

Ivani, E.G. (1999) 'Islamic Mediation Techniques for Middle East Conflict', Middle East Review of International Affairs, Vol. 3 No. 2 http:/meria.idc.ac.il/journal/1999/issue2/jv3n2a1.html, accessed on 23 February 2007.

IPT (The Investigative Project on Terrorism) (2008) 'Apologists or Extremists?' http://www.investigativeproject.org/profile/167, accessed on 14 March 2011.

IMFA (Israel Ministry of Foreign Affairs) 'UN Security Council resolution 242', November 22, 1967 http://www.mfa.gov.il/MFA/Peace%20Process/Guide%20to%20the%20Peace%20Process/UN%20Security%20Council%20Resolution%20242, accessed on 7 October 2012.

Jarabik, B. and Kobzova, J. (2011) 'European Neighbourhood Policy: addressing myths, narrowing focus, improving implementation', Centre for European Studies (Policy Briefs) www.thinkingeurope.eu/publications_policybriefs_bytopic.asp, accessed on 30 October 2011.

Jewish Israel (2011) 'Messianic Attorney Calev Myers' speech nixed at Durban 3 protest', 26 September http://jewishisrael.ning.com/profiles/blogs/messianic-attorney-calev-myers-speech-nixed-at-durban-3-protest, accessed on 21 January 2013.

JIJ (Jerusalem Institute for Justice) (About Us) http://www.jij.org.il/about.php, accessed on 15 June 2012.

Joffe, J. (2006) 'Germany and Israel: Between Obligation, Taboo, and Resentment" in European-Israeli Relations: Between Confusion and Change?', Gerstenfeld, M., *Jerusalem Centre for Public Affairs*, www.jcpa.org/JCPA/Templates? ShowPage.asp?DRIT=6&DBID=1&LNGID=1, accessed on 7 January 2009.

Jones, J. and Oborne, P. (2009) 'The pro-Israel lobby in Britain', *Open Democracy* www.opendemocracy.net/ourkingdom/peter-oborne-james-jones/pro-israel-lobby, accessed on 8 December 2009.

JURIST (2011) 'UK passes law limiting arrests under universal jurisdiction' http://jurist.org/paperchase/2011/09/uk-passes-law-limiting-arrests-under-universal-jurisdiction.php, accessed on 10 February 2013.

Kadary, N. (2007) 'The Balfour Declaration: A Watershed in the History of the Zionist Movement', *The Jewish Agency for Israel*, www.jafi.org.il/education/100/ACT/23zion.html, accessed on 23 March 2007.

Kagan, R. (2002) 'Power and Weakness', *Policy Review*, No. 113, June & July www.hoover.org/publications/policyreview/3460246.html, accessed on 18 May 2009.

Kantor, M. (2009) 'The story derive from age-old antisemitism', *The Swedish Wire* www.swedishwire.com/component/content/article/11-opinion/797-the-story-derives, accessed on 8 December 2009.

Karsh, E. (2005) 'European Misreading of the Israeli-Palestinian Conflict: Finnish Foreign Minister Tounioja – A Case Study', *Jerusalem Centre for Public Affairs*, Vol. 3 No. 2, www.jcpa.org/brief/brief004–27.htm, accessed on 23 February 2007.

———— (2009) 'What's Behind Western Condemnation of Israel's War Against Hamas?', *Jerusalem Centre for Public Affairs*, Vol. 8 No. 17, www.jcpa.org/JCPA/Templates/ShowPage.asp?DRIT=1&DBID=1&LNGID=1, accessed on 12 January 2009.

Kelman, H.C. (2011) 'A One Country/Two State Solution to the Israeli-Palestinian Conflict', *Middle East Policy Council* http://www.mepc.org/journal/middle-east-policy-archives/one-country/-two-state-solution-israeli-palestinian-conflict, accessed on 19 September 2012.

Kemp, R. (2009) 'Hamas, the Gaza War and Accountability under the International Law' (Joint International Conference), *Jerusalem Center for Public Affairs* www.jcpa.org/JCPA/Templates/ShowPage.asp?DRIT=0&DBID=1&LNGID=1, accessed on 19 November 2009.

Klaff, L. (2010) 'Anti-Zionist Expression on the UK Campus: Free Speech or Hate Speech?', *Jewish Political Studies Review*, Vol. 22 Nos 3 & 4 http://jcpa.org/article/anti-zionist-expression-on-the-uk-campus-free-speech-or-hate-speech/, accessed on 5 June 2011.

Knesset (2011) 'Israeli Knesset Ceremony in honour of the Evangelical Christian supporters of Israel' www.hhttp://hhceevents.blogspot.com/p/knesset-conference-jerusalem-22112011.html, accessed on 28 November 2011.

Koch, C. (2011) 'The Arab Spring is a real opportunity for Europe', *Europe's World*, www.europesworld.org/NewEnglish/Home_old/Article/tabid/191/ArticleType/ArticleView/ArticleID/21837/language/en-US/TheArabspringisarealopportunityforEurope.aspx, accessed on 21 October 2011.

Kohler-Koch, B. (1997) 'Organized Interests in the EC and the European Parliament', *European Integration Online Papers*, Vol. 1 No. 9 http://eiop.or.at/eiop/texte/1997–009.htm, accessed on 1 February 2011.

———— and Quittkat, C. (1999) 'Intermediation of Interests in the European Union', Working paper No. 9, *Mannheimer Zentrum für Europäische Sozialforschung* http://www.mzes.uni.mannheim.de/publications/wp/wp-9.pdf, accessed on 10 March 2011.

Korn, E. (2007) 'Disinvestment From Israel, The Liberal Churches and Jewish Responses: A Strategic Analysis', *Jerusalem Centre for Public Affairs*, No. 52, www.jcpa.org/JCPA/Templates/ShowPage.asp?DBID=1&LNGID=1&TMID=1, accessed on 23 February 2007.

Kratochvil, P. and Dolezal, T. (2010) 'The Roman Catholic Church and European Integration: A Study on the Limits of Schmitt's Political Theology', *SGIR Conference*, Stockholm. http://stockholm.sgir.eu/uploads/RCC%20and%20EU%20theory_Final.pdf, accessed on 10 March 2011.

Kuntzel, M. (2005) 'National Socialism and Antisemitism in the Arab World', *Jerusalem Center for Public Affairs* http://jcpa.org/phas/phas-kuntzel-s05.htm, accessed on 1 January 2011.

———— (2007) 'Hitler's Legacy: Islamic antisemitism and the impact of the Muslim Brotherhood' http://www.matthiaskuentzel.de/contents/hitlers-legacy-islamic-antisemitism-and-the-impact-of-the-muslim-brotherhood, accessed on 1 January 2011.

Landen, T. (2009) 'Sharia banking conquers Europe', *The Brussels Journal* http://www.brusselsjournal.com/node/3837, accessed on 10 October 2010.

Lapidoth, R. (2007) 'Security Council Resolution 242: An Analysis of its Main Provisions', *Jerusalem Centre for Public Affairs* http://jcpa.org/article/security-council-resolution-242-an-analysis-of-its-main-provisions/, accessed on 5 February 2013.

Lempkowicz, Y. (2006) 'EU freezes financial aid to Palestinians', *European Jewish Press* http://www.ejpress.org/article/5245, accessed on 19 October 2011.

Leustean, L.N. (2011) 'The Politics of Religious Lobbies in the EU' Summary of Findings, Aston University http://www1.aston.ac.uk/lss/research/centres-institutes/aston-centre-europe/projects-grants/religion-eu/#findings, accessed on 12 December 2010.

Levin, K. (2009) 'Is Israel Doomed?', *Front Page Magazine,* 23 January, www.frontpagemagazine.com/Articles?GUID=EABBD297–58AB-4E, accessed on 24 January 2009.

Levitt, Z. (2005) 'End Times Prophecy Events', *Zola Levitt Ministries*, www.levitt.com/essays/endtimes_events.html, accessed on 8 March 2006.

Lipman, J. (2011) 'Christians show support for Israel', *Jewish Chronicle Online* http://www.thejc.com/galleries/news-galleries/christians-show-support-israel, accessed on 12 February 2013.

Littman, D.G. (2010) 'How can the EU promote the "Universal Values" in the world community at large?', *New English Review* http://www.newenglishreview.org/custpage.cfm/frm/63288/sec_id/63288, accessed on 11 November 2010.

Loconte, J. (2008) 'The Decade of Appeasement', *The Weekly Standard*, 2 July, www.weeklystandard.com/Utilities/printer_preview.asp?idArticle=14705&R=139B, accessed on 3/19/08.

Luxmoore, J. (2005) 'Rethinking Christendom – The Church and the New Europe' www.secondspring.co.uk/articles/luxmoore.htm-30k, accessed on 22 May 2008.

Lyons, G. (2009) 'Hermeneutical Bases for Theology: Higher Criticism and the Wesleyan Interpreter', *Wesley Center Online,* www.wesley.nnu.edu/wesleyan_theology/theojrnl/16–20/18–06.htm, accessed on 20 April 2010.

Mandel, D. (2009) 'Winston Churchill – A Good Friend of Jews and Zionism?', *Jerusalem Center for Public Affairs* (Jewish Political Studies Review) http://jcpa. org/article/winston-churchill-a-good-friend-of-jews-and-zionism/, accessed on 16 February 2010.

Al-Manar (2011) 'Islamic delegation heads to Vatican to attend interreligious prayer' (editorial) www.almanar.com.lb/english/adetails.php?eid=32676&frid=23&seccatid=14&cid=23&fromval=1, accessed on 25 October 2011.

Marcus, I. (2007) 'From Nationalist Battle to Religious Conflict: New 12th Grade Palestinian Schoolbooks Present a World Without Israel', PMW (Palestinian Media Watch) http://palwatch.org/STORAGE/special%20reports/School Books_English_Final.pdf, accessed on 4 August 2010.

Marek Siwiec 'European Parliament/MEPs' http://www.europarl.europa.eu/meps/en/28380/Marek_SIWIEC.html, accessed on 5 July 2012.

Marquand, R. (2012) 'In a France suspicious of religion, Evangelicalism's message strikes a chord' *The Christian Science Monitor* http://www.csmonitor.com/World/2012/0712/In-a-France-suspicious-of-religion-evangelicalism-s-message-strikes-a-chord, accessed on 7 August 2012.

Massignon, B. (2003) 'Regulation of Religious Diversity by the Institutions of the European Union: from confrontation of national exceptions to the emergence of a European model', A paper presented at the annual meeting of *The Association for the Sociology of Religion*, Atlanta http://hirr.hartsem.edu/sociology/massignon.html, accessed on 7 June 2011.

——— (2010) 'Religious and secular mobilisations and counter-mobilisations in Brussels', A paper presented at the Does God Matter conference, Aston University www.aston.ac.uk/EasySiteWeb/GatewayLink.aspx?alId=82384, accessed on 7 June 2012.

Massing, M. (2006) 'The Storm Over Israel Lobby' (in *New York Review of Books*, 8 June), *The Shalom Centre* www.shalomctr.org/node/1127, accessed on 15 December 2008.

McCall, T.S. (2006) 'Israel: The Centre of Divine History', *Zola Levitt Ministries* www.levitt.com/essays/dh.html, accessed on 8 March 2006.

McGriff, D. (2007) 'Recognising Deception and Apostasy', *The Tribulation Network* www.the-tribulation-network.com/denemcgriff/Apostasy/recognising_decep tion, accessed on 5 May 2009.

McLaren, B. (2009) 'For points towards peace in the Middle East', *Sojourners* http://blog.sojo.net/2009/04/16/four_poins_towards_peace_in the_middle_east/, accessed on 18 May 2009.

MEMRI (2006) 'The Covenant of the Islamic Resistance Movement – Hamas' Special Dispatch, No. 1092, 1–9 www.memri/org/bin/articles.cgi?Page=archives& Area=sd&ID=SP109206, accessed on 27 January 2009.

Meyer, C. (2008) 'A return to 1815 is the way forward for Europe', *Times online*, 2 September, www.timesonline.co.uk/tol/comment/columnist/guest_contributors/article4656, accessed on 22 December 2008.

Miller, R. (2005) 'The EU's Palestine Problem', *TCS Daily*, http://www.ideas inactiontv.com/tcs_daily/2005/06/the-eus-palestine-problem.html, accessed on 1 September 2012.

——— (2007) 'Why the European Union Finally Sidelined Hamas', *inFocus Quarterly*, The Jewish Policy Centre, Vol. 1 No. 2, http://www.jewishpol icycenter.org/52/why-the-european-union-finally-sidelined-hamas, accessed on 13 December 2012.

Missler, C. (2001) 'Midrash Hermeneutics', *Koinonia House Online*, www.khouse.org/ articles/2001/341/, accessed on 8 March 2009.

Mordecai, V. (2004) 'The Judeo-Christian Alliance – Is the Messianic Era Beginning?', *Israel Today* www.changingworldviews.com/GuestCommentaries/ victormordecaiarticle1.htm, accessed on 11 March 2007.

Morris, B. (2005) 'Yasser Arafat worthy successor to Haj Muhammad al Husseini', *Eretz Yisroel.Org*, www.eretzyisroel.org/~jkatz/arafathusseini.html, accessed on 2 February 2007.

Myers, C. (2012) 'How to advocate for Israel' Youtube http://www.youtube.com/ watch?v=b36IG94R4Yc&list=PL8mGc4bTP6lKRMUXT1BV6Ynfu fezERVOv&feature=g-all-a, accessed on 5 October 2012.

National Intelligence Council (NIC) (2007) 'Non-State Actors: Impact on International Relations and Implications for the United States', *Conference Report* www.dni.gov/nic/confreports_nonstae_actors.html, accessed on 6 January 2009.

Noebel, D. (2009) 'Barack Obama's "red" Spiritual adviser, *World Net Daily*, 26 March, www.worldnetdaily.com/?pageId92833, accessed on 20 April 2009.

Nye, J.S. (2004a) 'Europe's soft power', *The Globalist*, 3 May www.theglobalist.com/ StoryIdaspx?StoryId=3886, accessed on 7 November 2006.

O'Donnell, C.M. (2008) 'The EU, Israel and Hamas' (working paper – section Middle East), *Centre for European Reform* http://www.cer.org.uk/sites/default/files/ publications/attachments/pdf/2011/wp_820–1475.pdf, accessed on 20 November 2008.

———— (2011) 'The EU and the EU should support the Palestinian bid for UN membership', *Centre for European Reform* www.cer.org.uk/topics/enlargement-and-neighbourhood, accessed on 21 October 2011.

Official Journal of the European Communities (2000) 'Charter of Fundamental Rights of European Union' (2000/C 364/01) http://www.europarl.europa.eu/charter/pdf/ text_en.pdfs, accessed on 2 March 2011.

OIC (1990) 'The Cairo Declaration on Human Rights in Islam' www.oic-oci.org/ english/article/human.htm, accessed on 10 October 2010.

Olive Tree Ministries (2008) 'Dual Covenant Theology', Understanding the Times Radio Programme, www.olivetreeviews.org/radio/mp3, accessed on 10 December 2008.

Ottolenghi, E. (2010) 'Squaring the Circle: EU-Israel Relations and the Peace Process in the Middle East', Centre for European Studies – Research Paper, http:// www.1888932–2946.ws/ComTool6.0_CES/CES/E-DocumentManager/gallery/ Research_Papers/1stDSBookSquaringtheCircleEU-ISRAELWEB.pdf, accessed on 12 November 2010.

Parker, M.A. (2007) 'Symbolic Politics and Europeanisation of Islam' in Swayd, S.S. (ed.) Islam: Portability and Exportability (UCLA Center for Near Eastern Studies) http://www.international.ucla.edu/cms/files/swayd_islam_portability.pdf, accessed on 1 July 2012.

Parsons, D. (n.d.) 'Christian Friends and Foes of Israel: What Motivates Them?', *Jerusalem Centre for Public Affairs* (Lectures Online) www.jcpa.org/indexph.asp, accessed on 19 January 2009.

Pasture, P. (2009) 'Religion in Contemporary Europe: Contrasting Perceptions and Dynamics', *Academia.edu* http://www.academia.edu/1262489/Religion_in_ Contemporary_Europe, accessed on 20 January 2013.

THE PRO-ISRAEL LOBBY IN EUROPE

Patterson, M. (2002) 'Will fundamentalist Christians and Jews ignite apocalypse?', *National Catholic Reporter*, October, www.natcath.com/NCR_Online/archives/ 101102/101102a.htm, accessed on 9 October 2006.

Paul, G. (2004) 'The Great Scandal: Christianity's Role in the Rise of the Nazis', *Council for Secular Humanism* www.secularhumanism.org/library/fi/paul_23_4. html, accessed on 1 April 2011.

Pawson, D. (n.d.) 'Revelation – (part 8 Rapture and part 9 The Millennium)', *SermonIndex.Net*, www.sermonindex.net/modules/mydownloads/viewcat.php? cid=528, accessed on 1 April 2009.

Pearce, T. (nd) 'Restoring the Kingdom to Israel – Part I and II', *Light for The Last Days* www.pwmi.org/11d004.htm, accessed on 19 September 2006.

Pfeil, H. (2011) 'The EU in the Arab Spring', *Open Democracy*, www.opendemocracy. net/h%C3%A9l%C3%A8ne-pfeil/eu-in-arab-spring, accessed on 21 October 2011.

Philips, M. (2007) 'Britain's Antisemitic Turn', *The Coordination Forum for Countering Antisemitism* (CFCA),www.antisemitism.orgil/eng/articles/25854/Britain% E2%80%99s_Antisemitism, accessed on 17 December 2007.

———— (2009a) 'Britain's surrender', *Wall Street Journal* (Europe), 20 January, www. melaniephilips.com/articles-new/?p=639&print=1, accessed on 20 January 2009.

Pijpers, A. (2007) 'The EU and Palestinian–Israeli Conflict: The Limits of the CFSP', *Netherlands Institute for International Relations* http://www.clingendael.nl/ publications/2007/20070911_cesp_paper_pijpers.pdf, accessed on 20 January 2013.

PMW (Palestinian Media Watch) 'About Us' http://palwatch.org/pages/aboutus.aspx, accessed on 5 October 2012.

———— 'PMW Research Center' http://www.palwatch.org/pages/impact.aspx, accessed on 5 October 2012.

Prasch, J. (2008) 'Stephen Sizer's November 23rd sermon', *Moriel Ministries*, 7 December. http://moriel.org/MorielArchive/index.php/news/uk/stephen-sizers-november-23rd-sermon, accessed on 8 March 2009.

———— (2008a) 'D. James Kennedy and Biblical Significance of the Modern State of Israel', *Moriel Ministries*, February 5. http://moriel.org/MorielArchive/index. php/discernment/israel/d-james-kennedy-and accessed 08 March 2009.

———— (2009) 'Stephen Sizer Contra Melanie Phillips', *Moriel Ministries*, 10 March. http://moriel.org/MorielArchive/index.php/news/uk/stephen-sizer-contra-mel ani-phillips, accessed on 8 March 2009.

———— (2009a) 'The death of reason and the return of Jesus' www.africanaquatics. co.za/_christian/_articles/death_of_reason_and_the_return_o.htm, accessed on 5 May 2009.

———— (n.d.) 'Midrash'(Miscellaneous), *Revival Theology Resources* www.revivaltheol ogy.gharvest.com/7_misc.midrash.html, accessed on 8 March 2009.

Quartet (2011) 'Middle East Quartet Statement', New York, September 23 www.consil ium.europa.eu/uedocs/cms_data/docs/pressdata/EN/foraff/124734.pdf, accessed on 30 October 2011.

Rettman, A. (2010) 'EU court strikes blow against Israeli settlers', *EU Observer* http:// euobserver.com/24/29558, accessed on 20 December 2011.

———— (2010a) 'Senior MEP quits Israel trip in propaganda row', *EU Observer* http:// euobserver.com/foreign/30095, accessed on 20 October 2012.

Revelation TV (2011) 'TV Debate: Has the Church Replaced Israel?' aired on 9 November 2011, www.calvinlsmith.com/2011/11/tv-debate-has-church-replaced-israel.html, accessed on 12 November 2011.

Robert, J. (2008) 'The Influence of Israel in Westminster', *The Palestine Chronicle*, 1–6 http://www.palestinechronicle.com/print_article.php?id=13821, accessed on 11 November 2011.

Rocha, D. (2009) 'British Ambassador in debate aimed at improving relations', *Arutz Sheva* www.israelnationalnews.com/News/News.aspx/134596, accessed on 8 December 2009.

Rodney, S. (1995) 'Truth: A Reply to Bruce', *Journal for the Scientific Study of Religion*, Vol. 34 No. 4, 516–520, web22epnet.com/DeliveryPrintSave.asp?tb=1_ug =sid+3D5CABE2–99B0–46, accessed on 7 March 2006.

Roughneen, S. (2008) 'Europe's Sharia question', *International Relations and Security Network*, www.isn.ethz.ch/isn/Current-Affairs/Security-Watch/Detail/?lng= en&id=92057–34k, accessed on 20 May 2009.

Rosen, E. (2010) 'Mapping the Organisational Sources of the Global Delegitimisation Campaign against Israel in the UK', *Jerusalem Center for Public Affairs* http://jcpa.org/text/Mapping_Delegitimisation.pdf, accessed on 29 September 2011.

Rosenberg, J.C. (2011) 'Epicenter Conference 2011' www.epicenterconference.com/, accessed on 20 December 2011.

——— (2011a) '2011 Epicenter Conference begins in Jerusalem' http://flashtrafficblog.wordpress.com/2011/05/15/2011-epicenter-conference-begins-in-jerusalem/, accessed on 20 December 2011.

Rubeiz, G. (2006) 'Religion and politics in the Palestine/Israeli conflict', *The Arab American News* www.arabamericannews.com/newsarticle.php?articleid=6329, accessed on 12 October 2006.

Rubenstein, R.L. (2009) 'Jihad and the roots of Europe's religious identity', *New English Review*, pp. 1–7 www.newenglishreview.org/custpage.cfm/frm/29722/sec_id/29722, accessed on 23 January 2009.

Rubin, B. (2011) 'Belgium: Half of All Muslim Immigrant Children Are Antisemitic', *The Right Side News* www.rightsidenews.com/2011051713549/editorial/world-opinion-and-editorial/belgium-half-of-all-muslim-immigrant-children-are-antisemitic.html, accessed on 10 July 2011.

Ryness, S. (2012) 'EU-Israel ACAA debate polarises MEPs but is passed by long-awaited plenary vote', *European Jewish Press* http://www.ejpress.org/article/news/eastern_europe/62638, accessed on 24 October 2012.

Saidel, N. and Joffe, E. (2011) 'British-Israeli Relations Increasingly Fragile', *Gatestone Institute* http://www.gatestoneinstitute.org/1767/british-israel-relations-fragile, accessed on 2 February 2012.

Sankowska, H. (2007) 'The ABC of EU peacekeeping abroad', *EurAktiv* http://www.cafebabel.co.uk/article/2762/the-abc-of-eu-peacekeeping-abroad.html, accessed on 22 February 2013.

Santayana, G. (2005) 'Prepare for peace and you will get war!', *World Net Daily* www.wnd.com/index.php?fa=PAGE.printable&pageId=31650, accessed on 1 December 2008.

Sari Essayah 'European Parliament/MEPs' http://www.europarl.europa.eu/meps/en/96682/SARI_ESSAYAH.html, accessed on 5 July 2012.

Schmale, W. (2008) 'A history of European identity', *Eurotopics* (Magazine) www.
eurotopics.net/en/magazin/geschichte-verteilerseite-neu/europaische, accessed
on 23 January 2009.

Sharon, M. (2004) 'A War Between Civilizations, The Agenda Of Islam Through
Fundamentalist Islam', *Focus on Jerusalem* (Library) http://focusonjerusalem.com/
awarbetweencivilizations.html, accessed on 26 March 2009.

Shay, A. (2012) 'Manipulation and Deception: The Anti-Israel BDS Campaign
(Boycott, Divestment and Sanctions)', *Jerusalem Centre for Public Affairs* http://
jcpa.org/article/manipulation-and-deception-the-anti-israel-bds-campaign-
boycott-divestment-and-sanctions/, accessed on 21 January 2013.

Shtauber, Z. (2005) 'British Attitudes toward Israel and the Jews' in Gerstenfeld, M.,
European-Israeli Relations: Between Confusion and Change?, *Jerusalem Centre for
Public Affairs* www.jcpa.org/JCPA/Templates?ShowPage.asp?DRIT=6&
DBID=1&LNGID=1, accessed on 7 January 2009.

Siedschlag, A. (2006) 'Neorealist Contributions to a Theory of ESDP', Presentation
at the II European Security Conference Innsbruck, University of Innsbruck,
Austria http://www.esci.at/papers/NR-ESDP.pdf.

Silverstein M. et al. (2002) 'Born-Again Zionists', *Mother Jones*, Vol. 27 No. 5, 56–62,
weblinks3.epnet.com/citation.asp?tb=1&_ua=bo+B%5F + shn + 1=db +
afhjnh + bt, accessed on 28 February 2006.

Sizer, S. (2001) 'The Jewish Temple in Contemporary Christian Zionism' www.
cc-vw.org/articles/temple.htm, accessed on 22 February 2007.

——— (2004a) 'Christian Zionism: The new heresy that sways America', *Greenbelt
04* www.cc-vw.org/articles/greenbelt04.htm, accessed on 12 October 2006.

——— (2009) 'Charles Freeman: Their real target is you, Mr. President', 17 March
http://stephensizer.blogspot.com/2009/03/charles-freeman-encounters-israel-
lobby.html, accessed on 28 March 2009.

Skinner, C. (2005) 'Response to a Christian anti-Zionist', *LMF Resources* www.
lmf.org.uk/response%20to%20christian%20anti20%zionist.htm, accessed
on 23 February 2009.

Sofer, R. (2008) 'Foreign Ministry fears anti-Israel mood in Germany growing', YNET
News www.ynetnews.com/Ext/Comp/ArticleLayout/, accessed on 1 April 2011.

Spencer, R. (2009) 'Geert Wilders: man out of time', *FrontPage Magazine* http://97.
74.65.51/readArticle.aspx?ARTID=33824, accessed on 10 November 2009.

Springford, J. (2003) '"Old" and "New" Europeans united: public attitudes towards
the Iraq war and US foreign policy, *Centre for European Reform* http://www.
academia.edu/247326/Oldand_NewEuropeans_United_Public_Attitudes_
Towards_the_Iraq_War_and_US_Foreign_Policy, accessed on 12 December 2011.

Steinberg, G.M. (1999) 'The European Union and the Middle East Peace Process',
Jerusalem Centre for Public Affairs, (Viewpoints) www.jcpa.org/jl/vp418.htm,
accessed on 30 January 2009.

——— (2004) 'Learning the Lessons of the European Union's Failed Middle East
Policies', *Jerusalem Centre for Public Affairs*, (Viewpoints) www.jcpa.org/jl/vp510.
htm, accessed on 30 January 2009.

——— (2008) 'Europe's Hidden Hand: EU Funding for Political NGOs in the
Arab-Israeli Conflict', *NGO Monitor* http://www.ngo-monitor.org/data/
images/File/NGO_Monitor_EU_Funding_Europes_Hidden_Hand.pdf,
accessed on 10 July 2012.

Stelzer, I. (1996) 'Christian Socialism in Britain', *Public Interest*, No. 124, 3–9 weblinks3.epnet.com/citation.asp?tb=1&_ug+sid + 36224AF7%2D9983% 2D41B3%, accessed on 7 February 2006.

Sugg, J. (2005) 'A Nation Under God', *Mother Jones*, Vol. 30 No. 7, 32–38, web11. epnet.com/DeliveryPrintSave.asp?tb=1&_ug=sid + ACDB7AB0–2A6A-4, accessed on 16 February 2006.

Sutherland, P. (2008) 'Europe and Its Values', *Christian Association of Business Executives*, 18 November, www.wpet.org/newsletter/HK%20Nov08%20Peter %20Sutherland.doc, accessed on 2 April 2009.

Talhami, G. (2000) 'Islamic Politics in Palestine – Book Review', *Middle East Policy*, Vol. 7 No. 3 www.mepc.org/journal_vol7/talhami.html, accessed on 1 December 2008.

Tellis, W. (1997) 'Introduction to Case Study', *The Qualitative Report*, Vol. 3 No. 2 http://www.nova.edu/ssss/QR/QR3–2/tellis1.html/, accessed on 3 April 2011.

Tibi, B. (2009) 'Islamists Approach Europe: Turkey's Islamist Danger', *The Middle East Quarterly*, Winter Issue, 47–54 www.meforum.org/article/2047, accessed on 28 January 2009.

Tobin, P. (2000) 'Liberal Modernist Theology', *The Rejection of Pascal's Wager* www. geocities.com/paultobin/liberal.html, accessed on 3 March 2009.

Tocci, N. (2011) 'The European Union and the Arab Spring: A (Missed) Opportunity to Revamp the European Neighbourhood Policy', *European Institute of the Mediterranean* www.euromesco.net/images/iemedeuromescobrief2.pdf, accessed on 21 October 2011.

Tortola, P.D. (2006) 'Christianity and International Politics in the thought of Reinhold Niebuhr and Herbert Butterfield', Paper presented at the Midwest Political Science Association, Chicago http://www.allacademic.com//meta/p_ mla_apa_research_citation/1/3/9/9/0/pages139906/p139906–1.php, accessed on 10 October 2009.

Trifkovic, S. (2006) 'An End-Timer on the East River: The Hidden Message of Ahmedinejad's U.N. Speech', *Chronicles – News and Views* www.chronicles magazine.org/cgi-bin/newsviews/2006/09/22, accessed on 15 December 2006.

Trochim, W. (2006) 'Theory of reliability', *Research Methods Knowledge Base* http:// www.socialresearchmethods.net/kb/reliablt.php, accessed on 3 April 2011.

Tossavainen, M. (2009) 'Swedish Reactions to the Anti-Israel Blood Libel Report', *Jerusalem Center for Public Affairs* www.jcpa.org/JCPA/Templates/ShowPage.asp? DRIT=1&DBID=1&LNGID=1, accessed on 19 November 2009.

Tovias, A. (2011) 'Adjusting to External Norms and Standards of the "West": The Case of Israel', *European Institute of Mediterranean* www.iemed.org/publicacions- en/historic-de-publicacions/papersiemed-euromesco/adjusting-to-external- norms-and-standards-of-the-west-the-case-of-israel, accessed on 21 October 2011.

Tucker, A. (2012) Why Israel (blog) http://www.whyisrael.org/2012/03/05/we-love- muslims-but-hate-the-religion-of-dhimmitude-2/#more-5596, accessed on 14 August 2012.

Vale, R. (2011) 'Is Europeanisation a Useful Concept?', *e-International Relations* http:// www.e-ir.info/2011/01/17/is-%E2%80%98Europeanisation%E2%80%99-a- useful-concept/, accessed on 20 January 2013.

Van Dam, R. (2006) 'Anti-Israeli bias in the European Parliament and other European Union institutions', *Jerusalem Centre for Public Affair* (Post-Holocaust and Antisemitism), No. 48 www.jcpa.org/phas/phas-048-vandam.htm, accessed on 16 November 2006.

Vidino, L. (2007) 'The Tripartite Threat of Radical Islam to Europe', *inFocus*, Vol. 1 No. 3 www.jewishpolicycenter.org/91/the-tripartite-threat-of-radical-islam-to-europe, accessed on 1 April 2009.

Vimeo (2011) 'Israeli Knesset International Conference' www.http//vimeo.com/36687613, accessed on 3 April 2012.

Vogel, T. (2009) 'Redesigning foreign policy', *European Voice* www.europeanvoice.com/article/imported/redesigning-foreign-policy/66221.aspx, accessed on 19 November 2009.

Volf, M. (2005) 'Christianity and Violence', *Speaking of Faith* www.speakingoffaith.publicradio.org/programmes/volf/index.shtml, accessed on 1 October 2006.

Vulkan, D. (2012) 'Britain's Jewish Community Statistics', *The Board of Deputies of British Jews* http://www.bod.org.uk/content/CommunityStatistics2010.pdf, accessed on 10 October 2012.

Wagner, C.D. (1998) 'Evangelicals and Israel: Theological Roots of a Political Alliance', *Christian Century*, 1020–1026 www.publiceye.org/Christian_right/Zionism/wagner-cc.html, accessed on 9 October 2006.

——— (2003) 'Bible and sword: US Christian Zionists discover Israel', *Challenging Christian Zionism* www.christianzionism.org/Article/Wagner06.asp, accessed on 10 April 2009.

Wallace, C.D. (2011) 'Foundations of the International Legal Rights of the Jewish People and the State of Israel: Implications for the Current Debate' in ECI San Remo Resources www.ec4i.org/index.php?option=com_content&view=category&layout=blog&id=85&Itemid=63, accessed on 10 October 2011.

Warraq, I. (2009) 'The Pious Fraud', *City Journal*, Vol. 19 No. 1, www.city-journal.org/2009/bc0229iw.html, accessed on 24 January 2009.

Weiner, R. (2009) 'The Virtual Jewish History Tour – Sweden', *Jewish Virtual Library* www.jewishvirtuallibrary.org/jsource/vjw/Sweden.html, accessed on 10 December 2009.

Weiss, T. (2006) 'European Security: Time to Move Beyond "Effective Multi-lateralism"', *The Henry Jackson Society* www.henryjacksonsociety.org/stories.asp?id=311, accessed on 10 April 2009.

Weissman, J. (2011) 'Leeds Messianic Fellowship: A Response to the British Methodist Report on Palestine and Israel' http://lmf.org.uk/wp-content/uploads/2010/08/Leeds-Messianic-Fellowship-A-Response-to-the-British-Methodist-Report-on-Palestine-and-Israel.pdf, accessed on 30 October 2011.

Whine, M. (2006) 'Islamist Recruitment and Antisemitism on British Campuses', RUSI Homeland Security and Resilience Department http://www.thecst.org.uk/docs/RUSI%20Homeland%20Security.doc, accessed on 6 November 2010.

White, B. (2011) 'Israel's advocates in the UK cosy up to Christian Right', *Ben White blog* http://pulsemedia.org/2011/09/15/israels-advocates-in-the-uk-cosy-up-to-christian-right/, accessed on 1 October 2012.

Wistrich, R.S. (2005) 'European Antisemitism Reinvents Itself', *The American Jewish Committee* www.ajc.orgatf/cf/%7B42D75369-D582-4380-8395./wistrich.pdf, accessed on 3 December 2009.

———— (n.d.) 'British Antisemitism: A Suitable Case for Treatment?' (Lectures Online), *Jerusalem Centre for Public Affairs* www.jcpa.org/indexph.asp, accessed on 19 January 2009.

Witney, N. (2009) 'Europe: Nice location, shame about the neighbours', *Europe's World*, www.europesworld.org/NewEnglish/Home_old/Article/tabid/191/ArticleType/a, accessed on 20 January 2010.

WJC (World Jewish Congress) (2009) 'Sweden' www.worldjewishcongress.org/en/communities/show?id=111, accessed on 10 December 2009.

Youngs, R. (2006) 'Europe's flawed approach to Arab democracy', *Centre for European Reform* (Publications – The Middle East) www.cer.org.uk, accessed on 11 November 2006.

YNET (2012) 'WJC to honor pro-Israel Christian leaders' http://www.ynetnews.com/articles/0,7340,L-4176219,00.html, accessed on 10 June 2012.

Zimmer, A. (2000) 'Corporatism Revisited – The Legacy of History and the German Nonprofit Sector' in Zimmer, A. (ed.) *The Third Sector in Germany* http://www.aktive-buergerschaft.de/fp_files/Diskussionspapiere/2002wp-sband03.pdf#page=82, accessed on 2 February 2011.

———— (2000a) 'Welfare Pluralism and Health Care: The Case in Germany' in Zimmer, A. (ed.) *The Third Sector in Germany* http://www.aktive-buergerschaft.de/fp_files/Diskussionspapiere/2002wp-sband03.pdf#page=82, accessed on 2 February 2011.

Zunes, S. (2006) 'The Israel Lobby: How Powerful is it Really?', *Foreign Policy in Focus* (Special Report), May 16 www.fpif.org/fpiftxt/3270, accessed on 5 May 2009.

———— (2006a) 'Was Hezbollah a legitimate target?', *Foreign Policy*, August 8 www.alternet.org/audits/40009, accessed on 18 October 2006.

Magazine, newspaper articles and other

Bates, S. (2006) 'Leading Anglican hits back in anti-Israel row', *The Guardian*, 20 February.

Butt, R. (2008) 'Archbishop backs Sharia law for British Muslims', *The Guardian*, 7 February.

———— (2009) 'Rabbis may halt Vatican talks over Holocaust-denying priest', *The Guardian*, 29 January.

Dempsy, J. (2011) 'A deepening rift between Germany and Israel', *The New York Times*, 7 March.

Der Spiegel (2006) 'Ahmadinejad interview', 10 April.

———— (2010a) 'The role of imam is different in Germany – Interview with Rauf Ceylan', 1 January.

———— (2010b) 'The man who divided Germany: Why Sarrazin's Integration Demagoguery has many followers', 6 June.

———— (2010c) 'Islam is Like a Drug – Interview with Hamed Abdel-Samad', 17 September.

Derfner, L. (2008) 'And you took me in', *The Jerusalem Post*, 9 December.

The Doomsday Code (2006) narrated by Tony Robinson, Channel 4 [documentary: DVD].

The Economist (2006) 'A dilemma over Hamas and its cash' (Middle East and Africa), February.

———— (2009) 'God and Berlin' (Europe), 26 March.

———— (2012) 'The Church of England: Hot and bothered' (Britain), 10 March.

Ekstrom, A. (2010) 'Israel and the Jews, two separate entities to Europe's radical right', *Haaretz*, 15 December.

Elboim-Dror, R. (2009) 'God's promise of land to Jews has deep pull on secular Israelis', *Haaretz*, 27 November.

Eldridge, M. (2009) 'Churchill and the Jews: An Assessment of Two Recent Studies and Their Contemporary Relevance' (research paper), *Olive Press*.

Engel, M. (2002) 'Meet the new Zionists', *The Guardian*, 21 November.

Ferrero-Waldner, B. (2007) 'The European path for Israel?', *Haaretz*, 26 February.

Fischler, F. (2002) 'The Role of the Catholic Church in the Process of European Integration' – Conference.

The Forsaken Promise (2006) Hugh Kitson, narrated by Ian Cullen, Eastbourne, Hatikvah Film Trust [documentary: DVD].

Freund, M. (2011) 'Christians For Israel: Missionaries to the church', *The Jerusalem Post*, 30 March.

Gale, G. (2009) 'Europe's Christians remember Evian 1938', *The Jerusalem Post*, June.

Glick, C. (2010) 'Making Israel's Case', *The Jerusalem Post*, 14 May.

God's Prophetic Agenda (2004) Watchmen on the Walls Video Ministries, Prayer for Israel, UK [educational: DVD].

Greenwood, P. (2012) 'EU move to upgrade relations with Israel', *The Guardian*, July.

Haaretz (2006) 'EU lawmakers want to ban Ahmadinejad from the World Cup', 1 June.

Hannan, D. (2006) 'How Europe unwittingly fuels bloodshed in Israel', *Daily Telegraph*, 17 May.

Hastings, M. (2006) 'Israel can no longer rely on the support of Europe's Jews', *The Guardian*, 20 June.

Horowitz, D. (2006) 'Evangelicals seeing the error of replacement theology', *The Jerusalem Post*, 20 March.

Israely, J. (2006) 'Ten questions for Romano Prodi', *Time Magazine*, 23 April.

Jerusalem the Covenant City Lance Lambert, Eastbourne, Hatikvah Film Trust [educational: DVD].

Kitson, H. (2005) 'The Forsaken Promise', *Prophecy Today*, Vol. 21 No. 5, 12–13 September/October.

———— (2007) 'What is Christian Zionism?', *Sword*, Vol. 2 No. 2, 18–19 March/April.

Lazaroff, T. (2012) 'J'lem lawyer lobbies EU on Palestinian human rights', *The Jerusalem Post*, 23 March.

———— (2009) 'EU's Solana: Don't drop two-state solution', *The Jerusalem Post*, 17 March.

Lefkovits, E. (2006) 'Congress forms Israel Allies Caucus', *The Jerusalem Post*, 27 July.

Liddle, R. (2009) 'Onward Christian Zionists', *The Spectator*, 11 January.

Lindsay, D. (2004) 'Ruth not Orpah: Let the Gentile Churches bless Israel', *Prophecy Today*, Vol. 20 No. 4, 12–13.

Maceoin, D. (2009) 'Marching for Hamas', *The Jerusalem Post*, 24 January.

Maltz, S. (2009) 'Darwin's dangerous legacy', *Sword*, Vol. 4 No. 2, 36–7.

McDonald, H. (2002) 'The beast is back', *The Guardian*, 15 December.

Monbiot, G. (2004) 'Their beliefs are bonkers, but they are at the heart of power', *The Guardian*, 20 April.

Morris, B. (2011) 'Arab Spring and Israeli security', *Anglo Israel AIA,* November issue, 6–9.

Oestreicher, P. (2006) 'Israel's policies are feeding the cancer of antisemitism', *The Guardian*, 20 February.

Philips, M. (2009) 'Beware the new axis of Evangelicals and Islamists', *The Spectator,* 4 March.

Prasch, J. (1997) 'Threat of persecutions of Israeli believers', *Moriel*, News and prayer letter, No. 10.

Ravid, B. (2012) 'EU foreign ministers pushing to label all settlement products', *Haaretz*, 3 October.

Rifkind, H. (2011) 'Gaddafi is done. Now for the difficult bit', *The Guardian*, 2 October.

Robinson, A. (2005) 'The problem of Post-Millennialism', *The Watchman*, No. 22, 14–19.

Sandell, T. (2009) 'A false icon', *The Jerusalem Post* (Opinion), 19 January.

———— (2010) 'Obsessed with Israel', *The Wall Street Journal* (Opinion Europe), 9 November.

———— (2011) 'A missed opportunity for the EU', *The Jerusalem Post* (Editorial), 21 March.

Sewell, D. (2002) 'A kosher conspiracy', *New Statesman*, 14 January.

Shenk, C.E. (1998) 'Jerusalem as Jesus views it', *Christianity Today*, October.

Sherwood, H. (2010) 'Chris Patten urges bolder EU approach over Middle East conflict', *The Guardian*, 18 July.

Sorko-Ram, A. and Sorko-Ram, S. (2004) 'Bless Israel, bless the world', *Prophecy Today*, Vol. 20 No. 3, May/June.

Stam, J. (2003) 'Bush's Religious Language', *The Nation*, 22 December.

Tucker, A. (2009) 'Speech to His Excellency Mr. Avigdor Lieberman, deputy Prime Minister of Israel and Minister of Foreign Affairs, at 11 November in The Hague, Netherlands', *Israel and Christians Today*, December.

Warraq, I. (2008) 'Why the West is Best', *City Journal*, Vol. 18 No. 1.

Weaver, M. (2010) 'Angela Merkel: German multiculturalism has "utterly failed"', *The Guardian*, 17 October.

Weber, T.P. (1998) 'How Evangelicals became Israel's best friend', *Christianity Today*, Vol. 42 No. 11, 39–49.

INDEX